GU _____ HE
_____ RS
POCKETBOOK

Got an idea...?
Grab a camera...
Go make a movie...
Get it out there...

BY

CHRIS JONES

ANDREW ZINNES

AND GENEVIEVE JOLLIFFE

info@guerillafilm.com   www.twitter.com/livingspiritpix

www.guerillafilm.com   www.chrisjonesblog.com

Join our Facebook group 'Guerilla Film Maker'

Continuum International Publishing Group
The Tower Building
11 York Road
London SE1 7NX

80 Maiden Lane
Suite 704
New York 10038

www.continuumbooks.com
www.guerillafilm.com

First published 2010
Reprinted 2011

ISBN 978 1 4411 8078 0

British Library Cataloguing-in-Publication Data

A catalogue record for this book is available from the British Library

THE GUERILLA FILM MAKERS COMMANDMENTS
(REVISED AND UPDATED)

Thou shalt striveth for excellence each and every day. Only through excellence can thou reacheth salvation

Thou shalt make movies, and keep making movies for only this way can one learn the craft

Thou shalt cast from thine mind the phrase 'it cannot be done'

Thou shalt surround thineself with positive and excellent people

Thou shalt respect the film makers who will come after thee and never burnest bridges that others may need to use

Thou shalt backup all data from cameras in at least three places

Thou shalt shoot hundreds of great stills

Thou shalt only shoot when thine screenplay is Oscar worthy

Thou shalt cut thine movie, then recut, recut and recut more

Thou shalt beg, borrow, blag but never stealeth, for this burneth bridges for others who follow

Thou shalt Twittereth these words regularly

Thou shalt Facebook and blog thine progress for thine followers

Thou shalt shareth with all film makers whatever thou learneth

ACKNOWLEDGEMENTS

Book Producer Judy Goldberg, for being so totally reliable and always available to help.

Production Manager Verity Budden, for stepping into the breach when needed the most.

In house editor extraordinaire, **James Barham**, for editing all those videos on www.guerillafilm.com ready for the book launch.

Thanks to **Lynn and Stan Morris** for their babysitting skills.

And of course our publisher **David Barker**, for staying cool...

But most of all we want to thank

YOU THE FILM MAKERS...!

...for being so inspirational, for pushing the boundaries of possibility, imagination, and occasionally the law(!)

YOUR FILMS ROCK...!

...and we cannot tell you just how much we look forward to interviewing YOU about YOUR amazing success in the next book... **So remember, AIM HIGH!**

Stay in touch, join the Facebook page, join www.guerillafilm.com and let us know how you are getting on,
AND MAKE AMAZING MOVIES!

Team Guerilla Film

CONTENTS

JOIN THE WEBSITE

www.guerillafilm.com

The web component of this book is a place where you can...

- Watch videos of film makers interviewed in the book.
- Listen to podcasts with film makers and experts.
- Download contracts and forms for using in your films.
- Find links to cool film making resources to help you make
  better films.

But it will be so much more. Our sincere hope for the website is that it will evolve alongside you, the film makers. So swing by and get involved... And check out our blogs at... **www.chrisjonesblog.com** and **www.guerillagal.com.** And join our Facebook group called **Guerilla Film Maker.**

THE GUERILLA
FILM MAKERS POCKETBOOK
LEGAL DISCLAIMER
READ THIS FIRST!

Nothing in this book should be construed as legal advice. The information provided and the sample contracts and documents are not a substitute for consulting with an experienced entertainment lawyer and receiving counsel based on the facts and circumstances of a particular transaction. Furthermore case law and statutes and European and International law and industry practise are subject to change, and differ from country to country.

The copyright in and to the sample contracts and documents in this book is owned and retained by the originator of the work ("the Owner"). These sample contracts and documents have been created for your general information only. The Owner, the authors of this book and the publishers cannot therefore be held responsible for any losses or claims howsoever arising from any use or reproduction.

www.guerillafilm.com

THE SETUP...
THE GUERILLA
FILM MAKERS

Q – What is a guerilla film?

GFM – It's a film made with no real resources. It's a question that we get asked a lot and there is no straight answer aside from when you are making a guerilla film, you know about it! Think 'no cash' and 'bending all the rules to get it done'.

Q – So what do you need to make a guerilla film?

GFM – With technology today, all you need is a good idea and the passion and drive to make it happen. HD cameras on phones, real time video downloading, access to all manner of first rate film education - if you feel film making is your calling, there really is no excuse now. In reality though, you are going to need a camera, some microphones, some lights, an edit suite and lots of time. You will also need a great idea that has been developed into a terrific script, a merry band of crazy people who are prepared to follow you on this journey, and a bunch of actors willing to risk looking like idiots when they deliver your dialogue!

Q – Why choose to be a guerilla film maker?

✉ info@guerillafilm.com   🐦 www.twitter.com/livingspiritpix

🏠 www.guerillafilm.com   🅱 www.chrisjonesblog.com

📘 Join our Facebook group 'Guerilla Film Maker'

WHAT DO YOU REALLY NEED?

Making films is fun and exhilarating, kind of like an addiction. But let's be clear, to make a successful career in this business is going to require guts, determination, passion, perhaps a little bit of luck... and, of course, some kit! So what do you really need to start making your movies, be they shorts, features, docos, virals or any other variant?

You are going to need a camera, the latest and greatest. Do your research. Ask around and see what others are using, but remember, the best camera to get is the one you borrow from someone else. The camera you buy for starting a film career will not be the camera you take through to bigger and more ambitious films in the future, so it's wise to not over invest in too much kit too early. You will also need microphones, lights, a car and loads of other stuff.

Rounding off your arsenal will be an editing system with good speakers – it could be Adobe Premiere, Avid, Sony Vegas or Final Cut Pro. The most popular system right now is undoubtedly FCP (Final Cut). You will also need a system to drive the software and lots of hard drive space. We would also recommend you keep your editing computer separate from your work computer.

GFM – Very few film makers we know would ever choose to be a guerilla film maker. They do it because they don't have any other way into the film business. Like us, when they started they did not know powerful people, are not related to anyone within the film business, and do not have significant wealth behind them - but they do have burning desire and a great story they need to tell. Then the little voice kicks in and they start thinking... 'You know I could do it with what I have, I mean I already have a camera, and I know someone who has a location I could use...' and before you know it, the ship is launched.

Film making is like being infected by a disease. For most of us, it happened at a young age when we saw 'that film' (insert your own movie here) and found yourself deeply impacted by the experience. That's like 'the bite'. Over time you start making little films and if you are lucky, you get bored and move onto a job that pays well! If you're not lucky, and you probably aren't as you are reading this, then you're infected for life. We love that old adage, *'film making is not*

1. Make lots of little movies. Learn the craft of putting images together with sound.

2. Ask for feedback and take it onboard.

3. Work on your sound, learn how important clean dialogue and the use of sound FX & music can be.

4. Act in other peoples films. You will find out how hard it is to be an actor – which will make you a better director.

5. Become a skilled editor – edit your own, and other people's films.

6. Shoot, edit and master to DVD a wedding video. Make money. Make people happy. Learn to shoot under pressure.

7. Make a documentary about your mum or partner doing the washing. Do it in a day.

taught, it's caught!' Sadly, all of us at the *Guerilla Film Makers Handbook* are also infected, so we welcome you with open arms.

Q – This is starting to sound pretty scary!

GFM – Let's keep it in perspective, the worst day being a guerilla film maker is better than the best day stocking shelves at the local supermarket. You really do get to chase your dreams instead of dreaming about chasing your dreams. And it's a marathon too. Over the six books we have now published, we have seen many film makers fall by the wayside, but those who commit to the long haul, usually make it all the way. We are seeing friends who have struggled for 15 years, finally get that break and are now directing fully budgeted movies. It's exhilarating. So guerilla film making is a jumping off point, not an ending point.

Q – So it's a long journey?

GFM – It can be. And it's frustrating to see people who are more connected or wealthier than you, get breaks that you feel you should have – but that is nothing to do with your own reality. You are not them, and they are not you. You need to use what you have, your skills, your ambition and drive, and not worry about anyone else. Focus is a key skill you must have.

It's also important to pace yourself too. Don't try and do it all too quickly, take your time to make lots of short films, go to festivals, make friends, share your movies, accept criticism, write lots of scripts, work on other people's films... There's lots off stuff to learn, and fun to have, before you tackle that big break out film.

There's a bunch of myths out there, and many of those myths evolved out of the film business of the nineties. But it's the Wild West out there now, the nineties are long, long gone, and no one can offer very specific film making plans or templates to follow anymore. You have to arm yourself and find your own path to the summit. And you do that by relentless training, getting in shape, and THEN and only then, making a big movie.

Q – Do you have both producers and directors on guerilla films?

GFM – Sure, but it's much more fluid than on budgeted films. One lesson we learned very early on is that if you want the luxury of directing, you must also learn to be great producer. You need to be part of that fabric, that decision making process, to control your own destiny.

We have interviewed film makers who have managed to make films entirely on their own, literally 'one man cast and crew'. But most are a couple of dedicated people, who work for a long time, often many months, with a dedicated cast and crew of five or ten people.

If you can, find a partner. Working with another person is so important as it makes you much more effective. With a partner, you can't go off on self indulgent whims, and often, the other partner is good at stuff you are terrible at, so the relationship is complimentary. You also have a shoulder to cry on which really helps, and if you know your partner is working late on a budget, you tend to work late on the script too, and so productivity of the team soars. Find a partner. We cannot stress this enough.

8. Go to local film festivals. Expose yourself to lots of different films, even if you don't like them.

9. Become a photographer and study how to capture amazing images. You don't need a crew or actors to learn this skill. Develop an eye for composition.

10. Work on other people's films, and learn at their expense. Find out about other short films being made in your area and offer yourself for free. You will learn and make contacts.

11. Ask experienced people if you can buy them a cheap sandwich for lunch. Ask LOTS of questions and let them ask about you.

12. Go to art galleries, the ballet, music concerts and the theatre. Expose yourself to as much and as varied art as possible.

13. No-one will ever just give you an opportunity. You have to make your own until you have 'value'. Then you'll have lots of opportunities.

Q – Do guerilla films always lead on to bigger films?

GFM – Of course there are no guarantees, but logic dictates that if you make a film, you learn something, and you take that new knowledge to the next film.

But climbing the ladder is not for everyone, and some film makers will get much more pleasure staying small, taking complete creative control over their movies, utilizing a very small setup (such as a bedroom with edit suite and a small HD camera kit), using the internet to get their films out there, and all the time, hold down another job and have a family in due course.

They may not make much money at all, but, and this is crucial, they are making films that really connect with huge audiences, and having fun too. Ten million hits on YouTube is both possible and a staggering statistic for these film makers. Not long back it would be inconceivable that a short film maker could ever reach an audience of that scale. We live in truly amazing and exciting times.

Of course, if you do get that 'ten million hits' on YouTube, suddenly other sections of the film business sit up and take note. They will probably ask you out to lunch to feel you out.

Q – What models for success are there?

GFM – It all begins with an understanding of what you are making. There are two basic steps in a film maker's life. Learning to make films, then making films to make money. Of course there is a crossover and you never really stop learning, but there is a basic ground floor of 'learning' you kind of need to reach before you can start engineering a business around making sustainable money.

The problems usually arise when a film maker thinks they are making a film that will attract sales, when in fact they are involved in a learning experience. Of course there are two important points.

First, there is a learning experience to be had by trying to sell your film, successfully or not (perhaps this is most valuable learning experience of all). And second, what the hell do we know! There is always that film that comes out of left field and sells a shed load of territories and copies. As Goldman says, 'no-one knows anything'.

PPP A STRATEGY FOR SUCCESS

People often ask how we got so much for free when making films, how we got crews to work such long hours, and why thay are all still our friends (mostly). The first thing to remember is that if 'we believe', it's much easier for others to believe too. So it all begins with what most people would call conviction and passion. Then add PPP – requests that are professional, persistent and polite.

So when you send out a letter, make sure that it's short, specific, concise, typo free and has accurate contact details. That would be a professional letter. In our office, we regularly receive a hand scrawled DVD in the post. That is NOT professional. Persistent means when they say no, you professionally and politely ask again, maybe in a different way. Or you ask someone else. Polite means always being gracious. It's hard to dislike anyone who is always smiling, calm and confident.

To recap... Set your goal then be professional, persistent and polite about getting there...

Q – Assuming I am ready for my first big project, what then?

GFM – What kills most careers dead is being shut down because the film maker can't survive the long haul. We can all do the sprint, but how about the marathon? So reduce your overheads, that means selling the nice car (that was bought on credit that you are still paying off), living at home with mum, cancelling the gym or your TV cable deal... Learn to live very cheaply. Second, make money from making movies. That could be working on film and TV crews, making video virals or music promos, even wedding videos. The idea is to stay away from a normal job that will suck your soul dry. And also stay away from a long term job in the business or you will get seduced into earning money and not chasing your dream (with the one caveat that this 'corporate ladder' approach does work well for some people).

One very successful model is making special interest DVD / films – like a film about railways or, as a friend of ours did, Scooters and Mopeds (www.scooterfilm.com). In these films, there is no story as such, just an engaging video about a niche group and their loves. The people interested in that niche will often pay over the odds for tailored and detailed content, buy extra copies for presents and even buy the sequel from the website before it's even made (as they all joined your Facebook group, you can stay in touch). If you are smart, using the film making kit you already have, you can make this film for little more than your time and basic expenses. Then you own that title and for the rest of time it could make you money. Do this several times over and you have a library of titles.

Of course, most of us don't want to make a special interest DVD, so this is a means to an end.

Q – What about documentary?

GFM – If you have a good idea and access to the subject, we suggest you really consider making a doc. Our *Guerilla Film Makers Documentary Handbook* is filled with case studies of people who just started shooting and ended up on the world stage. It makes a lot of sense. Of course all the same rules apply to documentary as they do with narrative – it's got to be a great story well told, with engaging characters and hopefully gripping sequences with a killer finale. Remember, you may have the kit already, so why not?

Q – What about narratives? Specifically shorts?

GFM – The world of short film making is thriving, largely thanks to the internet and people having just a few moments to watch something, either online or as an email attachment. Festivals have increased in their numbers too, so there are loads of places to get screened. Cheap cameras and kit mean that anyone can have a crack, which is great, but the flip side is that it's now more competitive than ever.

Short film sales are not good though. It is possible to sell a short, but generally, whatever money you spend making and exploiting a short, should be written off. It's not a business proposition, but it is still tax deductible! Think of shorts in terms of fun, learning, breaking new ground and most importantly, having some excellent work to show off your skills. And it's a fact, you can make a short film and end up winning an Oscar™. Every year it happens to one new film maker, so why not you?

Q – And features?

GFM – The world of micro budget features is now saturated. But it's still possible to break through. We suggest there are two ways to do this.

First, your film is so innovative and unusual, it captures the imagination of festival coordinators, journalists, studio executives, and the film starts to get a real buzz. This is VERY hard to engineer, in fact we suggest it's near impossible to manufacture that buzz. If it happens to you, it's probably about being in the right place at the right time with the right movie. Or you are just so darned unique and amazing that your talent cannot be ignored. But you really must be that special, and not just think you are because your mum told you so.

The second plan - you make a targeted genre film and adhere to those genre expectations – a good example of this approach is a micro budget British thriller called *Ten Dead Men* – an actioner with loads of punching, kicking and of course, ten deaths. It's simple, knows what it is and has sold tens of thousands of DVDs in the first few weeks of release. Apparently the acting is not amazing, but the fighting is. These guys do not need to recoup very much before they are out of the hole and making another film, with all their experience from the last film in their arsenal.

Genre is so critical for micro budget films. Along with that comes trailers, posters, key art, and of course a very tight edit. No-one likes to be bored, especially distributors in Cannes or at the American Film Market.

GOALS TO SET NOW

1. Whatever goal you set, put a deadline on it or it will become 'one day, some day' and you will never do it.

2. Get out of bed one hour earlier every weekday.

3. Read 20 shooting scripts downloaded from the internet by the end of next month.

4. Call a film school and ask for a tour, irrespective of whether you want to go or not.

5. Make a short film next weekend. Conceive between now and then. Shoot Saturday. Edit Sunday. Youtube Sunday night.

6. Watch a foreign language film every night for a week.

7. Go to a film festival in the next four weeks.

8. Make three phone calls you have been putting off today.

9. Read this book from cover to cover BEFORE putting on your shelf.

10. Write four pages of script every day for 25 days – then spend 25 days editing and rewriting. Now you have a first draft feature script!

11. Research a local film maker, director, editor, camera person, anyone(!) and ask them if can you buy them coffee in return for advice.

Whatever you choose to do, make sure you DO IT! Success lies in DOING IT, NOT TALKING ABOUT IT!

Q – Which would you choose?

GFM – All are great models. We have made genre features, Oscar ™ chasing shorts and controversial docs. For us, it's all about making movies, making sure those movies make some money back and then moving on to the next. Follow your heart.

Q – What mistakes do you seen film makers make?

GFM – Over the years we have seen hundreds of film makers come and go, some successful, others not. We have personally advised many of them too. Most mistakes are really not mistakes, more a misunderstanding of where they are in their own personal careers and journeys. All too often people invest too heavily too early, make big mistakes and find it hard to recover from those disasters. So take your time, make lots of films, make your mistakes when it doesn't matter and no-one is looking. When you are ready, take the money you can hustle and make the 'break out' movie that is worthy of your time and talent.

Q – What advice would you offer a new film maker?

GFM – Commit to every experience being a learning experience, take every opportunity, and make even more opportunities yourself. But do remember to have fun and enjoy it along the way, or your life will fall apart and your movies will end up being dull.

WORDS OF WISDOM FROM OUR FRIENDS

'If it is something YOU don't believe in, you won't have the passion and physical energy to get your shit together and convince a million people to believe it. You've got to feel it...'

CATHERINE HARDWICKE,
Director, 'Thirteen', 'Twilight'

'Stand your ground. I wouldn't be sitting here right now if I hadn't stood my ground and been a pain in the ass. Get people to work for you for cheap. Inspire your crew and actors and they will do anything for you...'

RICHARD KELLY,
Writer and Director, 'Donnie Darko'

These quotes are drawn from expert interviews in other books in the Guerilla Guides series.

The Guerilla Film Makers Handbook UK Edition
The Guerilla Film Makers Handbook US Edition
The Documentary Film Makers Handbook

Check out the website for details at **www.guerillafilm.com**

'Grab a camera, shoot on video and experiment. Robert Rodriguez said 'Every filmmaker has twenty bad films in them, so you might as well get them out of your system early'. Video is a perfect way to do that...'

STU MASCHWITZ, Magic Bullet

'The day that you go home early is the day that you become complacent...'

EDGAR WRIGHT, Writer and Director, 'Shaun of the Dead'

'Appreciate that the longer it takes, the more you can benefit from the journey. It is a marathon, not a sprint. You need to figure out who you are in the world if you are going to say anything valuable...'

DAVID YATES, Director 'Harry Potter'

'Treat making your film, however you're making it, not as a means to an end, but as the best film you're ever going to make. Do something you believe in, something you love, and enjoy it...'

CHRIS NOLAN, Director 'The Dark Knight'

'Be on the look out for good ideas – they are the one constant. Good ideas will take you anywhere you want to go, in any part of Hollywood. There was never a meeting or a place that I couldn't get into as long as I had that one thing, a good idea...'

**BOB KOSBERG,
Hollywood Pitch King**

'Don't take no for an answer. Be tenacious and believe in the projects you are pushing and the filmmakers you are shepherding. Be resourceful and leave no stone unturned when you are trying to get a project off the ground...'

KEYA KHAYATIAN, Hollywood Agent, UTA

'Spend a lot of attention on your first twenty pages. It has all been seen before, so the secret is saying it in a different way...'

JOHN OBRIEN, Writer

'Write and keep writing...'
ROBIN SCHIFF, Writer

'Make your own film and understand that you can't and shouldn't compete with Hollywood. Even if you had an unlimited amount of money. Make the film you want to make...'
ED SANCHEZ, Director, 'The Blair Witch Project'

'You can turn a great script into a bad movie, but you cannot turn a bad script into a great movie...'
ELLIOT GROVE, Raindance

'Listen to everyone. Listen, listen, listen. Listen to everything they have to say, then forget it all and go and work it out yourself. Because the filmmaking process is changing so much that every 6 months everyone is wrong again...'
CHRIS ATKINS, Film maker

'If you can get a picture of who you are, through other people's eyes, you'll save yourself so much time. It will free you, it will liberate you, so that you can spend your time on that area to which you're most suited...'
STUART HAZELDINE, Writer and Director

'It sounds corny, but don't give up. If you really do believe in it and yourself, then keep going...'
MICHAEL McCOY, Independent Talent Group

'Don't be afraid to push boundaries. Learn from the past, but don't live in it...'
GEOFF STANTON, Agent

'I would say this to everybody starting out – do what you are told. Put your armor on, because your ego may well get bruised...'
OLIVIA WILLIAMS, Actor

'Any time there's an option of taking an easy way out by producing shoddy work, remind yourself of your standards and remember that keeping to them will set you apart from the crowd. Not that many people do this, but not that many people make it to the top...'
ROB HALL, Assistant Editor

'Learn to talk about yourself and your project in one minute or less. Check your ego at the door. Never have more than two screaming, yelling, freaking-out meltdowns per movie. Enjoy this experience, you never know how many more of these you might get to do...'
RICH HULL, PGA

'Don't give up...'
JOHN SCHMIDT, Content Film

'Take a job, any job and work hard. Work as if it's your last job...'
**DEREK ROBERTO,
Production Co-ordinator**

'Choose to be in this industry because you are passionate about telling stories in a cinematic form. Don't do it for money, it won't work out. It's a tough field. Be prepared for a long involvement...'
**PAUL SESSUM,
Agent**

'Wear comfortable shoes...'
GREG JACOBS, First AD

'Travel around the world, experience different cultures. Fall in love. Break up. Get into therapy. Read books. Find the scripts of great films and read them, then watch them to see how they made the leap from page to screen...'
ERIC STOLTZ, Actor

'Stay open and be flexible and roll with the punches. Don't let your ego get the better of you...'
SUSIE DeSANTO,
Costume Designer

'Working on a film is like being in an orchestra. Depending on what is taking place, sometimes certain instruments have a solo, and when it's your solo you need to be ready...'
JUDY LOVELL,
Make-up Supervisor

'Make it entertaining. It does not matter how serious the subject matter, how wordy it is, just make it entertaining. That is what it is all about...'

JASON THORP, Fox FX

'Don't be afraid to ask. Most people are flattered to be asked for their knowledge and expertise in an area. None of us got anywhere completely on our own – we all ask for help...'

SANDRA HEBRON,
London Film Festival

'If you have a great script and a great little scene to send out to five companies, you will get five calls. So, story, story, story is the key...'

LEIGH WHANNELL,
Writer and Actor, 'Saw'

'It's affordable to make your own feature film in your bedroom now, and make it as good as anything Hollywood is doing So why not just do it? It really is as simple as that...'

JULIAN RICHARDS,
Writer and Director

'The best thing anyone can do is translate a story to the rest of the world no matter what format is used...'
DAVID HAYS, E-Film

'It takes persistence, hard work and if you're not prepared to fight the good fight it's better not to start. When you're told 'no', find a different door to knock on...'
TOM ORTENBERG, Lionsgate

'Have the courage to quit a job that is taking up your time from making your movie...'
DYLAN KIDD,
Director 'Roger Dodger'

'It is very easy to get intimidated and cowed as a first time film maker when you are working on a set with people who are much more experienced than you. You start questioning yourself. But you must remember that you're putting your own voice to it. You must stand your ground without being an asshole...'
CHRIS KENTIS,
Writer and Director, 'Open Water'

'I don't think I have ever met a successful film maker that was not obsessed with the craft...'

JAKE WEST,
Writer and Director

'Be very courteous, it's amazing how far good manners will get you in this town...'

JEREMY BOLT, Producer

'Be absolutely determined. For all the ups and downs, over 6 years, whatever it took to get Dog Soldiers made, there was never a point where I thought, this isn't going to happen. I always knew it was going to happen, it was just a question of when...'

NEIL MARSHALL, Director
'Dog Soldiers', 'The Descent'

'To make a great film, you need life experience, so travel and engage in life. Working in a coal mine is better than learning the Avid at age 18. Life experience is huge in becoming a great filmmaker...'

NINA SEAWEY,
The Documentary Center

'This is your film. Trust your gut. Make your voice heard. Even after you sell the film, never be afraid to speak out on decisions that are being made – you know your film better than anyone...'

SHEENA JOYCE, Producer,
'Rock School'

'You've got to love it or you aren't going to make it. And surround yourself with some key people. Worry about the things you have control over and keep your eye on things you don't understand.

ADRIAN BELIC, Producer,
'Genghis Blues'

'There are thousands of good films made and why some are more successful than others, no one can say. You need luck to be in the right place, at the right time, together with the right people...'

LUC JACQUET,
Writer and Director, 'March of
the Penguins'

'Think big but keep your overheads small...'
CATHY HENKEL,
Director, 'The Man Who Stole
My Mother's Face'

'Don't take no for an answer. And you have to be more passionate about the story than anyone else because they're not going to care. You have to make them care...'

**BRIAN HERZLINGER,
Director, 'My Date with Drew'**

'To me, what you need is an idea and the ability to wake up every morning and deal with that idea and the many facets of bringing it to life...'

**STACY PERALTA
Director, 'Dogtown and Z-Boys'**

'I think documentary encourages filmmakers to be very flexible in their approach. To not go into subjects with a thesis all carefully worked out. They have to be open and on a voyage of discovery themselves and take the audience with them...'

NICK BROOMFIELD, Director

'While it's much easier to make a documentary, it's much harder to get them seen. So if you want that to happen, you have to be doubly thoughtful about what it is...'

MICHAEL APTED, Director

CHAPTER ONE
SCREENPLAY

THE GUERILLA FILM
MAKERS POCKETBOOK

Q – When you have no money or experience to make a film, how can you use the screenplay to your advantage?

WRITING A FEATURE FILM
BLAKE SNYDER

Blake – In any filmmaking endeavor no matter the budget, concept is king. Time and again it's been proven that no amount of money thrown against a project with a vague or uninspiring concept will succeed. If we look at *The Island* as an example, it had Michael Bay, Scarlett Johansson and Ewan McGregor. It had $150 million in budget and another $50 million in advertising. And it made just $32 million domestically because the audience didn't know what it was. Answering the basic question, "What is it?", takes no money at all and doing so is the first step to success.

Q – What advice would you give on choosing a concept and moving forward with it?

Blake – I'm a great believer in pitching. Go to Starbucks, pitch to civilians and see if their eyes light up. If the person you're pitching starts pitching back with ideas to improve it, then you know you are on to something. Further, I think all ideas need to have irony in them. Those are the ones that stand out. And your idea needs to be primal. The ones that work on a caveman level work the best.

Q – How would you go about creating a good structure and plot?

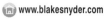 www.blakesnyder.com

WHAT MAKES A GREAT STORY?

It may seem counter-intuitive, but cameras and microphones are the least important things about filmmaking. What about actors, crew and money? All very important – especially the last one, but no, they do not make or break your film. Ironically, the most important thing is both the cheapest and most elusive item – your script. Without a great script, you have nothing.

A great story has fantastic characters through which the narrative is told. People watch movies for people – and that is why they are more important in the long run than the plot. Great characters mean your audience will have personas that reflect themselves and their passions, troubles, hopes and dreams. We want to identify with them and watch them overcome their problems. And we want great villains. They show the worst in all of us and are best when that 'worst' is something with which we sympathize.

A great story also has a plot that always feels fresh, new and surprising. The greatest sin you can commit as a storyteller is to bore the audience. You must grab the audience from the get go, and never let them go. You must keep the stakes rising, the jokes coming fast and furious and the drama always at a fever pitch. If you can do this, the rest will sort itself out. Good luck!

Blake – In my book *Save the Cat*, I have the Blake Snyder Beat Sheet, which contains the 15 beats that are in every story. It's a process of transformation – the hero starts out one way and ends another. If you put your hero through the obstacle course of those 15 beats, he will transform. A new device that I have created to help fulfill the transformation is called the Five Point Finale. This covers the five main points of Act 3 that all heroes go through in order to achieve a resolution. One thing to keep in mind is that these things work because they hit us on a gut level, so if you are shying away from structure because it's formulaic or hampers your creativity, you are misleading yourself.

Q – What do you suggest as ways to help write great characters?

Blake – The most important thing about any character is that they are pushed all the way back. When we first meet them their world has to be pocked with problems, which are usually 1000 different things masquerading as fear. The

1. It's easy to overwrite dialogue. Beware.

2. Speech comes in short sentences with simple words. Eavesdrop on a conversation in a café for research.

3. We often speak in metaphor and euphemism. Let the reader get the subtext of your point.

4. On the nose dialogue feels stilted. Avoid it.

5. Don't overuse punctuation marks.

6. Read your dialogue aloud or have a friend read it for you. You will see what sounds bad or is running long.

7. Don't be afraid of minimal dialogue or even no dialogue. A lot can be said in silence.

8. Rewrite!

story will be about how they get rid of those fears and problems. This will lead to conflict, which will lead to drama, which will get our attention. I think a trap that most filmmakers fall into is that they say, "Transforming isn't the way I envisioned it." But that is exactly what the audience *wants* to see.

Q – What is theme to you and what are some helpful ways of finding it?

Blake – Theme is the lesson learned by the hero. In my beat sheet I have a theme statement, which is a moment on page 5 where someone turns to the lead character and says something like, "He who has the gold makes the rules." At that moment the hero doesn't understand what that means – that is the theme. In the Pixar film *Cars*, on page 5 someone turns to Lightning McQueen and says "Racing ain't a one man deal, Lightning." That's the theme there. He's selfish to begin the story and he's selfless by the end. That is the lesson he learned. Many times you want to anchor theme to plot where in the course of the story there will be a debate whether the theme is true or not. All good movies are an up and down ripple of looking at every side of the theme. Theme is tied to and explored in the B story, which is usually the characters the hero meets in Act 2 in his new world. It can be the love story or the mentor relationship. These are the people who are teaching the spiritual lessons to the lead character.

Q – What are your opinions on finding your voice and writing good dialogue?

Blake – Finding your voice is a key element of a screenwriter or filmmaker's career. To me it is what do you do better than anyone else. What can hurt a screenplay is on the nose dialogue or a scene or

story premise that seems cliché. Just like your idea has to have irony, your characters need to be ironic and when they speak they must do so with irony. We want to be surprised by everything that happens.

Q – Are there any creative traps that writers can fall into and how do you get out of them?

Blake – Not knowing who your audience is. If your story is only interesting to you and a handful of people then you have a problem. The best way to avoid this, and most screenwriting issues for that matter, is go through all the steps I outline in *Save the Cat*. Get the idea, create a logline, pitch it, test it, break it out into the 15 beats, make sure the hero transforms, make sure the idea is big and grand enough, are there enough problems, make sure there is a spiritual reason for taking this journey, make sure there is a moral – if you can deliver those things, that's what makes a difference.

Q – Are there any mistakes that you see which drive you crazy?

Blake – I have a rule in my classes – no voiceover, no flashbacks, no dream sequences. I think those are crutches for a lot of beginners. Not that they don't belong in scripts, but if you can do without them it is a better exercise of your skills. Also not listening to criticism drives me crazy. Whether it's a friend, a civilian or someone in your writing group giving you a critique you need to listen to them. Feedback is a big part of filmmaking and if someone early on can give you a clue that something is amiss, you should pay attention. Now it's possible the feedback is wrong, but you should listen to it. And many times it's the message beneath what they are saying that is the true issue.

Q – Do you have any advice for new screenwriter/filmmakers?

Blake – This is the Golden Age for low budget filmmaking. You can start with a Youtube short and become a star and thereby break into the Hollywood system. You can make a short film, get into Sundance and then have a career making movies. There has never been a more democratic time. Even if you want to keep your movies small and idiosyncratic, you can market them that way and make a living doing it. Everyone is always looking for talent.

NOTE - Just weeks after we interviewed Blake, sadly he passed away.

WRITING FOR LOW BUDGETS
GENEVIEVE JOLLIFFE

Q – What makes a script suitable for low budget production?

Gen – I have written and collaborated on screenplays made for as little as ten grand, all the way up to a multi million dollar project that we sold to Warner Bros. Of course both are about a great story well told, but with the low budget feature, there is a huge amount of practical stuff that can just make your life easier. Right now though it's never been easier and cheaper to write and make a film.

Q – What kind of practical stuff makes you life easier?

Gen – When I made my first film, an actioner called *The Runner*, I learned heaps about script and logistics. Stuff like, keep your crew in one place. This means tailoring a story that can be told in one or two locations. A great example of this would be the movie *Bound*. I also learned that writing 'night time' or 'it's raining' in the script was great to visualise at the word processor, but a nightmare during production. So keep your locations minimal, and reduce any night time or atmospherics.

---

gen@guerillafilm.com   www.twitter.com/guerillagal

www.crazeepictures.com   www.guerillagal.com

Join us on Facebook at 'Guerilla Film Maker'

Keeping your characters to a minimum helps too, as there are less actors to deal with, and that means less makeup, costume, catering, cabs etc. This also forces you to be a better writer as you can't rely on script contrivances so readily. It really all does need to come from deep down inside the characters. And actors love that, so it's a win/win strategy. Cheaper production, better writing, better performances.

Q – How long should a low budget screenplay run?

Gen – Don't you mean how short? Really, it needs to be as short as you can make it. 80 to 90 pages is a good rule. If you have a 125 page script, it's either hugely overwritten or too big for your budget. So you need to cut.

Q – How do you cut a script without damaging it?

Gen – Ironically, most stories work better when trimmed down. It's like a distillation process. I rewrite every sentence and see if you can get the same message and information over, but in fewer words. Usually, I can.

You can also merge characters too, as often in the subplots, characters can perform multiple story functions. Three sisters become two for instance. It sounds weird when you have spent months on a script, but it's better you try it now than the producer and director getting a hacksaw out over lunch when they realise they just can't shoot it. I have heard of people being advised to just reformat their script to make it shorter, which I think is stupid. Stick to the standard format then you know where you stand.

WRITING LOW BUDGET

1. There's an inevitability that your script will be a little dialogue heavy. Make it fascinating.

2. Keep your characters to a minimum. See if you can cut or merge multiple characters into one.

3. Keep your locations to a minimum and preferably in places you can get for free.

4. Write something that can be shot during the day and outside. Less need for lighting setups. In the woods for instance.

5. Set the story in the present so there is no need for period or futuristic costumes and props.

6. Keep your script to 80-90 pages. It's less to film.

CONT...

7. Avoid visual effects, even if you are a whizz on After Effects. It all adds time and no-one is impressed by VFX, only great stories.

8. Avoid explosions, car crashes, etc. unless you are prepared to 'cut away' instead of showing the action (which can work very well).

9. Avoid snow, rain, mist and even exterior night if possible.

10. Avoid using animals or children. If you have to use kids, get older ones to play younger.

11. Audiences will watch anything, no matter how cheap, as long as the story keeps them engaged.

12. All these limitations MUST become your allies and inspiration.

Q – What concepts work best for low budget films?

Gen – More often than not it's a character study – so choose a really fascinating character. We made a serial killer thriller and the writing was so much easier because hey, he's a serial killer – whatever he says, it's gonna be interesting! We also pulled huge amounts from research and put it into the mouths of the characters and into the plot. Choosing really fascinating characters makes your life so much easier. So the story can be about interesting people stuck or locked into a single or limited locations.

Of course you can drift away from this model, but every new location, prop, situation, character etc., stretches your budget even further. Locations like 'the woods' or 'your uncles' country house' are great as you don't need to do any dressing. And when it really comes to it, almost any story can be told in the woods. Try it with your idea now. Can it be told in the woods? That kind of lateral thinking will also help make your story a little more unique too.

Q – What if you have a big event like a car crash?

Gen – We made a film called *Urban Ghost Story* and it had a spectacular car crash in it, but the whole film revolved on what happened in those few seconds. It was pivotal to both the setup and resolution, and so we did it properly with a professional stunt team. It was surprisingly cost effective for what we actually got on film. But in many other circumstances, I would say, can you play the scene as a memory? We the audience hear the sound while the survivor of the crash

SCRIPT DOCTOR
JULIE GRAY

... are things to think
...hoosing a story?

...o have an original and entertaining idea. I think a lot of new
...n that. Writers should get a logline down on paper and be
...movies are similar to this idea? When did they come out? Do I
...e twist on this idea? Really test that idea out before writing the
...yourself so much heartbreak later.

...e tips that you would give for creating a solid structure

...h great characters because structure is closely woven to
...ment. A character is going to experience an arc of change and
...sformation side by side with your structure, you will see a clo...
...at hero's journey. For example, the *call to adventure*, which i...
...ent, will happen around page 10. Your first act break, which is
...ter enters this new world from which they cannot return until
...ir arc, occurs around page 30 – so the connectivity of charac...
...ture is pretty closely tied. Ask yourself – are things getting

...iptdepartment.com   ... www.justeffing.com

...ptdepartment.com

...cebook page 'The-Script-Department'

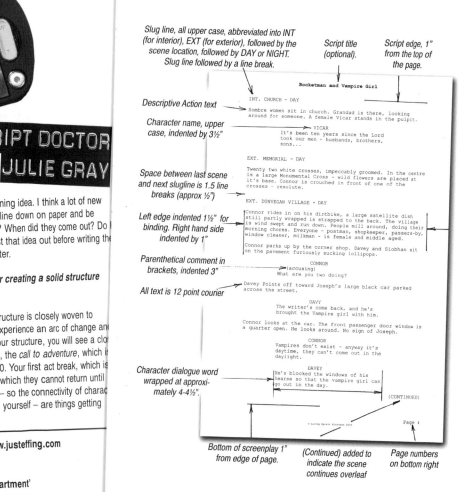

Slug line, all upper case, abbreviated into INT (for interior), EXT (for exterior), followed by the scene location, followed by DAY or NIGHT. Slug line followed by a line break.

Script title (optional).

Script edge, 1" from the top of the page.

Rocketman and Vampire Girl

INT. CHURCH - DAY

Descriptive Action text →
Sombre women sit in church. Grandad is there, looking around for someone. A female Vicar stands in the pulpit.

Character name, upper case, indented by 3½"
                    VICAR
          It's been ten years since the Lord
          took our men - husbands, brothers,
          sons...

EXT. MEMORIAL - DAY

Space between last scene and next slugline is 1.5 line breaks (approx ½")
Twenty two white crosses, impeccably groomed. In the centre is a large Monumental Cross - wild flowers are placed at it's base. Connor is crouched in front of one of the crosses - resolute.

EXT. DUNVEGAN VILLAGE - DAY

Left edge indented 1½" for binding. Right hand side indented by 1"
Connor rides in on his dirtbike, a large satellite dish still partly wrapped is strapped to the back. The village is wind swept and run down. People mill around, doing their morning chores. Everyone - postman, shopkeeper, passers-by, window cleaner, milkman - is female and middle aged.

Connor parks up by the corner shop. Davey and Siobhan sit on the pavement furiously sucking lollipops.

Parenthetical comment in brackets, indented 3"
                    CONNOR
              (accusing)
          What are you two doing?

All text is 12 point courier
Davey Points off toward Joseph's large black car parked across the street.

                    DAVY
          The writer's come back, and he's
          brought the Vampire girl with him.

Connor looks at the car. The front passenger door window is a quarter open. He looks around. No sign of Joseph.

                    CONNOR
          Vampires don't exist - anyway it's
          daytime, they can't come out in the
          daylight.

                    DAVEY
          He's blocked the windows of his
          hearse so that the vampire girl can
          go out in the day.

Character dialogue word wrapped at approximately 4-4½".

                                        (CONTINUED)

© Living Spirit Pictures 2005

Page 4

Bottom of screenplay 1" from edge of page.

(Continued) added to indicate the scene continues overleaf

Page numbers on bottom right

remembers, and maybe weeps? You get the emotional impact of the crash for the cost of one close up and a car crash sound effect. And again, this limitation gets the actors all excited too, and so you end up with something that connects with audiences more authentically and deeply.

Q – Any other script or story tips?

Gen – Sure. Things like, *'four policemen burst in'* should be changed to, *'two policemen burst in'*, to *'two plain clothed policemen burst in'*, to *'the characters hear the sound of the police bursting in'*.

We also learned in our serial killer thriller that you can have characters tell stories of big events in their lives, and you kind of get the production value of that event as the audience imagines it as they talk. Kind of like that scene in *Jaws* where Quint talks about his boat going down during WW2 and the men getting eaten one by one by the sharks. Great scene!

Audiences love mystery too – you don't need to show them everything. What was really in the bag in *Pulp Fiction*? Use that to your advantage. I know cinema is all about 'show don't tell...' but occasionally you can 'tell compellingly and don't show...'

Buy into the fact that you are making an exploitation film, in the true sense of the phrase – you are exploiting the resources you have around you. So do you know

WHAT IS A GENRE SCRIPT?

'Genre' refers to a group of films that are similar in tone, setting, topic and / or format. Examples would be 'comedy', 'horror', 'thriller' or 'action'. Genre films have conventions and audience expectations, like the body count getting higher and higher as a horror film moves along.

Watch some of your favorite films, of any genre, and you will start to get a feel for the patterns, rules and expectations of the genre. With this blueprint in mind, you can start structuring your own genre film – just remember the genre conventions may be recognizable, but your story, characters, location and events should be as original as possible.

anyone with a boat? Can you h...
OK now your film is set on a bo...

Q – What common mistakes d...

Gen – Perhaps the easiest one t...
over writing. Simply, there are too...
used.

And then, not getting into the stor...
your script is 120 pages long, from...
I would suggest that you could cut...
the first 40 pages. Often we don't...
setup, back story and explanation....
it as a writer, but we the audience '...
we just don't need it all explained to...
complex back stories can be distille...
single word and a look. I know it's a...
as much about the gaps and silences...
words.

All of this is a product of not rewriting...
believing that draft 1 or 2 is just peach...
to shoot.

Q – What advice would you offer a fil... embarking on their first feature with... budget?

Gen – It's always about the story. Alway...
back to that foundation. Fascinating cha...
doing compelling stuff, with a little myste...
in to keep people guessing about what wi...
happen. If you get that part right, you cou...
it on a cell phone and you will still win awa...
an agent and get work. Just make a comm...
to never be dull.

Q – Wh... about wh...

Julie – It's cruc...
writers struggle...
critical; what ot...
really have a u...
script. You'll s...

Q – What are... and plot?

Julie – It star...
character dev...
if you lay tha...
connection w...
your inciting...
when your c...
they comple...
arc, plot and...

 julie@...

 www.t...

Join c...

worse and worse? Is each scene really forcing the next scene to occur like dominoes?

I tell writers to remember that when we go to the movies, we want to see a story with a beginning, a middle and an end in such a way that we get resolution or satisfaction. So when thinking about your plot, you want to think about whether you're really delivering on that promise of change, redemption and closure. Things start out one way, then they get worse and worse until your hero finds a way to overcome, and become a new person in doing so. Real life is nothing like that. That's why we go to the movies.

Q – What are some tips on writing good action lines?

Julie – Be as pithy as possible. Writing a screenplay is a bit like haiku – truncated but highly evocative. Make sure your "voice" comes through in the writing. That means a reader can really get a sense of your personality when reading your script. You want to avoid writing more than four action lines in a row or there will be too much black on the page and that's harder for people to read. You don't want to write action that is blow-by-blow and too detailed. Use shorthand. That's what screenwriting really is. Shorthand with personality. If you are writing a particular genre, your action lines take on that genre. So thriller and horror action lines should read scary and exciting, comedy action lines should read funny, etc. Never write dry action lines.

Q – What are some great tips for writing dialogue?

SCRIPT EDITING

1. The art of screenwriting is 'saying the most with the least'.

2. Your script will be improved by a judicious edit. Trust us on this.

3. Try rewriting every sentence but with fewer words.

4. It isn't about great prose, but it should jump off the page. Fewer words often say more.

5. Try cutting out entire sentences. Does it still work? Is it better?

6. Take feedback and act on it – you will know in your gut if it's right.

7. Get some actors or friends to read the script aloud. It's a wake up call for sure!

8. Get to the action as quick as possible.

9. Remember. Less is more. Always.

WRITING NARRATION
(the bits between the dialogue)

1. Film is a visual medium so write ONLY what can be seen. Beware of phrases like 'he feels sad...'

2. Keep narration to three lines or less. If you go over, start a new paragraph. This makes for a faster read.

3. Don't overwrite. Keep it short and snappy.

4. Spice things up. Use onomatopoeia - i.e. 'ROOOAR' instead of 'a lion roars'.

5. Short sentences. Create tension.

6. Italicizing, <u>underlining</u> or **bolding** make things stand out. But don't overdo it.

7. Let your audience know where your characters are geographically to avoid confusion.

Julie – Dialogue should sound natural. One of the best exercises to sharpen those skills is to eavesdrop on conversations and listen to how people talk. People rarely say exactly what they mean. People use sarcasm. People joke. People can be overdramatic. So listen to the beats and the pauses and the subtext. If there is one thing that will kill your script and drive readers crazy, it is stilted, on the nose dialogue that is overly expository and doesn't reveal anything more about the character. You can have fun here. You can write characters with specificity as to how they talk. Dialogue tells us where your character is from and who he or she is – do they have habits? Are they from the South or another country? Are they pedantic? Are they an intellectual person?

Q – Would you advocate a table read to look for problems?

Julie – Yes. They are a great way to hear your script's flaws. Most writers get too close to their work. They think it is all there on the page. But having actors read your script is a different story. The things that are not working will stand out in living color and the things that are working will be so seamless.

Q – What do you see most often that drives you crazy in a new writer's script?

Julie – The thing that annoys me is the BOSH script. That's "Bunch Of Stuff Happens." These tend to be stories that have a soft premise which is entertainment-speak for a plot without tension, conflict or originality.

Q – What does a script consultant do and when should they be engaged?

Julie – A script consultant gives you notes and feedback on your script that goes beyond script coverage at a production company. That coverage is designed to weed out the good from the bad. A script consultant tells the writer what's working, what's not working and gives suggestions on how to fix it. My advice is to first get some feedback from some trusted friends and colleagues who are at least somewhat familiar with the world of film. Just to get a gut reaction. Next, if you have any friends who are in the industry and have some credibility, I would get their feedback. Then ultimately it is best to go to a consultant because they are not your friends. They are not going to bullshit you. They will tell you how your script stands up against others they have read in the genre including those that got made. They will tell you if it is commercial. If you wrote something identical to *Memento*, they are going to tell you it's just like *Memento* and therefore not going to do well in the marketplace. The range of cost is great. It can be as little as $85 to $300 to thousands of dollars. So you have to research and choose the analyst or the company that fits your vibe and budget.

Q - Is networking important for writers, and film makers?

Networking is crucial. Film is a very social business. You need to be meeting industry professionals who may be in a position to help you out down the line and you also need to be meeting your peers and fellow writers. Meeting other writers can be a great way to grow your network; you can get notes, feedback, advice and support through other writers. Meeting industry professionals can pave the way for

8. Use metaphors to get your ideas across.

9. Avoid repeating phrases or words. Buy a thesaurus!

10. Read your narration out loud and you will see when things are running long.

11. Look at your pages. If it looks dense, get aggressive and start rewriting or cutting.

12. Read professional screenplays to get a feel for how your script should read and look.

DO NOT underestimate how long it takes, and how hard it can be, to write a great script... And your movie can only be as good as the screenplay...

meetings, referrals or even landing representation. If you're not a member of a writer's group, consider forming or joining one. Online forums can be rich with information but beware those anonymous individuals who may be misleading at best and scathing at worst. In person networking is much more powerful, over all.

Q – What advice would you give a new filmmaker?

Julie – Watch a lot of movies that you love and want to emulate. This will help you learn about the craft. And never take the screenwriting aspect too lightly because if it's not on the page, it won't be on the screen.

"JAWS" (SEE PAGE TO RIGHT)
THE 'CLASSIC' THREE ACT STRUCTURE

We tell stories in one basic way, which has survived since we lived in caves. It will have a beginning, a middle and an end - the three act structure. There are many other so called 'script models', but this one is about the best place to start.

We have used JAWS as an example script as it is so well structured. For more on 3 Act Structures, read any of Syd Field's great books.

Act 1 (the beginning): lasts about ¼ of the running time of the film. Here we meet the characters including the villain, get to know the world and set the tone of the film (comedy, horror, etc.). You can have a prologue to help set up back-story before getting into the main portion of the film. Halfway through there will be an inciting incident that gets the story moving. You end with the Act 1 break, which is an event that launches us into the rest of the story.

Act 2 (the middle): lasts about ½ of the running time of the film. This is where your characters try to achieve the goal that has been set-up at the Act 1 break. Obstacles will be thrown in their path by external forces or their own internal misgivings, which they must overcome. At the midpoint of the film, there is a reversal of action. This means the heroes will have achieved some goal but in doing so it leads to bigger problems. ¾ of the way through Act 2, there is generally a power shift where the hero begins to weaken and the villain gains power. This ends at the Act 2 break where the hero is at their weakest and the villain is at their strongest.

Act 3 (the end): lasts about ¼ of the running time of the film. Everything comes to a head here. The hero must pick themselves up after the end of Act 2 and take on the villain for the climax of the story. They may or may not succeed, but the important thing is that they grow from the experience.

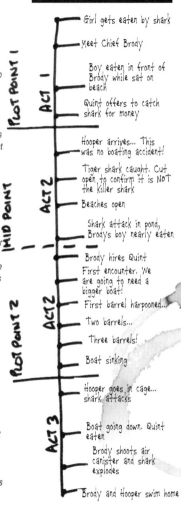

PLOT POINT 1

ACT 1

- Girl gets eaten by shark
- Meet Chief Brody
- Boy eaten in front of Brody while sat on beach
- Quint offers to catch shark for money

ACT 2

MID POINT

- Hooper arrives... This was no boating accident!
- Tiger shark caught. Cut open to confirm it is NOT the killer shark
- Beaches open
- Shark attack in pond, Brody's boy nearly eaten

ACT 2

PLOT POINT 2

- Brody hires Quint
- First encounter. We are going to need a bigger boat!
- First barrel harpooned...
- Two barrels...
- Three barrels!
- Boat sinking

ACT 3

- Hooper goes in cage... shark attacks
- Boat going down. Quint eaten
- Brody shoots air canister and shark explodes
- Brody and Hooper swim home

WRITING A SHORT FILM
CHRIS JONES

Q – You have written and made both shorts and features, why go back to shorts?

Chris – Writing *Gone Fishing* was a tactical move, to make a high quality film and try to win an Oscar™.

Q – How did you approach the script?

Chris – Like every script I have ever written. I avoided it for a great deal of time, terrified of failure. But at the same time, kind of stewing in the ideas. The first draft came out very quickly. I did three further drafts thereafter, working with several other writers who I gave carte blanche to edit and write whatever they liked. Of course, I could re-edit what they added later, but both Guy Rowlands and Martin Gooch both added amazing material to the script. I just kept it all shepherded so it stayed within my vision. Each draft was about a day's work, with a week or two of stewing between. Feedback from friends was vital too.

Q – Have you read lots of other short scripts?

✉ chris@guerillafilm.com   🗨 www.twitter.com/livingspiritpix

🏠 www.livingspirit.com   🅱 www.chrisjonesblog.com

📘 Join our Facebook group 'Guerilla Film Maker'

EXTERNAL VERSUS INTERNAL

The best stories are dramatic. And the best way to achieve drama is to create obstacles, problems and dilemmas, which your characters much overcome. There are two basic places where these can come from – the external world of a character and the internal personality flaws of a character.

External obstacles come from the villain. Either they are directly set up by them (such as destroying your best weapon) or come about from one of their actions (having to cross a minefield because the villain destroyed the easier path across a bridge).

Internal obstacles come from a character's personal demons such as a fear of flying, impulsiveness or low self esteem from an overbearing parent. A character must attempt to overcome these issues throughout the story in order to grow as a character.

Overcoming external problems can instill confidence in a character to face their internal issues. Likewise, coming to terms with an internal flaw can give someone the empowerment to take on external obstacles.

Chris – Yes. Most of what I read is overwritten. To say they are also cliché is also true but a little unfair as cliché's would get written out in later drafts. So I guess what I see is generally overwritten and underdeveloped. If only the writers would commit to a couple of redrafts! I also see that there are two broad camps of short film. One is about entertainment and a broad message, the other is about observation and interpretation and is a rarefied experience. Of course there is huge variance between these two models. I would put *Gone Fishing* very much in the entertainment camp.

Q – Did you read many books on short screenplays?

Chris – I had a look at some but I did not find much useful in them. A micro budget short film should really be conceived, shot, edited and up on youtube in a few weeks. Too many short film makers think of their short film as a ticket to the big time. It can be of course, and that's what I tried to do, but I was doing that

with three feature films behind me – and it took a
year of hard work too. You can't 'get it' from a book
or a course, you really only learn the craft of
screenwriting by hammering the keyboard, getting
it to set, getting it in post and finally putting it in
front of an audience. Do that, then read books and
do courses. Then make another film, and so on.

**Q – What is the difference between writing a
short and feature?**

Chris – The big one is the scale of the project. Not
the story you tell, but the fact that it's 15 pages
and not 120. You can read it over coffee, and
remember the whole thing! With a feature script,
so much time is spent dealing with domino effect
changes to the script. Of course that happens in
shorts, but it's not the same, mainly because you
don't have so many subplots and characters. I
have to say, after working in features, it was a joy
to write a short. There is a myth that writing a
great short is harder than writing a great feature.
Utter nonsense, propagated by people who have
never written features no doubt!

Q – Is there a story format for shorts?

Chris – I suppose so. By their very nature, shorts
tend to be a little avante garde and experimental.
And so they should be. It's too big a risk to make
those 'out there' creative choices on a feature, but
a short is much more disposable if things go
wrong. So short film makers can and do take more
creative risks.

I have seen a number of basic story formats. Many
follow a character through a moment in their lives,
where a choice needs to be made, kind of a
minimalist plot that is big on character. Others

follow a more traditional three act structure and tell well conceived and executed narratives. The twist in the tail is always an audience pleaser, but it must be done well.

For me I have read too many scripts set in inner city environments with 'young people issue-tastic' narratives. I guess it's a symptom of the emerging film maker group and the fact that many may be in film schools in cities. Nothing wrong with it, but I would always choose to be different.

Q – Are there clear genres too?

Chris – Yes. For instance, there is a thriving and very 'out there' horror short film scene, complete with ghettoised film festivals and fan bases. All the same questions asked of features get asked of shorts though, especially when programming at a festival. What kind of movie is it? What's it called? Do you have a poster? Who is in it?

When you roll the whole thing into one package – complete creative control, fast turnaround, the ability to tell stories that would never get made as a feature, film festivals waiting with open arms, and ultra cost effectiveness - shorts do look very attractive.

Q – So what makes a great short script?

Chris – Conflict and controversy always play well in short films. As a writer, you have no commissioning editor or sales agent breathing down your neck so that can be liberating. You really do have creative control, and so you can go to greater extremes. The shorts I have seen that have worked very well often take a contemporary issue and then push it to the logical ends.

6. Try to get both sides of the story. It will make your doc seem less biased.

7. You need obstacles and villains to create drama – otherwise you are making a promotional piece. They can be people, things or institutions. For the latter, try to get a person to represent it.

8. If the doc is following you, then you must grow as a person.

9. When choosing someone's story to follow, make sure they are open, honest and will tell you all.

10. Documentary filmmaking is fiction filmmaking backwards. You make pictures and then create the story in the edit room as opposed to following a script and making the pictures afterwards. Hire a great editor!

Personally, I don't like those films, but I do see that it is great story telling and that it can open doors and launch careers.

I think minimalism is also a trait of shorts – it is of features too, 'write the most with the least', but I think shorts in particular, work well when told in a very minimalist way. Audiences are really paying attention when they watch a short simply because it's such an unusual story format for most people. And so you can take greater story risks and allow people to find the narrative, rather than laying it out in front of them, which sometimes happens on features.

Q- What advice would you offer someone writing a short script?

Chris – Choose a great subject, something about which you are passionate. Write from the heart, then re-edit and re-draft. Keep refining the script, it's almost impossible to do too much of it, and it always comes back to haunt you in the edit if you don't. I would also get to some festivals and watch loads of shorts in a theatre, ideally not online as it's not the same. Most of all though, get out there and do it, and commit to the next film being just 'the next film' and not the 'highlight of your career'. Do it and move onto the next.

Finally, I would suggest you try and get involved in editing a film. You will be amazed at how much you can take out, and when you see other short films, you will also be amazed at how much the film makers often chose to leave in. You will then learn to take it out at the script stage and save resources.

Q – You have an online course about making shorts?

Screenplay formatters
1. The industry standard is Final Draft, but its not cheap.
2. Celtx has a free script formatter that can be downloaded from www.celtx.com and works on PC, Mac and Linux.

Chris – Yes, when we made *Gone Fishing* and got so close to the Oscars, we documented it all and filmed a two day workshop about the journey we undertook and what we leaned. It has proven very useful for film makers and I am delighted that we have helped them make better choices and better use of limited resources. You can check it out at www.gonefishingseminar.com

CHAPTER TWO
PLANNING

THE GUERILLA FILM
MAKERS POCKETBOOK

Q – What is the job of a producer on a low budget or short film?

Gen – It's largely blood, sweat, grit and determination – it's about keeping the whole project going when there are no real resources. When I am producing, I work closely with the whole team and everyone helps out with whatever is needed, be it a new location, actor, prop or just a cup of tea. It's all hands on deck! Even the director gets their hands dirty.

Q – How does it all begin?

Gen – Often out of necessity. Someone just has to start solving problems. For many film makers, myself included, producing is part of just getting the job done. Unless you know anyone more qualified who is willing to work for nothing, it usually means that you are the producer. That said, there does need to be a dividing line between the director and producer, assuming they are not one and the same – which is possible but not recommended due to workload, especially during the shoot.

gen@guerillafilm.com   www.twitter.com/guerillagal

www.crazeepictures.com   www.guerillagal.com

Join our Facebook group 'Guerilla Film Maker'

Producing a low budget film is a crazy mix of production management (organizing people and stuff), line producing (getting great deals), juggling problems, not going to sleep for 2 months, haggling with agents, sweet talking policemen, acting as cast and crew therapist and pretty much anything else you can imagine! You are constantly flitting between problems in a state of crisis management. It's all a product of working with inexperienced people (oneself being one of those people!) and having no real resources to dip into when it goes wrong – and it always goes wrong!

Q – Is it better to work with a partner?

Gen - In my experience, guerilla film projects evolve out of relationships, so yes I have always worked with a partner, sometimes producing, sometimes writing, sometimes directing. A project has a much better chance of making it to set if a producer and director collaborate from a concept level as everyone is so much more invested and acting as one unit. When you team up with a 'complimentary' partner, all sorts of magical stuff begins to happen. When you are down, they are up. If you are good at writing, but hate accounts, they are good at accounts and hate writing. It's about finding someone who compliments your skills and you compliment theirs. If you then both have drive and a shared vision, then that's when the magic happens, and it can happen VERY quickly.

Q – How do you fund a film?

Gen – We have always sought and found private investment and that has worked very well for us. It's about getting passionate about the project as people tend to invest in the film makers more than the film. But it's essential you are honest with people about your experience and the likelihood that they could lose money. The chances of success are very slim – but every few years there is a breakout film like *Paranormal Activity*. The chance that yours is that film is very small, but... it could be the one. Only time will tell.

The kind of deals we have cut with investors have varied, but in the end, the simplest is always best. We ended up with a simple 'loan agreement' that said, you loan us $10,000 to make the film (usually as a group of investors making up that ten grand) and when we sell the film, every dollar that comes through the door will be split 50 / 50 between us (the film makers), and them (the investors group). We also added a clause that said we could deduct reasonable expenses

FORM A COMPANY?

1. If you are learning film, or if you only intend to share your work with friends or on YouTube, you may not need to create a company.

2. If you want to sell you film and make money, you will need to do accounts and may also want to form a company.

3. Keep your receipts. Even movie tickets could be claimed against tax.

4. Call an accountant and ask for a free one hour consult. Ask for a free consult with a local bank manager too.

6. Seek advice from anyone you know who runs their own company.

7. Take a book keeping course.

8. Forming a company sounds great, but it's a lot of hassle and costs money. Make sure it's the right choice before doing it.

too, like annual accounts and some running costs, but they must be reasonable costs.

Q – Should you start a company?

Gen – Yes. As you can begin to offset all your camera and editing equipment against tax, you look more professional with a company (with business cards), and perhaps most important, you are now learning 'how to run a company' - and the business side of film making is as important as any creative aspect of film making. It's usually the creative stuff we have fallen in love with, and so we tend to avoid the business side. Doing accounts is just not as much fun as writing a script - well not in my books! But like a script, you need your accounts to be done properly or your whole empire will collapse.

Q – What equipment does a producer need?

Gen – Not much really. A phone, a computer with internet and a printer / copier. That's pretty much a mobile 'production office' and you can setup business almost anywhere there is power and Wi-Fi. You don't need any special qualifications, contacts or equipment. Just passion, a great idea and the ability to convince people it is such a great idea that they should get involved too.

Q – From what I have read about other film makers and how they have made their films, it seems that producing is like operating in constant crisis. Is it really that bad?

Gen – It can be! The key is adequate planning and realistic goals. You spend your time constantly projecting into the future to anticipate problems and deal with them before they blow up in your

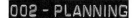

face. And of course there are so many variables on a film shoot that this is almost impossible – but the very act of projecting forward and figuring out solutions prepares you for the unforeseen. Try and surround yourself with helpers who can protect you from smaller problems. Big problems will of course work their way up the chain of command until they land in your lap, but smaller ones should be dealt with by the people who surround you. That way you can devote yourself to the big issues and not get entangled in time consuming and often over emotional smaller problems.

Q – What makes your life easy?

Gen – Having the story based in as few locations as possible. Minimal cast means less hand holding and ferrying around. A tight script with no baggage that wastes resources. Of course enough money to pull it off always helps, but most of the time the ability to make the movie with *what you have* is all the money you really need. The cliché is true at every level of production – *'there is never enough money, time or light'*. Don't wait for money, take the plunge and go with what you have, but be smart about how you use it.

For me, the thing that is most important is the knowledge that the concept, genre, casting and the execution of all of our resources, will result in a picture that is marketable. I know from experience that film making is a long haul and you need to be able to sell your work. It's not something that is negotiable or to be embarrassed about – it should be up front and centre stage. We MUST sell this movie.

Q – What advice would you offer a new film maker?

Gen – Learn all the different skills and jobs in the film making process, such as sound recording, production management, editing, writing – all of it – as early in your career as possible. You don't need to be an expert in each, but you do need a good understanding of as much of it as possible. This will give you a great foundation from which you can deal with daily problems during a production.

Aim high – many film makers fail because they are just not ambitious enough. But be smart in that ambition too. It must be achievable and you must have a strategic plan that you can execute right now, or at least in the very near future.

Most important is to just get out there and keep making movies and learning.

FUNDING
CHRIS JONES

Q – How much should I spend on a film?

Chris – That depends on you, your film and where you are currently sitting in your career as a film maker. Generally, a trend we have seen over and over is that people spend too much money, too early in their career. They make a great short and think they are ready for a feature, and then they get a lot of money based on that short, and end up messing up their big break. You don't want to do that as, by definition, you can only make a 'first feature film' once, and people rarely give you a second chance.

The nightmare scenario is going into a meeting and pitching a great idea only to be asked how your last film performed, then having to tell them, 'it made no money'. I hear it over and over: 'If only I knew then what I know now, and if only I could have that first chance again, I would do it all differently.'

Pace your career and make a strategy whereby, when you find real money (and you will), that you can spend that money wisely on a film that will serve both your career AND your investors. Before taking any big money, I suggest most new film makers should produce a micro budget feature for $1,000 so that they get the experience of story telling in 90 minutes. It's so very different to making shorts.

---

chris@guerillafilm.com

www.twitter.com/livingspiritpix

www.livingspirit.com

www.chrisjonesblog.com

Join our Facebook group 'Guerilla Film Maker'

THE PRODBLEM WITH DEFERRED FEES

One way film makers have kept budgets down, is to offer 'deferred fees'... 'work now and we will pay you from the profits'. We don't recommend deferred fees. Not because we don't feel you should not share in the success of your film, but because your film is most likely not going to make any money. And even if it does, it will be a small amount. Only one in a thousand films becomes a Paranormal Activitysuccess.

But for the outsider looking in, because you are a great sales person and you push your film out there, your film might look like it could be the next Paranormal Activity. And if that happens, you will get calls from irate crew members chasing their deferred fee from a perceived pot of gold that just doesn't exist. It makes for very bad future relationships.

If you must do deferred fees, make all your accounts transparent so that people can really see the state of play. That usually silences any complaints. If a crew member is insistent on a deferred fee, they may be getting involved for all the wrong reasons. It may be wise to move on.

Q – Where do you get money for low budget films?

Chris – I wish I had a straight answer. I could cite you literally hundreds of films where the financing has utilised a different model each time. And with social networking, it seems anyone can reach anyone else now. And that relationship could lead to your next investor, contributor or sponsor.

Q – Give us some ideas of how to fund a film.

Chris – First off, for low budgets, the best money to raise is the money you don't spend. So keep your budget down by being a cunning producer. Second, have a mix of funding ideas operating in symphony. There are online websites for people to make donations, but you'll struggle to raise any significant money this way. Have a go, but unless your idea really motivates a large group of people, you're going to struggle. Everyone is now trying 'crowd sourcing' like this, and once everyone is doing something, it's time to look elsewhere.

I definitely suggest you should look to friends and family for small 'family sourcing' donations. But keep those amounts of cash small and manageable. You

*1. Where possible, fulfill
any promises made. It
may not always be
possible to fulfill a
promise (one of the
disadvantages of low
budget film making), but
make it a priority to do so
at almost any cost.*

*2. Regular updates can
be delivered on a secure
website or emailed
PDFs.If the line of
communication goes
cold, so will the investor.*

*3. Press - this is great for
keeping people happy.
Everyone associates
press coverage with
success, but beware, this
may produce a false
sense of financial returns
on the part of the
investors.*

*4. Several low budget
pictures have allowed
investors to act in the
film in return for cash. It
works and everyone is
happy. Beware of
problems if their scene is
cut - make this possibility
known in advance.*

don't want to take any money that you must pay
back, as owing money to friends and family is a
terrible weight on the creative soul. Plus, you may
need to go back to them for more money in the
future.

And for myself with these small donations, I am
always very clear that there will be no financial
returns. It is not an investment. It's a contribution (I
don't like the word donation either, for me it feels a
little too beggar like).

***Q – Why would anyone just give a film maker
some money like this?***

Chris – You have a lot to offer. With blogging,
webisodes and social media, you can take a
contributor on an amazing creative journey. Plus
you can offer credits on the film, a copy of a
signed DVD, tickets to a swanky premiere, set
visits, posters etc. To most people, if they know
you, if they believe in YOU (not the film), they will
be prepared to risk a small amount of money on
what will give them the nice fuzzy feeling that they
are helping, as well as a good story to share with
colleagues and friends.

The psychological distinction is that they are
buying 'an experience' and not donating to a cause
or investing in a business. So £50 or £100 is still a
lot of money for people to just 'give', but if you
deliver on what you promise, they will get value for
money – it's the same price as an expensive night
out on the town, or a birthday present for a loved
one. And once one person is hooked, encourage
them to invite all their friends too. It grows virally. I
do feel film makers need to move beyond the
ghetto of other film makers on Facebook and in
the Twitterverse. I see a lot of film makers asking

film makers for money! And I cannot stress how vital a 'personal connection' can be with this model.

Q – What about investors who put in cash?

Chris – Yes, getting back to where money comes from. There are all manner of legal entities into which people with money can invest cash, get tax relief or some other benefit, but for that you will need to be setting up a production company and hiring lawyers and accountants, all of which costs money. If you are ready for that structure in your career and if you can raise that extra money, then it's a good idea.

For others, we have operated investment as 'a loan' with a premium. It's a straight deal where an investor puts in say $1,000, and if the budget is $10,000, they get 10% of the investors share. It's simple. Then from sales of the film, from the very first dollar, we split it 50/50 between the film makers and investors. So the investor in this example would get 5% of all gross receipts from the very first dollar. This works because it feels fair, it's very simple and easy to remember. There is an example contract on the www.guerillafilm.com website, though you MUST get it looked over by your own lawyer and accountant before utilising.

To help, we have always created a document about the film, the company, the film makers, added photos and artwork, budgets, schedules etc., and passed that around. It isn't a direct invitation to invest, more a kind of 'what we are doing' pamphlet. Creating that document always helps organise your thoughts, set goals and deadlines, and excite others. People often read it

5. Treat them as a VIPs and introduce them to the cast and crew. They are, after all, the people who funded your dream.

7. All correspondence should be impeccably presented. Checking spelling, formatting and accuracy before sending out should be second nature but often isn't.

8. If things are going badly, let them know. Investors would rather know things are going badly than hear nothing at all.

7. Give them a credit at the end of the film.

8. A micro budget feature film is a VERY long term investment, maybe 15 years. Consider how you are going to manage that commitment.

9. Above all, be honest and stay in touch.

and ask 'How can I help?' In this day and age of the Internet, it's a good idea to print it on nice glossy paper too, it will make you distinct.

Q – How much contact with the production do you need to give investors?

Chris – Well if you are doing a good job for your crowd sourcing people, such as running the blogs and Facebook pages etc., most investors will be happy with that. Remember, they are investing in you - the film maker - and not so much in the film or business itself. So they want to feel connected. If you want to offer more sensitive financial details, set up a private area of your website where they can log in and view details online. You want to minimise how much work you need to do to service their expectations as that can eat up resources, and you want to be using those resources to cast your film, rewrite the script, design a poster etc.

Q – Should you start a company?

Chris – If it's a commercial proposition, yes. If it's a learning project or a film that you are using only as a calling card – maybe…maybe not. You should get insurance and open a dedicated bank account though, just to keep everything clean.

Q – What is the real chance of an investor getting money back?

Chris – It's a tough marketplace out there, and films are selling for shockingly small amounts of money. There are so many films available it has become a buyer's market. If you focus on targeted theatrical releases which you manage, DVD sales which again you manage, and then work hard for TV deals, and international sales, you should make some money back. But of course, the more you spend, the more you need to recoup. There is no easy answer to this. Sales agent Julian Richards, whose interview is in the sales section of this book, offers an insight into the real value of a film, not the mythological value.

Q – What about grants, arts bodies and government money?

Chris – There is money out there, all over the world. But my experience of that kind of funding has never been great. It usually comes with lots of strings attached. It could be tax benefits, but you need to shoot it in a specific place, or it could be funding from an arts body, but you need to tell a specific story. And

CREWING UP... WHERE TO FIND CREWS

Whether you are shooting a camera test, an Oscar™ contending short or a micro budget feature, you will need a crew.

As your film making ambitions and productions grow, so will your crew needs. At the same time so will your relationships with other film makers, and those relationships lead to crews who are looking for experience right now. Relationships and personal referrals from other film makers are by far the best way to find crew, but you need to be in the game to build those relationships, so get going now. There are plenty of resources on the web too, such as Mandy.com, ShootingPeople.org and Craigslist.org. Use them and share any new resources you find with your community.

At the most basic level, you simply need help. It could be switching lights on and off or making tea for an actor, all the way up to operating Steadicam or performing complex stunts. So why would anyone help you? There are two main reasons. First is experience (they get to learn while you pick up the cost of their education). What if they screw up? Well that's why they are doing it for free (or next to nothing). The second reason is for a credit as they are building their resume. There is a third reason too, which is simply that people love making movies. It's kind of an addiction.

There are some crew members who will need to commit to the long haul too. You may need help in your office months before the shoot, and these guys would be what we call 'production assistants'. They help fix any problem thrown up by the production. You may need an editor too, one who may need to commit to months of work. Editors and PAs are special crew who become close allies on your journey, so choose wisely.

It's important to treat you crew with the utmost respect. You are a new film maker, so you are going to be underfunded and inexperienced. Shit will happen. It's how you deal with it that counts. This is why planning and prepping is so vital to your success. It's a small world and word gets around if you behave like an idiot.

when any kind of committee gets involved, it will probably take longer to make, and may end up becoming a pale reflection of what you set out to do as so many other people end up 'having their input'. It does work well for some film makers though, so you should pursue it and create relationships. It just hasn't worked for me in the past.

Q – What mistakes do you see over and over?

Chris – The same mistakes we have all made, because we fall passionately in love with our films. We believe completely, and ultimately promise too much. That's why I don't like doing deferred fees now. It sets up film makers to create poor relationships three years down the line. Just be careful what you promise your investors (and crew are investors if you offer deferred fees). I find a good way to express it would be, 'There is a good chance you will lose your money, a good chance you will get some of it back, a smaller chance you will get it all back, and very small chance that this could go through the roof and be the next *Paranormal Activity*.

Perhaps the biggest mistake is taking money from sources that, if you cannot repay, will cause you serious problems. So convincing a family member to mortgage a home, or using your credit cards heavily, all are very bad ideas. And I know film makers will continue to do this! So you have been warned!

Q – What advice would you offer a new film maker?

Chris – There is a fundamental contradiction at the heart of funding a low budget movie if you make one assumption – *you need to pay back the money.*

First, there is never enough money, time and light to get the movie produced in the way you want. Second, the more you invest, the more likely it is you won't fully recoup your budget. It's a dilemma that has no direct answer. You must find your own way to make this equation work for you, your investors and your backers.

Be aware that you are wearing rose tinted spectacles when it comes to your film. In reality the relationship between you and your film is more like dating a crazy person. At first it's thrilling, but can quickly become very hard work if you don't manage your own expectations, and those of others around you. Just remember to enjoy it and have fun.

CREWING UP... HOW BIG IS YOUR CREW?

One of the biggest expenses on any film is that of your cast and crew. Just feeding, transporting and equipping them eats a sizeable chunk of any production budget. And then there is the pay! So the question becomes, how big is your crew? There are several major departments on any film. They are always headed up by the Producer and Director...

1. Production and organization – *Headed by the producer, with production assistants, assistant directors (who co-ordinate between the office and set), location managers, runners, script continuity, drivers and catering. Can include the writer and Director once production begins.*

2. Camera & lighting – *a department that can expand rapidly as camera formats move up the quality ladder. Includes lighting cameraman, camera assistants, focus pullers, grips (moving the camera), gaffers (lighting).*

3. Sound – *Usually a two person team of sound recordist and boom swinger.*

4. Design – *Covers make-up, costume, production design, location dressing, props, set dressing, special effects. Often the most neglected area for low budget productions, and that neglect often shows too!*

5. Cast – *That's the actors, and they do need special treatment.*

6. Post Production – *Editor and edit assistants. There may be conduits between Camera and Sound and Post Production to facilitate the movement of the footage (sound and picture). There may also be someone who is dedicated to backing up and archiving data, especially if you are shooting digitally and capturing files and NOT to tape.*

Whether you are a crew of two or an army of thirty, you need to cover each and every department base.

DOING DEALS
IVAN CLEMMENTS

Q - How do you get great deals?

Ivan - I should preface this with the fact that you need to be passionately driven by the project that you are involved in. If you are not sold on the project, then how can you sell anyone else? Pick up the phone and start talking to people. It's amazing how much people want to help in this business. And everyone is very forgiving of naiveté. It seems to me that almost everyone has been through mountains of crap to get where they are. Unlike school, where inflicting the same pain on newbies as was once metered on them is held in high regard, peers in the film business seem to actually want to help. How mad is that?

Q - How do you deal with the fear of picking up the phone and cold calling?

Ivan - Making the first call is always the hardest. It's a bit like approaching someone you fancy. You're full of excitement but you fear rejection. Just take the plunge. If you get rejected first time, remember, there are plenty of others to try. Have you seen the size of the *'Knowledge'* in the UK? Or the *'Hollywood Creative Directory'* in LA? Both are big directories, really big. Another great way to look at it is not that it's cold calling, but rather rapport practice (thanks to Gary Craig for that).

Q - Why would anyone give you something for free?

ivan@withitfilms.com

Ivan - I never view it as getting something free. I prefer to view it as relationship development. What you're saying to whomever you are trying to get to collaborate with you is this, 'roll with me on this and you'll get my future business and referrals'. And you better be good on your word. If a lab gives you an unbelievable deal, make sure you go back to that lab with paid work. This will give you credibility and the word will spread. Go bad on your word and people won't let you use their toilet let alone notice that you're alive.

Q - Why do you think others don't get such great deals?

Ivan - I'm not sure really. I can only tell you what I do to achieve results. Be funny. Most of the time this business is merciless if you're not on the creative side. Make someone's day with a giggle and you'll get miles ahead. Lift spirits, cajole, be cheeky, ask for the moon always, always be VERY thankful for whatever you get. Make them feel like merciful gods. People like to feel that they have done something amazing for someone else. Don't you?

Q - How do you know what to ask for? If it costs 100 grand, how much should you try and get it for?

Ivan - Something I learnt early on is never to pay rate card. If you've actually got money to spend, you should be able to get at least 40% off that quoted rate. That was minimum for me. 50-60% is achievable. It's not unusual. Here's a deal I negotiated with a well known film stock company which we'll call Major Film.

DOING DEALS

1. Don't buy it or rent it, borrow it from a friend.

2. Be polite but unreasonable in your request for what you need. Be flexible too. People usually want to help.

3. Offer to pay upfront for a bigger discount.

4. Ask for advice first, then ask if they can help. That way, when you ask for help, they already have a relationship and they also know that you have no money. Their advice will probably be useful too!

5. The more prestigious your film, the more you can get deals. So aim very high in your concept, shooting formats and casting.

6. Always pay your bills on time. Other film makers will follow in your footsteps.

CONT...

I needed 100,000 feet of 35mm stock. Rate at the time was 24p per foot which came to £24K + tax. At the time, this was way beyond anything I could afford. I invited the chief sales exec for a drink in a bar on Wardour Street, central London. I began by talking about HIM and his life (we later on became good friends). I definitely wanted to go with this company as they were much more friendly and accessible to guerrilla film makers like myself. After a few drinks we drifted into the deal. I said 'look Joe (real name withheld), I'm only doing this deal with Major Film because of you. But I'm absolutely flat broke'.

'So Joe', I continued 'How about this? I've got £8K I can give you today if you can defer the balance till we hit profits and the VAT until I get that back next quarter?' It was the ballsiest ask I'd made so far, but also the easiest in a way as I had no choice. There was no more money. Joe laughed, 'you've eaten the ass out of my trousers.' We shook on it and I bought another round.

Q - What helps sell the deal?

Ivan - Yeah, this is where you can get really creative. Get a great DP who's looking to break out of commercials and into film. They're usually wealthy and will happily work for free. Then when you go to hire equipment and lights, mention who the DP is and that he's agreed to use them exclusively on the next few jobs if they'll give you a major deal. Or, if you've managed to land a known actor, use that to attract a great DP or other great cast. I got a top class camera operator on my second film simply because he'd done several huge Hollywood movies and had a month to kill. Sell the sizzle of your project and people will come. Sometimes they'll work for peanuts and

---

7. If you cannot pay your bills, stay in close contact with the folks to whom you owe money.

8. Communicate over the phone as much as you can, or better, in person. And only use email to follow up. Email is not an ideal way to ask for help.

9. Give gifts to those who really helped – a cheap bottle of wine works wonders. Make friends and keep friends for the next one.

10. Offer credits and tickets to the première, but don't expect people to be wowed by this nowadays.

11. If you get paying work, offer those who helped you out with paid work or rental. Look after those who have helped you by paying back the debt.

12. Get it in writing.

13. If you get a free deal on kit, they will still want you to have insurance, so it's never really free.

sometimes even free or deferred payment. As a guerrilla film maker, you've got to be creative. Tell a DP you've got an A lister gagging to play lead role (unfortunately the actors often pull out at the last minute – but by then everyone is committed).

Q - Where do you find investors?

Ivan - This is the harder side of getting your film made. You've got the great script and now you need the finance to make it. Unless you're independently wealthy and can finance the project, you're going to have to raise the finance elsewhere. And there's no easy answer to finding investors. Family and friends. Network through them, they usually know someone who knows someone. I personally prefer private investment as you are in control of the project. If you go for public money sources, like the Film Council in the UK, or other deals in other

E-FAIL...
HOW TO MAKE ENEMIES AND ALIENATE PEOPLE!

'Write a long email about your amazing film, send it to someone you have never met, and it's sure never to get read.

Most people send an email when they want help. That's all well and good, but... people help people they know. People they like. People they feel a connection with. That's one reason why nepotism exists. So you need to get to 'know' the people who can help you – and that's why networking is so very important in this business.

Sending an email is the least effective way to make a new connection. Email is primarily a tool for short introductions, short fact based communications, and of course, gossip. Yet some people write pages of information about their film, making astonishing requests at the end, and all without knowing the recipient personally! Those emails are headed for the delete button.

Pick up the phone. Write a letter. Drop in and say hello. Offer to buy coffee, a drink or lunch. Create a real world personal connection where you can really interact.

BUDGET AND MONEY

1. You will go over budget! So plan for that.

2. There are no rules. You can get everything for free if you work hard and people like you. Try before you buy!

3. It's easy to cost out kit. Make a spreadsheet and add it all up.

4. People are harder to cost, as they come and go, and will want feeding and transport. Keep a close eye on these costs.

5. Be meticulous about keeping records and check everything. Get a left brained friend to help.

6. Always get a receipt.

7. Pay your bills promptly. If you can't pay promptly, call and explain.

8. Don't forget post, sales, PR and festivals. They cost too.

countries, there are always strings attached and hoops to jump through. But if you're happy with that, all well and good.

Q - What were your biggest mistakes as a producer?

Ivan - Underestimating the catering budget. I can't tell you how important this is on set. On my first feature, where the money was tight, I had near rioting because of the poor quality of the food. I acted fast and all was ok. FEED YOUR CREW PROPERLY!!! Especially the camera crew or you're likely to find a dolly wedged somewhere fairly unpleasant.

Though I successfully made two features with people working for deferred fees (the only way I managed what I did), I would advise not taking this route as it takes away some of your power. You're reliant on good will and have to work that much harder to keep everyone on your side. From their point of view, they don't have to take any shit, and can walk any time. On my second film, I had to constantly replace camera crew and gaffers because they had to take paid work when it came up. Praise your crew as often as possible. Everyone wants to hear they are doing a good job. On set it will often become VERY stressed and from time to time, people will blow. Let them do it, and let them do it to you if possible and simply soak it up and don't react. Walk away once they've finished and talk to them later. It's usually momentary and in time will seem insignificant.

Q - What advice would you offer a new film maker?

Ivan - That's rather a broad question. First, obviously read GFMH! Do any of Chris' courses while he still has a chance to do them. Do Dov Simmens. Read Robert Rodriguez' 10 minute film school which is free online. Then get to it. Set a date that you're actually going to start principal photography no matter what.

Raise as much money as you can and actually start filming. Make a feature first, don't waste time with a short unless you have a very good reason for doing so (you can read all about why Chris and I decided to go down the short route in his book).

Features are much easier to sell than shorts. But seriously, get or write a great script that means something to you, challenges values, makes people think. You will only learn the true craft of film making by doing it. It's wonderful, fulfilling, scary, heartbreaking, back breaking, exciting, fun...the list goes on. And I can't get enough of it. Good luck to all of you.

THE BEST MONEY YOU RAISE IS THE MONEY YOU NEVER SPEND!

BLAG IT, BEG IT, HOWEVER YOU DO IT, GET IT FREE!

Q – Production Assisting - what are the challenges?

Judy - First of all – leave your pride at the door! Whether it's your first job out of college or you're 40 years old and you've given it all up to finally pursue your film making dreams, you must be prepared to do <u>anything</u> and <u>everything</u> that's asked of you. Even if you're clearly over qualified. On low-budget films the lines between roles can easily become blurred as you'll always have a fraction of the crew you'd expect on bigger budget productions. So if it's just you and the runner in the office and the runner has been sent out on an errand, then while he or she is away, people will look to you to get the coffee, organize lunch or photocopy call sheets even though it's not technically part of your job description.

On small productions the troubleshooting and problem solving can often become very personal. The last production I worked on we shot in approximately 8 locations but only paid for 1. We utilized over 40 extras and only paid for 10. And the majority of props and dressing came courtesy of the crew. At the end of the day a lot of our resources came from the production team calling friends who had houses, or friends who were actors and getting them along for a sandwich and a fun day out. So when you overhear the producer and the director talking about how the hell they're going to find a Labrador puppy or an electric guitar for that crucial scene tomorrow – don't be afraid to tell them about your dog loving friend Dave who's in a band. It might not always work out but you will be seen as someone with ideas who wants to help and this can only ever be a good thing.

judy@lobster-snyder-productions.com   www.judysyoyo.com

Q – Aside from production problem solving, what else should you be doing?

Judy - In a busy production office it's imperative that you keep your eyes and ears open at all times. Even if you're knee deep and engrossed in complex travel itineraries or battling to get tomorrow's call sheet finished, LISTEN to what's going on around you. More often than not what's being discussed in the office WILL involve you and, either what you're doing today, or what you'll need to be doing tomorrow. I cannot stress enough how much it will make your life easier by paying attention to each and every conversation within your earshot. Once your ears become attuned to the environment, it will become like second nature.

Similarly, always be aware of your surroundings. Keep an eye on who has gone where and with whom. So when the producer calls in a terrible flap because he can't find the director – rather than shrugging your shoulders and looking vacant, you can tell him immediately that the director just stepped out to the bathroom. Also, always be sensitive to the hierarchy on set and the importance of certain situations. For example, if the director is in the middle of an intense conversation with the producer, this is not a good time to interrupt. Unless, of course, you have the lead actor stood in front of you demanding to see the director! It's important to learn and recognize what is important and what's not. You will make mistakes in the beginning, everyone does and generally everyone will be forgiven for them ONCE! Learn from that first time and don't ever make the same mistake again, people under pressure are never *that* forgiving.

Double and triple check any document you have prepared before it is distributed. Mistakes are made when you're tired and complacent, especially when working over old templates (this happens a lot with call sheets and travel itineraries). And I guarantee that however thoroughly you think you've checked a document, you will always find another mistake the second you hit the 'send' button. A great PA will make OCD their friend!

Q – What advice would you offer a new PA?

Judy - Always ALWAYS, carry out every task (no matter how menial) quickly, competently and with a smile. Being good at your job and easy to work with is what will get you hired again and/or a great recommendation for that all important 'next job'.

PRODUCTION MANAGEMENT
ANDREW ZINNES

Q – What is the job of a production manager?

Andrew – My job is to run the production office and make sure that all the departments have whatever they need to make the film. I also keep track of the budget.

Q – What kind of office would you put together?

Andrew – Do it out of someone's home so you don't spend any cash on office rental. Then all you need is a good internet connection, a decent computer and decent cell phones. The key is to stay organized. Keep your casting separate from your location files. Make sure you have a good receipt file. And try to stay digital so you don't have tons of paper lying around.

Q – What are some prep things you can do to keep costs down?

---

 zee@guerillafilm.com   www.crazeepictures.com

 www.script-tonic.com

74

Andrew – The biggest thing is to go through the script and see if there are any trouble spots. Animals. Kids. Rain. Snow. Lots of extras. Crazy props. Expensive locations like city parks or docks. Elaborate stunts or special effects. I make a list of these things and then talk to the filmmaker to see if we can cut or alter them in a way that gives the same effect. So a city park becomes a friend's backyard or a car chase becomes an on-foot chase with a fistfight at the end.

Q – What legal forms and documents do you need to have?

Andrew – For low budget films, not many. You should have a basic location release, talent (actor) release and maybe a vehicle release. If you sell the film to a mainstream distributor, they will want to see those things. You can find sample documents on www.guerillafilm.com.

Q – Do you deal with insurance or permits?

Andrew – I do. But for movies at this level, it probably won't be an issue. You need insurance for renting equipment or for going to certain locations. Avoid locations that want permits and insurance.

Q – How do you stay on budget?

Andrew – Always haggle. Start by politely asking for everything for free and then go up from there. Offer them credits, publicity or a promise that you will use their services exclusively for the whole day or shoot. I once got a 70-ton crane for free because the guys who owned it liked the idea of it being in a movie.

Q – What common mistakes do you see?

Andrew – Not budgeting enough time in prep so I can get all the elements sorted out. I can get just about anything the production needs, provided I have enough time.

Q – What advice would you give a new filmmaker?

Andrew – Don't give up. For every day that you feel like you want to reach for the whiskey bottle, there will be day in the future when you can't believe people are paying you money to do what you do.

Q – Should I use friends as actors?

J.J. – Only if the script is about your friends, as then you're not asking them to do anything that isn't themselves. But when you ask them to be something other than themselves, and when they have no training, you are not going to get what you want.

Terry – It's like asking your friends to help you move. You save all that money, but sometimes your friends don't show up or they break your glass coffee table because they're not professionals. No, you want to hire real actors and hopefully actors who do things other than act so they have experiences from which to draw.

J.J. – You already have a relationship with your friends with defined roles. If you ask them to be in your film, you are changing the relationship, asking them to something that is unusual. That can create resentment and a hostile work environment. When you bring in professional actors that are excited about your project, they want someone to be in charge and tell them what to do.

Q – What are the first steps to starting the casting process?

 nitrocasting@gmail.com

J.J. – You want to use breakdown services or use free online casting websites. You don't have to be in New York, LA or London. Things have really changed now where everything is online. It used to be that you placed an ad and then got all these 8x10 envelopes with pictures and resumes. That has gone.

Terry - Some good ones in LA are Now Casting, LA Casting, Backstage West and East and in the UK, Casting Call Pro. They want you to list with them because you are getting work for their subscribers.

J.J. – Then the next thing you do is break down your film by making a list of every role you need filled. And then on these services you list the role, the age range and the character's description. If you need a Native American or someone really tall, you list that. Actors are always scouring these sites and even if the role doesn't pay well, but it's a good role, they will do it because it's a good building block.

Terry – They will travel to work with you. They will take a week off to do it. And if you find someone far away who makes your $200 film look like $2 million, you can't put a value on that.

Q – When you are sorting through all those headshots, what should you be looking for?

J.J. – Your first call is the picture itself. If you see someone that looks like what you think the role should look like, then that's number one. When you flip over the picture and look over their experience, you can garner a lot from the directors they've worked with and the venues where they've played. If you aren't familiar with that kind of stuff,

CASTING & ACTORS

1. Cast actors, not your friends.

2. Schedule enough time to find your actors, they are the most important thing to get right on set. Make the investment.

3. If you can get help from a casting director, do it.

4. Agents are tough to deal with. Their job is to get good jobs and good money for their client. They will see you as neither, even if you think your script is great.

5. There are lots of online casting services – some useful, some not. Google them all.

6. Actors are different creatures, don't ever expect them to behave like crew.

7. Work with actors as much as you can, on shorts, exercises and other peoples films. It's important to be around actors so you are comfortable with the way they can 'be'.

8. The bigger the name, the more they MAY need to be 'handled'. Don't be surprised at special dietary needs, picking up and dropping off and general diva like behavior.

9. Be honest about working conditions and pay BEFORE the auditions.

10. Remember to engage with actors and don't just sit behind the camera barking orders.

11. Beware of offering actors different deals. If one gets more than another, it can lead to anger. Everyone should be there to be part of the dream and not for the cash.

then look for someone who has some experience to help. Look for someone that has some training.

Terry – An actor that has another discipline like playing the guitar or piano – something you can see and do – is amazing. An actor that can speak another language is amazing. Even if they have no experience and are just taking acting classes, that's enough. I kind of want to meet that person and see what they are about.

J.J. – Sometimes actors will cram in every activity they have ever done in their life in order to make up for lack of experience. That's not necessarily a good thing. You want to see marketable skills.

Q – What's a good way to organize the casting?

J.J. – You want to look at each part together. Let's say that your parts are Suzie, Kip and Renaldo. You want to look at all your Suzie's together, all your Kip's together and all your Renaldo's together. Then it is fresher and easier to compare each person-to-person and more likely that someone is going to stick out in your mind.

Terry – Have a place for your actors to sit. Don't treat them like cattle. Give them five more minutes than you expect in the room. They are actors. Number one: actors feel. So if you put them in a stressful situation, they aren't going to act for you. Number two: actors talk and bitch. They might get one audition a week and they will put all their energy into it and if it's an awful experience, they get on the phone with every other actor they know or they update their Facebook and they say you are an asshole. And your rep is mud.

J.J. – About the audition itself, if you are low budget, you need to see less people and take more time with them. If you are a big budget film you can see tons of people and afford to make a mistake if you get something wrong. You can always recast and catch up. On a small budget, you don't have that luxury. So taking more time with each person, you get a chance to let the actor act, which they love because they feel like they are working. You get them to read the monologue or the scene and then you give them adjustments. Then you can see how they react and communicate with you. That will inform you as to if this is a person you can and want to work with.

Terry – You are trying to find a thoroughbred rather than just a horse. If you have an eight-hour day and you see 100 people, you are not going to see anything rise above the average. No one is going to break the mold. But 25 people in 8 hours and one person breaks the mold – that's worth your whole movie.

Q – What is good feedback to give an actor during an audition?

Terry – Always improvise. Throw the script away. Or if there is a significant script, have them read it, then give them the conflict in the scene and have them just go off. If they can do that then they can show up on the day and be great. There are a lot of great technical actors, but if you throw them into a hotel room in Fresno and say *'I need you to cry right now'*, with all these grips and hot lights around, they fold. Check their range. After they have done their first take with their own choices, give them something that is 180 degrees different. If the scene is that they are crying on a riverbank because their brother is dead, then the next time

12. Do not cast from your bedroom! Find a professional location.

13. Actors can drop out for many reasons, so keep backup actors in your folder. Do not burn any bridges.

14. Learn to spot both real talent when it's in the room, and actors who will be troopers – you will need both.

15. Film auditions as after seeing 300 people, faces tend to merge.

16. Keep on casting until you get the 'right' actors and not just 'some' actors.

Get the right cast and your film will almost make itself! SPEND TIME AND RESOURCES CASTING

tell them to do it while they are laughing because they've been on speed for four days. If they can pull it off instantly, then that is someone you want to work with.

Q – When would you videotape an audition?

J.J. – Do it for callbacks. It's too much work for the first round. The other time to do it is if someone has to see the actor and they can't make the auditions.

Terry – Actors are sensitive. If you have no camera in the room for the initial meeting, the actor will be himself or herself and be charming. At the callback, the actor has had a few days to prepare and is ready for the camera.

Q – What is the best way to hire an actor?

J.J. – The director should make that call because then their first real interface is very positive, as they want them to be in their show. But you must have specifics to appear professional. Tell the actor the role you want them to play and when you think they will be shooting. Tell them they will have a script by a certain date. If you are paying them, tell them how much. It doesn't have to be concrete, but you need to have a general idea.

Q – What should you do if you want to go after an actor that is known?

J.J. – You have to do research and find out who their agent or manager is. But it's a process and you have to have all the details of your project – your budget, your shoot dates, the plot – because you are going to go through a screening process. You start with the lowliest person in the agency and if you clear them, then you get bumped up a level. You have to establish that you are real and not making something in your backyard. Call early in the morning, early in the week. Have a website presence as they are going to check up on you. Give them a one sheet of what your project is. There are people wasting their time all week long with useless projects so if you are on it then you stand out. The actors want to work with you – you just have to get through the representation.

Q – What are the biggest mistakes that you see that drive you crazy?

Terry – An actor having an awesome audition and not shutting up afterwards. An actor should do a great job, shake your hand and leave.

BUILDING RELATIONSHIPS

Low budget film shoots are notoriously hard work. When casting, be clear about conditions, pay and expectations (anything like nudity, swimming, driving, extreme night shoots etc.). When speaking to actors on the phone to arrange a casting, repeat this information so they cannot later claim they were unaware.

Almost all actors embrace low budget shoots (if they know what they are getting into), but some can become difficult and make your life hell – especially if you are disorganised and unclear about what you need (and with the best will in the world, inexperience and under funding are a deadly combination). Once you have started shooting, you can become prisoner to their whims and needs – what you do? You can't fire them. Listen to your instincts BEFORE you commit to a casting choice.

Above all, stay friends. No matter the shit that goes down, always rebuild the bridge, hug and makeup. You may need them for a reshoot.

J.J. – Not spending the time to think about what you want. If you just cast a wide net, then you are wasting time. You can change your mind, but at least you had a thought to change.

Q – What advice would you give a new filmmaker?

Terry – Take an acting class. Find out what it's like to be on the other side so when you come back behind the camera you will have a better ability to talk to actors and see their talent.

**LOCATIONS
KATHY MCCURDY**

Q – Most new filmmakers can't afford a set or studio, so they must shoot on location. What does this mean?

Kathy - Deciding on where to shoot isn't just determined by budget. One also has to consider what the needs of the story, script, and schedule are. If you are shooting a walk and talk with no special effects, action sequences, etc. then it's often better production value and more cost effective to shoot on location. A dressed house or back yard, a dressed office space or industrial area can often be found for low cost especially when little impact on surrounding area is possible.

Q - What should you consider with regard to sound, light and power?

Kathy - When tech scouting, don't forget your sound department! If shooting in a kitchen, restaurant, bar or commercial space make sure any refrigeration equipment, air conditioning systems, exhaust or fans are turned off or unplugged for that low rumble will end up on your soundtrack. Check to be sure telephone ringers are off or unplugged. For exteriors, note any construction in the area or industrial plants - things of that nature.

They will make shooting exteriors frustrating and expensive when you hit post-production. Note what time of day the scene takes place in the script and

kpmccurdy@yahoo.com

LOCATION LOCATION LOCATION

The central idea of a micro budget film will often be set in, or revolve around, a single location. And that location should be one that you have in your back pocket – be it uncle Albert's boat, the neighbor's cabin in the hills or a disused warehouse that your friend owns. In short, find a location and design a film around it.

This will help with a number of crippling problems.

First, you will probably get the location for free, or for very little money, and often without difficult questions about insurance, access, shooting times etc. You will also keep your cast and crew in a single place, and moving a cast and crew is a great way to waste time and spend money. Finally, you'll also get access at all times, even for reshoots many months down the line.

remember to note where the sun will be at the location on the day you will be there. Note if any buildings or objects will block the sun and create shadows or the need for additional lighting. Also consider if the sun is blasting out the location the grip department will want to load silks and frames on the truck. As far as power considerations, the only location power options are plug-in 'house' power or tying in to a larger source of power at a location, typically a commercial building. The former source is used for 'kinos' lights or 'practicals' and the latter requires a licensed electrician, insurance specifics and careful practice. When building a production day, try to keep your locations as close together as possible for large company moves eats up a lot of time and money.

Q - Can you get multiple uses out of one location?

Kathy – Depending on the script, you might be able to use multiple rooms in the same house. So you could get your bathroom, kitchen and bedroom scenes, etc. all in one place. You can also dress a room for something else. So a living room could become an office waiting area, the back yard becomes a park and the front doorway could be the entrance to another house or an office building. In a commercial space, you can make a hallway look like just about any hallway in any other building. The same goes for elevators. And remember, there are other

1. Shooting on location
can be a major
advantage as you will
have to do minimal set
work, merely dressing.

2. Space can be a major
problem as even the
biggest of rooms will
become sardine like with
a full crew.

3. Shooting outdoors
can be a problem as
there is no way to
control the weather.

4. Always try and get
permission to shoot
wherever you intend to
be. Sometimes, if you
can foresee problems, it
is best to simply dash in,
shoot, and get out as
quick as possible. If
someone turns up to
find out what is
happening, try to get
them interested and
involved, and claim
complete ignorance.

things you can use from your locations that go
beyond creative needs. You may be able to get
crew parking, catering and offices and staging for
green screen in a parking lot of your location.

**Q - What is production value and how can a
good location help you achieve it?**

Kathy - Production value is the term used to
describe value for money as it appears on the
screen. The right location can offer great
production value. A practical location has a reality
and a feeling that a set on stage can't duplicate,
which is especially true of exteriors. On screen
will be a depth, a layered visual experience, and
an atmosphere that can further define a character,
explore story, further the plot and open up a script.

This is as important for blockbuster Hollywood
special effects movies as it is for ultra low-budget
first-time filmmakers. In the former, it makes the
fantasy worlds more real and believable; in the
latter it gives a gravitas and a professional look to
the overall work. For example, *The Blair Witch
Project* was really creepy - the forest was an
integral part to the story, character development,
and overall tone.

**Q - Should you try to get permits or permission
when you are low budget?**

Kathy - Filmmakers should always follow all laws
and regulations for filming in the area they have
chosen. This will protect you in case of accident,
lawsuit or emergencies. Film permit authorities
have forms to fill out or the film liaison will ask
specific questions in order to determine what will
be needed to ensure public safety as well as that
of the film crew. They typically want to know if you

are using a generator, how many people in your cast and crew, how many and what type of vehicles you have, where you will film, park your crew, park your working trucks and park your base camp. They will want to know your hours of operation and prep and strike days and plans. They will want to know all contact info for the company and what activity you will be doing - stunts, SFX, pyro, etc.

Many low budget films don't have money for permits in the budget. If not, take steps to creatively address the issue with the writer and director. For example, if the script calls for a scene on a boat at a dock in a city marina and you can't afford that - examine the essence and purpose of the scene and ask if there is another, less expensive way to achieve that – can that scene be set in an harbor office?

Q – Can you reduce the cost of shooting on location?

Kathy – Spend a lot of time prepping as you can avoid costly mistakes by learning as much about a location as possible. Film during regular hours in residential areas and during non-business hours in commercial areas. Shoot multiple scenes in one location. Keep crew-parking close to avoid the need for shuttle vans. Communicate accurately and timely to your crew with all pertinent information regarding safety, rules and regulations, and location-specific needs. Reduce or eliminate night shoots in residential areas. Also expense goes up with the amount of crew, extras and activity. Locations in cities tend to be more expensive than rural areas unless it is some kind of landmark or preserve.

5. Getting to and from difficult locations can be very costly in terms of time - one hour travelling is one hour less shooting.

6. Use movement orders. This is a piece of paper with a photocopied map (the route picked out with highlighter pen), explicit directions and mobile phone numbers for those who get lost.

7. Facilities for the crew on location can be a problem - a place to eat and sit will be needed, and a toilet must be provided - you can't ask your star to squat in the bushes.

8. Closing down streets is difficult. The police will be as helpful as they can, but they have crimes to stop and don't relish the thought of holding the hand of a new producer.

9. When choosing a location, don't forget the sound.

Q - How can you avoid damaging a location? What if you do mess something up?

Kathy - Use layout board, bubble wrap and mats to protect floors, wood, and wall coverings on interiors. I've seen camera people put tennis balls on tripod legs for the same reason. Minimize crewmembers inside a location and allow appropriate prep time and set up time for each shot so folks aren't rushing. That's when accidents happen. Ask crewmembers to remove utility belts with swinging hammers/clips and other metal object on them if filming in tight quarters. Monitor proximity of set lighting equipment and grip equipment to sprinkler systems. If the sensors register the heat given off by this equipment they can turn on the sprinklers, soaking your set, crew, and equipment as well as causing water damage to the location.

If something does get damaged, note it immediately and document it with photos and witnesses for insurance purposes. Encourage your crew to bring such things to the attention of the location manager or member of the producing team so that the producers are not blindsided later on by an irate property owner or worse - lawsuits. Be proactive in arranging for the damage to be repaired.

This can save you money and your nerves and those of the property owners. Make sure you have insurance and all your locations are named as additional insured to cover yourself in the event of major damage. Most damage is of the sort that can be repaired with little fuss so just make sure to be on top of it.

10. Film crews trash locations. Clean up after yourself, leave muddy boots outside, ban smoking inside etc. Remember, you may need to return to the location if there is a problem.

11. Think creatively - many locations can double for several different parts of your story. This will minimise the time you waste moving between places.

12. Beware of the cool location that is impossible to either light or get cameras into, buildings with big windows cause lighting problems, turrets with narrow stairwells are tough for carrying kit, anywhere in big cities will cost you simply in parking alone.

Q - Are there any tricks to getting locations for free?

Kathy - Be honest, up front and transparent. Have proper insurance and show the location owners that you are a professional and serious filmmaker. You might not have a budget, but you have your integrity and passion - show it and prove it. Explain what you want to do, why you would love to have the privilege and honor of filming at their property and what you can offer in return - insurance protection, a meal with the crew, and your undying gratitude. Maybe invite them to a screening, give them a copy of the final film if the location features prominently, perhaps contact the local paper and sing the praises of the establishment or owners. And always write a thank-you note. Good manners are always in style.

Q - What information should you give the director and the rest of the crew about a location?

Kathy - Safety requirements like hard hats, protective eyewear, appropriate shoes, etc. Some properties have sensitive needs like neighbors whose property should be avoided or business owners with deliveries or events happening during filming. This all needs to be communicated to your crew in a timely manner. If a property owner does not wish to be involved in the filming be absolutely certain to inform your entire crew to keep themselves and their equipment off that property. Obviously, the crew will need to know where to park, where their working trucks are, where base camp is and where bathrooms/catering/extras holding are located.

SCHEDULING
CHRIS JONES

Q – What is scheduling?

Chris – When you write a film, it unfolds, scene-by-scene, page-by-page, in a specific order. When you shoot a film, you rarely shoot it in that same story order. Often you need to shoot all the scenes in one location together, all the scenes with an actor on the same day and so on.

With very rare exceptions films are shot 'out of sequence', and the shooting for any production is called the schedule. When it goes wrong, or is not planned out well, your shoot can turn into a logistical nightmare.

Q – Who creates the schedule?

Chris – On big projects, it's often the first assistant director, or another member of the production staff. But on a small film, or short film, it should really be the director and the producer. Directors need to be involved as they have the specifics of how they want to shoot each scene in their head. They will also be forced to bite the bullet on how they physically approach the film (up until now it's been in their head, without actors throwing tantrums, rain, traffic and short days). Almost every director complains there is not enough time, money or light – and

---

chris@guerillafilm.com   www.twitter.com/livingspiritpix

www.livingspirit.com   www.chrisjonesblog.com

Join our Facebook group 'Guerilla Film Maker'

SCHEDULE AND BUDGET ARE GOLDEN

If the screenplay is the blueprint of the film for the director and actors, then the schedule and budget are the blueprints for the production team. In fact, the budget and schedule should be considered scripture! When a director disregards the need to stay on budget and on schedule for a guerilla film, life can get pretty painful very quickly because there is no more money!

Shooting late every night, or throwing in extra shoot days that should be 'days off', is all possible, but it will impact on both cast and crew, and over a short period of time the quality of their work will suffer and they will slow down. Shooting over schedule is just plain counter productive. On the flipside, we have visited sets where astonishingly, the production wraps early most days! This is also a problem as either the production has over scheduled and therefore is wasting money, or more likely, the director is not getting enough coverage (shots).

Work on that schedule almost as hard as you worked on that script, and then go back and work some more on that script too (ideally cutting out six pages and the car crash!)

that's true, but your job is to come out the other end with a completed film, irrespective of those limitations.

Directors doing the schedules will be forced to compromise their (often) over ambitious visions, and lose some battles in order to win the war of coverage. They should be compromised into shooting a scene in three shots instead of the seven they had planned in their head, BUT also keep the resources for the most important scenes when they really do need those seven shots for added impact. It's about choosing battles.

Q – What do you use to create a schedule?

Chris – There are some software tools out there, and I am sure they are all excellent, but I have found writing down the information on small cards, laying them out on the floor, and then arranging them in order to be the most efficient way. You kind of always need the big picture, and you can't get that on a computer screen. And no-one has any difficulty in understanding a card system. It's cheap, easy and very efficient. Once you have your shooting order, you carve it up into days and type it all out in a document on a computer, before printing and distributing to the crew.

Q – What information is on those cards?

Chris – Everything you need to know from a logistics perspective – scene number, location, day or night, interior or exterior (remember interior can be shot at night by blacking out windows), weather conditions, special props, vehicles, special effects, weapons. And, of course, all the actors (characters) and extras, plus special notes such as 'Jim's clothes are wet from scene 26'. When the director does this breakdown, lots of information that the production team might not come up with may be revealed. If an actor has an availability problem, maybe scenes can be split, shooting one actor against one wall, another actor against a different wall in another location? It's hardly ideal but it will get the job done.

Q – Scene numbers? What if there is a rewrite after the schedule is completed?

Chris – It's a headache for us all. So many variables make the schedule a work in progress until the very last shot. Maybe an actor won't sign up until the last moment, maybe they have certain dates they cannot do, maybe a location falls through at the last minute, maybe it just rains... All these things will change your schedule as you shoot. But by far the biggest headache is script rewrites.

Typically, the film makers hold on to stuff in the script that should be cut, and only in the final few days of prep do they really accept they need to be pruned out, and maybe new scenes, with new numbers, will be added.

Of course you cannot reformat your script as all your old scene numbers will change, and so you will need a new system, where scenes may be called 26B or 14C for instance, and they will be added to the schedule. Those new pages of script should also be circulated to cast and crew on paper that is not white - typically pink pages are the first colour to be used and denote this is a script change from the final 'locked draft' – and subsequently a whole rainbow of coloured pages may end up being used to accommodate more rewrites. The real lesson is to cut the script hard and merge scenes BEFORE circumstance and budget force you to cut – no-one wants a 3am rewrite under pressure.

HOW LONG WILL IT TAKE?

Simple dialogue scenes can move quickly. If you have just two characters facing each other while talking, you can shoot a master, and their close ups quickly.

Complex dialogue scenes move more slowly because having multiple characters may mean multiple camera / lighting setups. Also, you have more people to cover with close ups. If you know how you plan to edit the film later, you can shoot specific shots and leave what you know you won't use. However, this may limit your options in the edit if it does not work as planned.

Action scenes - especially those with stunts, take longer than you will expect as aside from setup time, they may need to have many different angles for editing. Stunt scenes take even longer because they must be planned down to the smallest detail, always putting safety first.

Cutaways and establishing shots - Close ups of newspapers and sides of buildings really make your film flow and take very little time to shoot. If you don't get them during the primary shoot, get a skeleton crew together and pick them up on weekends after principal photography wraps.

Night and Rain - The rule of thumb is that it will take you four times as long to shoot any scene that involves night or rain. Rewrite avoiding both if possible.

Day or Night - You may be able to shoot interior night time scenes by blacking out windows and vice versa. Always try and block locations together, then block day or night scenes within that location together, then see how that fits with other elements like actors or special props etc.

Track and Cranes - Any time that you move the camera other than on the tripod or on your shoulder, it will take twice as long because of setting equipment.

Production - It takes time to move trucks, equipment and people. Changing costumes and sitting in make up slows people down. Sets may need to be redressed and cameras reloaded. Then, there is lunch! Factor these things in.

Remember the Golden Rule... STAY ON SCHEDULE!!!

91

Q – How do you go about arranging those cards?

Chris – I begin by putting locations together, as moving a full cast and crew is very time consuming. Then you consider the day/night aspect and put all the day scenes together and night scenes together. You also consider if there are any other story locations that could be shot in the same physical location (shooting in a house is one location, but could you dress a room to look like an office? Or use the back garden for a woodland? Can you shoot more 'story' locations in one 'physical' location?) That's the first pass.

Then you look at the actor / prop / special requirements aspect. As a rule you want to hire actors, special effects guys, expensive cranes and the like, for as few days as possible, and so you kind of group those people and things together. That starts to change the schedule. Of course you want to minimize production moves, and so you start to get creative.

Very quickly you may realise that you could do with a rewrite to accommodate ideas that were great at the keyboard, but a nightmare in execution, especially when you have no money. This is where it's vital to have the director involved so that you can say..."Sure, if you really need it you can have it, but you will need to cut 'X' amount from the schedule, so tell me now what that is..." Very quickly they may come round and agree to a rewrite, or they will fight their corner as they feel what they are asking for is actually essential.

Q – How long will it take?

Chris – For a feature, about two days to get a good solid first schedule – but there will be constant tweaks.

Q – It sounds like a nightmare!

Chris – It's one reason why many successful low budget films are shot in one physical space, even if the story is set in a few locations. It's just a smart way to spend your very limited resources. If you plan a film with the location in mind (which ideally you have before you even think about making the film) you can spend most of your money on the screen instead of moving people between locations. Planning is essential to a successful shoot.

Q – What should a film maker look out for when scheduling?

Chris – Creative people are always optimistic – in their imagination it will always be sunny, there will be no traffic, the shoot will not fall behind, there will be ample parking etc. So have plans in place for when your Spidey senses start tingling. The big problems are always stuff like there is too much night shooting (where everyone is tired, you work in the dark and get half the shots you need), or there is rain in the script. Shooting in moving vehicles can be problematic and costly and it really adds very little value to the story – could that scene in a moving car be shot on a park bench? Or an even more appropriate and do-able story location? Of course you don't want to rip the guts out of the story by sanitizing everything, you need to find the right balance. Often the easy way to deal with it is to say, OK if I had to deal with this myself, with this much money, what could I actually achieve? Maybe it's time to cut the three elephants from the script, unless it's a film about elephants!

Q – What advice would you offer a film maker?

Chris – Bite the bullet weeks before you shoot. Go through your script and rewrite to make it cheaper and easier. You have limited resources and you don't want to squander it on things that really do not impress audiences – they want a cracking story that keeps them connected to characters and their dilemma – and that's really about what happens and to whom, not so much where it happens, or if its night or raining. And remember, a schedule is NEVER completed.

REWRITE FOR THE SHOOT

1. Before getting to set and finding out you don't have enough money, time or light, bite the bullet with a script rewrite.

2. Don't waste precious resources by filming redundant sequences that you will cut in post production. Cut now.

3. Listen to advisors and your gut niggles about stuff you suspect should be shortened or cut.

4. Don't fight it! We promise, your script can be shorter!

5. Merge minor characters into a single one. Try it!

6. Try merging scenes into one location. Does it really need to take place in several locations?

7. Rewrite night into day, write out the rain, unless you REALLY need it.

8. Do all of this as soon as you can, ideally BEFORE scheduling.

Q – What insurance might I need for a low budget film? What is the basic package?

Paul – There are two aspects to this. First is equipment. If they get their equipment from a supplier, say Panavision, they may get half a million worth of kit for free, and their budget may only be three thousand – maybe it's a short film to be shot over a weekend for instance. Panavision are going to need insurance and won't let the film makers take the equipment without seeing a valid insurance policy. Not only will they need the equipment covered for things like loss, damage or theft, but secondly, they will also need 'loss of rental' cover to compensate Panavision for their loss of rental if, for instance, the camera has been damaged, needs repairing and cannot be rented out for two months. So a short film might need to purchase a minimum premium cover, and that could be a very large percentage of their overall three thousand budget. It's a real problem for them and I acknowledge this.

In the UK, film makers will also need what's called 'public liability' insurance, to protect the public and property should something happen (usually for £5m). Often locations will require this insurance in place before they allow a crew in. By law in the UK, the film makers should also take out 'employers liability' to protect the employees of the production company, with cover of £10m.

paul@pdc-media.co.uk

94

In the USA they have similar cover for public liability (or CGL as it's known) which will also be needed. If they are hiring crew, workers compensation may be necessary too.

Some film makers choose not to take out insurance if they perceive that they can get away with it, especially in America where it is even more expensive. Often they have bought their own cameras too, and so then the risk is entirely theirs for equipment hire should there be a problem with their camera and equipment.

Q – What usually happens on those films, where everyone is working for free, with half a million's worth of equipment and only a few thousand in the bank for production?

Paul – They make a lot of calls and piece it together from several brokers, often without being sure that they have the right cover. I often suggest that they buy the equipment rental insurance from the company who is giving the kit to them for free as these companies usually have that facility. They may also hire a freelancer who buys annual insurance, and so their equipment is already covered (a sound recordist with their own sound recording equipment for instance).

Q – Could they enter into a co-production with a bigger company in order to sit under their umbrella insurance?

Paul – Yes that is possible. There is also 'material insurance' too, which would insure digital data and film negative. We are moving more digital now, and if a production has adequate data backup built into the budget and schedule, it's rare for anyone to make a claim for loss of data.

Q – Do you look at any paperwork?

Paul – Yes, I read the script, look at the budget and schedule, so that I can make a better assessment. I try and stay in touch with the film makers and nurture a relationship with them so as to keep good communication channels open. Often I advise people to put in well thought out contingency plans into their strategy rather than buying insurance.

Q – What about dangerous stuff in films?

STARTING A COMPANY: If you're making a film and using other people's money, then it's always a good idea to set up a company through which the entire film production will be put through. Accountants and lawyers are very expensive, so we suggest you buy a good business start up book in which 95% of your questions will be answered. You will then be able to calculate what type of company is the best for you. There are several different company formats you can set up depending on what country you're in and also for what purpose. i.e. in the UK, you could set up a limited company which gives you just what it says, limited liability in the event of a disaster. In the US, you could set up an S-corp, which offers limited liability, being taxed as a partnership and taxed only once, not again through a company tax. For more info on this, check out the US edition of The Guerilla Film Makers Handbook and/or consult with an accountant or lawyer. Bear in mind there are additional fees for having a company and depending where you are, can be expensive (i.e. in California, you must pay $800 for the privilege of doing business there.) In addition you have to submit audited company accounts each year.

Reclaiming Sales Tax: In certain countries you can reclaim the sales tax on your purchases through your company. In the UK, there is VAT (value added tax) on every purchase (with some exclusions such as food, books etc.) If you've set up a company, then you can become VAT registered and reclaim the VAT. However, you will also have to charge VAT on invoices on any sales to UK companies and individuals. In Australia, the sales tax is known as the GST (goods and sales tax) and they have a similar system. In the US, it's on a state by state basis on whether you can claim your sales tax or not. The taxman isn't too fond of filmmakers as until you've made sales on your film, you will always be reclaiming VAT / sales tax. And in many cases, your film sales are done with companies and individuals outside the UK and therefore you're not required to charge VAT. Hence, make sure your accounts are always in order, NEVER cook the books for the VAT man or you could go to prison.

Depending on the scale of your budget, other tax relief schemes are available for the prospective investor, such as in the UK the Enterprise Investment Scheme (EIS), the UK Film Tax relief which is provided by The Department for Culture, Media and Sport (see the DCMS website.) In America, different states offer tax benefits if you shoot there.

Paul – Health and safety is important and risk assessments are needed now, and they need to be done properly.

Q – And how do documentaries differ from narrative drama?

Paul – Documentaries can be more work and we have to be careful, especially if the subject matter is contentious. Errors and Omissions cover should be considered. If you were making a documentary about pharmaceuticals for instance, you may have problems as those companies have deep pockets and may take legal action against the production. So we need to be more vigilant and considered with a documentary.

Q – What is E and O insurance?

Paul – Errors and Omissions Insurance – it's a policy that covers libel, slander, defamation, breach of copyright etc... and is now needed should you want to get your film distributed in the bigger territories like the USA and UK. The BBC now requests an E and O policy on new productions for instance. The problem is that it can cost $12,500! Many indie film makers just can't afford that and so they buy the E and O cover at the very end, when they have a sale of their film in place. Then they either get some money to cash flow the purchase, against the sale with a broadcaster for instance, or they build it into the deal with the distributor or sales agent.

Q – What advice would you offer a new film maker?

Paul – Talk to people in the business, people with experience, and get some recommendations of who they would use. Call a few people specialist insurance brokers and see who you develop a good relationship with. It's often better to spend a little more to get the right broker, than it is to penny pinch. Also check what you are covered for as I see many film makers thinking they are covered, when in fact they have not really read or discussed in detail what and what is not covered.

The problem to always remember is that while insurance is not key to the making of a production, if claims do occur, they could potentially put the film-maker out of business.

FISCAL SPONSORSHIP

If you can get non-profit status in the US, any money given to use is tax deductible to the donor. It's best to join an organization that has 501 c 3 status rather than become a non-profit yourself. The donor makes the donation to the non-profit and they earmark it for your project. That way you can still make money off the film. Everybody wins! This works well for documentaries, but there's no reason it can't work for fiction as well.

THE BUSINESS PLAN

If you're seeking investors, then it's a good idea to have a business plan. It's also good to have to make you look at your project and really know it well. In this small document you will list a synopsis, wish cast list, your company and who's in it, your background, any crew, a plan on how you will make the film, when, where and for how much and a cash flow etc. How much is it going to cost, where is that money going and when do you need it, when you're going to shoot and for how long etc. Then you need to look at, who will buy this film, is there a market for it, what precedents are out there to show it can be done. Remember investors will be people who believe in YOU, what YOU are doing, and are excited by being involved in your quest, and can afford to lose their money if it comes to it.

LEGAL PROBLEMS TO LOOK OUT FOR

1. Make sure you get all your paperwork in place and have a chain of title; talent release forms, all contracts with investors, actors, crew, stills photos, music etc.
2. Make sure you have all the rights you need for copyrighted music, stills and video footage: you have the rights forever, you can edit an actor's performance, it's for all media worldwide etc. In the US, check out Fair Use laws that allow you to use these things for free in some cases.
3. Remember if it's the other side drawing up the contract, everything will be in their favor – so make sure you do the contracts to make sure you're protected.

CHAPTER THREE
PRODUCTION

THE GUERILLA FILM MAKERS POCKETBOOK

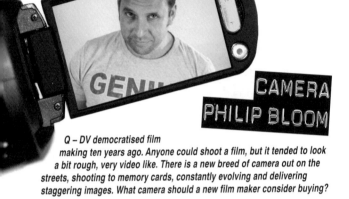

*Q – DV democratised film
making ten years ago. Anyone could shoot a film, but it tended to look
a bit rough, very video like. There is a new breed of camera out on the
streets, shooting to memory cards, constantly evolving and delivering
staggering images. What camera should a new film maker consider buying?*

Philip – This is a question that I get asked all the time. *'I have X amount of
money, I want to make a feature or short film, what camera should I buy?'* It's
difficult to answer. If someone says they want a cinematic look, with filmic depth
of field, with interchangeable lenses, and for it to be affordable, I would suggest
one of the new HD DSLR cameras, such as the Canon 5d MkII or Canon 7D.

These are not the most practical cameras to use, but light wise, you can shoot in
places that a traditional video camera can not. I've owned many of the low end
professional cameras such as an EX1, Z1, and HVX200, and the problem they all
have is the size of the chip behind the lens. They are comparatively small and so
the ability to get filmic images, with the background out of focus (so as to draw
the attention to the subject in the frame) is next to impossible. This is one of the
factors that distinguishes HD DSLR cameras, they have very large chips which
produce these very filmic images.

---

help@philipbloom.co.uk   www.twitter.com/philipbloom

philipbloom.co.uk   philipbloom.co.uk/blog

www.facebook.com/philipbloomfilms

Finally, cameras that can capture truly film-like images are now available to anyone with a credit card! Buying a camera 'off the peg' is just the beginning as there is a lot of extra kit to consider adding to your arsenal, lenses, supports, filters etc. (see later in this interview).

The most important element to get right is of course your camera person. It's an old maxim but it's as true today as it's ever been – 'it's not the tool, it's the person who uses it...' Your film will look amazing if you find someone who is good at lighting, framing, working with costume and make-up, working with production design and making actors feel good on set etc. Don't fall into the trap of thinking that just by buying the camera and the kit, somehow you will be transformed into a better film maker. You need to get out there and make stuff.

Before 'buying into' any camera system, we recommend renting a full kit for a weekend and shooting a project – short drama, music video, simple tests. Get a feel for it and find the problems before you invest heavily.

Q – So the size of the chip is in direct correlation to the depth of field?

Philip – Yes. The smaller the chip gets, the more depth of field you will have, to the point where on very small chips, almost everything is in focus.

Q – For clarity what is 'Depth of Field' and why is it such an attractive thing?

Philip – Depth of Field is one of the most important tools for a Cinematographer and a Director - it is used to draw attention to something within the frame. It gives you the ability to knock the foreground and background out of focus and draw the viewer's attention to the subject (by virtue of it being the only part of the frame that is in sharp focus). If you look at a shot where everything is in focus, in a busy restaurant for instance, and you want to focus on one character in the story, we could be distracted by everything else going on behind and in front of them. The image might be distractingly busy (this is what you get with video formats with small chips). With a controlled shallow depth of field you can decide what you want to 'see' in that frame. That is something that has been very difficult to achieve with smaller cameras.

Some of these HD DSLR cameras create really lovely images and have great progressive film modes too, they do look very filmic. Of course, the problem is, the more shallow depth of field you have, the more of a nightmare it is to shoot, because you have to get into focus pulling. If an actor moves, they may go out of focus, so you need someone to keep it in focus by 'focus pulling'.

Q – Some of your videos on Vimeo show that amazing depth of field, where you have shot footage at night, on the street, with available light and where the subject's eyes are in focus but their nose and ears are out of focus. It looks very cinematic.

Philip – Yes. But I would never shoot drama with that kind of depth of field unless the actor is like a statue. All they would need to do is breathe and then they would dip out of focus. Unless I am desperate for light, or am losing light, I would be shooting f2.8 most of the time, because at f1.2 or f1.4, even if they just sway slightly, you have a depth of field that is so narrow, that it will probably go out of focus.

Q – It is spooky the amount of parallels between this new breed of camera and how films used to be made pre-digital. Interchangeable lenses, video assist (not full HD output), 12 minutes on the chip which kind of equals one mag of film. There is a certain discipline required to shoot effectively with these cameras that is similar to shooting film. Do you think that is a positive thing?

Philip – I think it is hugely positive. I would never shoot any film without any proper back up from a professional level crew, even when I'm shooting corporate documentaries.

Q – The compact flash cards used by these cameras are cheap. Should you shoot, copy to a laptop, erase the card and shoot again, and so on?

Philip – I have never erased a card during a shooting day, that scares me. I suggest buying as many cards as you will need for a full day shoot, then backing up to at least two hard drives, ideally three, before erasing the cards.

Don't buy the super fast cards as they are more expensive and don't make any difference when shooting HD with these cameras. The only time it makes a difference is when you come to dump stuff off the card and onto a computer, then it is quicker, but you pay a premium for that speed. I would suggest using standard SDHD Class 6 8GB cards, and buy many more than you think you will need. You are better off investing in more cards, than faster cards.

When shooting, don't get confused, make sure every card is clearly labelled, use them sequentially, label the boxes, make notes in a notebook so you have a record of what you have shot and on which card. You don't want anyone erasing the wrong card!

The great thing about digital is that it is usually only human error that causes problems, and you can put procedures in place to deal with that. I make four backups of everything, and so the chance of losing anything is very remote. The most important thing is to check every copy.

Q – Let's assume the film maker has a cheap camcorder that they are messing around with, shooting short films and exercises. But now they are going for a big project, what should they be investing in?

Philip – The cameras are relatively cheap, but everything else you will need does start to add up. These are not ergonomic cameras, they are a nightmare to use handheld without any assistance. You will need to find a way to stabilise the camera. The good old-fashioned way is my favourite - a tripod. There are some great affordable Steadicam like solutions out there too, such as the Glidecam 2000 HD. There is a steep learning curve to using it but you can get some incredible results. There is the hand-held rig made by Zacuto that I have used that is very good. There are others too - any sort of hand-held rig will help.

Q – What about the viewfinder?

Philip – The optical viewfinder on these cameras does not work because it has a mirror box system. It is purely for taking photos. All video is shot through the live view mode and displayed on the back of the camera. This is the only way that you can view it on the camera without using an external monitor. That LCD screen on the back is not high resolution and any sunlight hitting it is going to make it hard to see anything. To improve this, I use a Zacuto Z Finder which sticks on to the back of the camera and gives you a view finder which enlarges

DEPTH OF FIELD

This refers to the area in the frame that will appear to be in focus. If you have very little (shallow) depth of field, then not much is in focus, whereas a lot of depth of field means almost everything is in focus. Shallow depth of field is effective with close up shots as the subject appears to be pulled out of the background. However, in these situations focus is critical 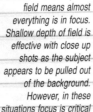 for you can lose it very easily. Large depth of field is great for establishing shots. Two main items affect depth of field, the length of the lens and aperture setting. Here are some rules of thumb to follow...

Length The shorter the lens (wide angle) the more depth of field you will have, and conversely, the longer the lens (telephoto) the less depth of field you will have.

Aperture The more light you let through the lens, the more depth of field you will have. So, at F-2 you will lose almost all of your depth of field while at F-22 you will have great depth of field.

By combining different focal length lenses and changing the amount of light reaching the lenses (either through lighting or with filters) you can manipulate the depth of field for creative purposes.

that screen to the equivalent of 100inches in your eye. It is slightly pixely, but it does give you the ability to see focus (costs about $400). It is the most essential thing I have used with these cameras. I have shot a number of things hand-held with one lens and the Z-finder. Nothing else. It also gives me stability because I've now got points of contact on the camera - my left hand on the focus barrel, my right hand controlling exposure, my elbows tucked in, and my eye is pushed up against the view finder. This gives me a very solid, stable system.

The other hand-held rigs help even more so, by pushing the camera into your body. It is very much like having an old camera on your shoulder, it gives you weight. So if you are doing a hand-held you have got to support it. If you can make your own homemade rig, great, better still, buy yourself a good one.

Q – Is shooting hand-held a problem?

Philip – You have to be careful when shooting hand-held because of the 'rolling shutter'. Because of the way the camera captures the image, if there is any significant movement such as the camera moves quickly or something passes through frame quickly, you can end up with skewed lines (you can view examples at www.guerillafilm.com). This is a limitation of the camera, but with care, it can be avoided or minimised.

Q – What should we be looking at for a small, affordable, lighting kit?

Philip – Just because these cameras have incredible low light abilities, people assume you don't need to light anymore -though you can light in a more subtle way. Happily, you don't need to carry around huge lights anymore, but you will still need to light your scenes if you want them to look attractive. Some people are using practical lights - lights that appear as props in a scene. If you are looking for professional lights, I like my Kino Divas, which are fluorescent lights with switchable tubes from daylight to tungsten. They are cool lights, so they don't heat up. Many other smaller lights are great too, whether you buy or rent.

Another very important piece of kit is a set of ND (neutral density) filters, so you can control the amount of light entering the camera, and therefore increase or decrease the depth of field. The best solution is to get 'variable ND filters'. Buy the biggest filter available and buy step down rings so that the filters will fit all your lenses. A manual follow focus is also good addition too so an assistant camera person or focus puller can shift focus easily.

SHOOTING HD DSLR BASIC KIT

1. Camera Body, ensure it has latest firmware and can shoot 24P, 25P and 30P. Check forums for latest information.

2. Buy the best lenses you can afford. A good lens should last your entire lifetime.

3. Buy the best tripod you can afford. A good tripod will also last decades and is arguably the most useful piece of support kit.

4. A variable ND filter set, so you can manage shutter speeds and depth of field more easily.

5. Lots of memory cards - 8gb or 16gb and no larger. Better to buy lots of smaller ones than a few larger ones. Label and number sequentially

6. Viewfinder. To convert the LCD panel on the back of the camera into a true viewfinder.

Q – It's starting to get expensive, and we haven't even discussed lenses. Maybe you should buy yourself a 7D or a 5D with a good zoom lens, and use it for cutaways and tests, but for a big project, rent a full camera kit?

Philip – It is interesting to see the increase in rental companies who are supplying full kits, and yes they are very affordable to rent. And as you said, let's not forget the most important thing, decent lenses. The cheap lenses that you are going to get thrown in with the camera are no use to anybody. They are slow lenses and therefore useless in getting shallow depth of field. Canon make some really good zooms, their f2.8's are optically incredibly sharp. The 16 to 35, 24 to 70 and 70 to 200 are three beautiful lenses that you can easily shoot a whole feature film on. Just those three lenses, though each one costs around $2,000 (give or take). It depends on your budget. Alternatively, there are other great makes out there - Sigma, Tokina and Tamron all make very good zooms. The key thing if you are going to buy a zoom is to buy a constant aperture zoom. That means it is f2.8 all the way through the zoom range. There are a couple out there that are f4, but I prefer the f2.8 because of that extra bit of light you may need. You could survive on zooms, there is nothing stopping you if you want to, and it's probably the most affordable way to do it.

If you are going to get a set of Primes which have a fixed focal length, then you are going to need to start with something pretty wide, say a 20mm for wide shots, maybe even wider if you want to get something epic. Then a 35mm, a 50mm and an 85mm, maybe even a 135mm and a 200mm for very long lens work. I love shooting with prime lenses, not zooms - it's a really great discipline and it makes you think a lot more about the shot. Zooms can make you lazy.

Q – With Primes you are able to shoot with lower light because there is less glass?

Philip – Yes, they will give you the ability to shoot in lower light. Then you return to the issue of focus which is critical as there is such shallow depth of field. It's no problem for those shots where there is little movement, then you can get away with shooting really wide-open apertures.

Q – You can record sound on these cameras, but it is not ideal.

Philip – The thing is, we can tolerate bad images, but you can't tolerate bad sound. If someone showed me a film that was badly shot but you could hear it clearly and it was engaging, I would get into it. Sound has to be one of your biggest considerations. Without a doubt, for a drama, you have to get a Sound Recordist, they have got to do it properly. Also there is no timecode on the files on these cameras so there's no true link between sound and camera.

Q – So buy a clapperboard?

Philip – Yes! Though there is software out there which does not even require a sync point. As long as you record a guide track on the camera with the built in mic, it will analyse the wave forms and sync it up for you automatically. Get someone to record sound separately, someone who knows what they are doing.

Q – What about frame rates? 25fps, 24fps, 30fps?

7. *Clapperboard. You should record separate sound and use camera sound as a guide track only.*

8. *Hand held camera support, so you can operate the camera 'on the shoulder' like a film camera.*

9. *LCD monitors, one for the DP, one for the director (or hook up to laptop – see interview).*

10. *Glidecam 2000 or other low cost Steadicam system for smooth camera movement.*

11. *Spare batteries and chargers.*

12. *Lighting kit. Whatever you can lay your hands on will help, and this kit should grow over time.*

13. *Consider pro flight cases for your investment.*

14. *Keep an eye on the internet for cool new toys and gadgets.*

Philip – If it is going to be on the web then it doesn't matter, you can shoot any frame rate. It comes down to what you think looks best. If you are going to put it onto DVD in Europe, the simplest way will be to shoot 25p. If you are in the States, you can shoot 30p, or 24p and later convert it for DVD. If you are looking to put it onto Blu-Ray then I would shoot everything at 24p because Blu-Ray can handle 24p.

Q – If you shot 24p, when you came to making your UK DVD, would you just speed it up to 25p?

Philip – Yes. It would work fine.

Q – I guess it is about working out your post production work flow and making a choice based on that, not basing it on some vague understanding on what the output should be at the end?

Philip – Absolutely.

Q – Staying on frame rates, how do you get in-camera slow motion?

Philip – You can shoot 50p and when playing back, slow it down to 25p. That will give you very nice slow motion. When you come to the edit, you change the meta data header from 50p to 25p, that changes the rate at which the computer plays the footage back. With FCP and Cinema Tools it's very easy.

Q – Do you think it is important to have an external preview monitor?

Philip – The external monitor is one of the biggest problems I have come across with shooting HD SLRs. As soon as you plug a monitor into the camera you lose your LCD screen.

You have 2 options. You can make yourself a powered HDMI splitter – which must be powered. You can rig battery power for when you are not near a power supply. You plug your HDMI lead into that, then one monitor for yourself, the camera operator, and one for the Director. An unpowered Y-splitter will not work. The only problem is that if you're going handheld and want to use that LCD screen, you're screwed as plugging the HDMI cable into the camera, switches off the LCD. There is currently no way of having an HDMI lead plugged in and having the LCD screen active, but there is a solution. If you plug a USB lead into the camera and feed that into a laptop, that will provide a live image of what is being recorded and keep the LCD screen working. That is the most affordable way. Especially if you are going handheld, get yourself a nice long USB lead!

Q – How do you approach Post production?

Philip – The key thing with getting those files off your cards and onto your computer is making back ups. And one backup is not enough as hard drives fail. You can automate the backup process with software to make life easier.

The file format is the next most important thing to figure out. If you are shooting a finishing format that has a very efficient compression, but it's also impossible to edit, you will need to convert it. You can do this in both Avid and FCP very easily, though whatever software you use, conversion can be slow (slower than real time). Most of the HD DSLRs shoot these formats and may need conversion.

Q – What mistakes do you see new film makers making when it comes to this kind of technology?

Philip – Someone wrote on my blog, *'Now that cameras are out there that produce such incredible picture quality, that everybody can afford... how can the pros stand out?'* People actually think that it's the tool and not the craftsperson! I have seen beautiful footage and awful footage shot with the Canon 5D, the same with the Red camera. It comes down to how you use the camera, your lighting, your framing, composition, your story-telling.

Q – What advice would you offer a new film maker?

Philip – Don't be scared by these cameras. It is a learning curve, but the principles are exactly the same. You need to get to know the camera and get around its limitations. The 5D mark 2 is Canons first generation camera that shoots HD video. As time progresses, so it will get even better. And there are many companies out there making great kit to support these new technologies and communities that grow out of it.

Also, film as often as possible, practice, practice, practice. Experiment - you will learn so much. You will screw up on things like your lighting and your sound, but you will learn from that experience.

SOUND
ADRIAN BELL

Q - What is your job?

Adrian - As a sound mixer I record mainly dialogue and some sound effects for films.

Q - Who's normally in your crew? How many?

Adrian - Three - a boom operator plus a sound maintenance engineer and myself. As you go down the scale in production size you'd end up with just the two of us, myself and a boom op. If it's micro budget it would just be the one sound mixer with a bag over his shoulder, winging it documentary style.

Q - Are there disadvantages if it's just the one sound mixer?

Adrian - You will lose time running around getting radio mics on and you'll need to think ahead so that you are not regularly needing extra bits of equipment. Also, it's difficult to mix radio mics while booming at the same time.

Q - What kind of equipment do you use?

Adrian - A hard drive recorder, an eight track mixer, four radio mikes, a couple of boom mics and maybe a couple of extra mics to plant or hide on set. If it's very low budget I'd record onto a hard drive field recorder. Or I could go straight in to the camera if it's a video format, then add a four channel mixer and carry it all

---

 www.adrianbell.net   mail@adrianbell.net

over my shoulder. One boom mic and say, two or three radio mics. This is similar to how I record documentaries too.

Q - Are producers surprised at how much equipment you have?

Adrian - Yes, most are blown away with how much we have! When we roll up at the location we hear, *'What on earth have you got a van like that for?'* They get it when you start using it all, as you get into the nitty gritty of production.

Q - Isn't it simpler to shoot it all on radio mics?

Adrian - Not necessarily, but recording with a multitrack recorder does offer the flexibility of recording everything separately on location, and we're getting into the habit of recording everything separately. The boom is recorded separately and all the radio mics are recorded separately and we also supply a two track mix which is used for the cutting copy for the editor. But you would not be doing that on a micro budget film as you wouldn't have the equipment or the extra crew.

Q - Is it best on a low budget film to focus on getting two really good tracks of audio, rather than four, six or eight?

Adrian - Yes, definitely. One track for boom and the other for mixed radio mics. I would always recommend trying to get the best sound on a boom mic first, but that obviously has limitations on the shot.

Q - Do most sound recordists come with their own kit?

Adrian - Yes.

Q - What are good quality microphones?

Adrian - Condenser microphones which are powered by 48 volt phantom power. Sennheiser gun mics, Schoeps gun mics. As far as recording dialogue, I use Sennheiser MKH 50's or 416's and maybe a Sennheiser MKH70 for exteriors if there is a lot of background noise. That's got a bit of colouration to it, so it's not as rounded as a 50 or 416. We also use a Schoeps CCM41 & CCM8 stereo kit for recording atmos and effects. Sennheiser MKH 50's or 416's as well as Schoeps CMIT mics, great for dialogue. These are my staple mics, but there are a number of other manufacturers mics to consider too. Experiment and listen!

1. Hire the best sound recordist you can. Inexperienced sound recordists may be paranoid and request further takes when they are not needed, or not know how to fix problems.

2. Everyone is a perfectionist. Learn to recognise when the sound is good enough.

3. When looking for locations, bear the sound in mind. Traffic and planes are usually the biggest culprits, as are air conditioning units. Most natural sounds can be covered up and disguised in post-production.

4. Blimps and barneys are good at filtering out most camera fan noise, but they will not get rid of everything.

5. Always get at least 30 seconds of room tone at each location so your dub mixer can lay down a decent ambient track.

Q - is there ever a problem with interference?

Adrian - We always have a rule printed on page one of the call sheet on all the shoots I've worked on, where we don't have phones on set. All phones must be switched off. If you use good quality radio mics they will almost certainly be licensed, which will cut down on interference.

Q - If the location is too noisy, is it wise to re-record the performance for sound only (ADR style) in a silent environment, directly after the take, with the actors still in the moment of the performance, but without the watching picture?

Adrian - Yes, if time permits and if the artist is happy to do it. We will always try and re-record that piece for sound only (no camera) because that artist has the emotion of the scene in their head. This creates a version of the sound that is clean and has the right emotion. The editor can often edit it to fit the sync dialogue later. If they turn up to do it four months later in a studio, they'll be in a different frame of mind.

Q - When on location do you find that everybody thought about lighting and beautiful shots, but nobody thought about the sound?

Adrian - Every time (laughs!) Ideally there would be a technical recce, so I would already be aware of any potential problems.

Q – What problems do you find with cameras?

Adrian - Many cameras are very noisy (laughs!) Hi Def cameras and their accessories are notoriously noisy with fans. Where possible, switch off all fans on equipment that's on set.

Q - Any problems with cast and crew?

Adrian - If you're working with a very unhelpful DP, you can have problems with lighting shadows due to boom shadows. Then you might have a situation like the shoot I'm on now, where we were asked to shoot close up and wide shots simultaneously. This meant there was no way we could get a boom in. Which for me, meant that the sound was going to be compromised because the only sync sound that would be useable would be on radio mics. It's always good to liaise with the costume department to find out what they're going to be wearing. Leather jackets are a pain in the bum, silk blouses are notoriously difficult.

Q - What are sound recording levels and why should you bother with them? I mean, on my camcorder I have automatic levels...

Adrian - It's absolutely imperative to line up your equipment, especially with digital recording kit. You must make sure you have the levels lined up at the start of the day's work and at various points along it. This means you line up your recording equipment with your camera equipment and wherever it's going from thereon in, and that you clearly mark at what level you've set your line up to so everyone knows along the post production chain what it's set to. If you don't do that, you'll encounter many problems in post. You might even record unusable sound or not record anything at all! Check those meters!

Q - How do you deal with very dynamic performances?

Adrian - My priority as far as dynamic range is concerned, is to not over record, so I would always

6. Post sync dialogue (looping / ADR) is a pain and expensive. Try to avoid it by either getting it right during the take or 'wild' (non sync) without the camera rolling, so it can be dropped in during post.

7. If you cannot use a boom mic due to space constraints, try using lavaliere mics hidden within the set (like a flowerpot or table lamp).

8. If you can afford it, try using more than one boom mic to record the sound so that you are completely covered. Also, get as many wireless lavaliere mics as possible for your actors.

9. Never say 'We'll fix it in post' unless you have no other options.

10. Listen to your sound recordist when they tell you there is a problem.

Recording device - DAT and solid state recorders semi-pro machines are affordable to buy, never mind rent. Beware of non professional connectors that don't deal with the rigors of film making.

Headphones -Essential to use high quality 'cans'. Enclosed earpieces mean you hear more of what is being recorded.

Tie Clip Mic - Concealed on actors when a normal mic isn't appropriate. Radio mics are expensive but good. Beware of interference with cheap ones.

Directional Mic (powered) - Several mics produce excellent results and a nominal hire charge will get you the best mic available. Sennheiser 416 is a good workhorse.

Large Diaphragm Mic - Ideal for recording foley sessions or close mic singing. No use on a film set.

Camera Mic - If shooting digital you may have a camera with a mic. This mic is useless for production sound but ideal for recording guide tracks for sync only.

Jammer / Baffle - Fits over the mic to protect it from wind. Usually comes with a 'furry' jacket that reduces wind noise even more. Essential.

Cables - Must be high quality and shielded. XLR cables are the professional norm. Get long ones to feed your sound to the camera.

Batteries - Batteries must be replaced regularly. You can't wait for the battery to go down as quality might be compromised.

Boom – The pole used to get a mic over the actors and kepy just out of shot.

Mixing Desk (e.g. SQN) - On complicated jobs where multiple mics may be used, you may need a small portable mixing desk.

under record rather than try and get more volume out of a quietly spoken artist. Yes, there are 'audio limiters' on the camera and on the mixer, but you try not to use them.

Q - Would you ever record the same performance on two channels, one recorded much lower than the other?

Adrian - Quite often I record two or more mics on one actor, and set them at different levels. One for the whisper and one for the shouts!

Q - Most people think of the mic being on a boom over the actors and radio mics hidden in clothing, but are there other places where you place mics?

Adrian - We can put microphones anywhere. We have mics specifically that we use for planting around the set. It might be in a flower vase, in the visor of a car, or behind the ear. Sometimes we go into theatre mode where you put mics in the hairline rather than on the body.

Q - How do artists respond to radio mics strapped to their ear?

Adrian - A lot of them have done theatre before. They may not have seen it in film, but generally they're ok with it. Again there's a lot of liaising between costume and makeup and if they have hairpieces it's a lot easier.

Q - How important is the clapperboard to the sound recordist?

Adrian - I think even in the digital / time code age, the clapperboard is the single most important piece of equipment on set today. Not only is it the easiest method of syncing sound and picture rushes, even with automatic time code synching but it's also fundamental to on set discipline. It's a mark that makes the crew quiet, and the actors know instinctively when they're on.

Q - You mentioned time code. What is time code and why do you use it?

Adrian - Time code is a reference signal that should be the same on both the cameras and sound equipment, and is used to help sync rushes. On lower end equipment, both camera and sound, there is no timecode so you would need to use the old school method of a clapperboard.

Q - If you are shooting HD, you have an audio track on the camera, so why not just put the audio onto that audio track?

Adrian - Generally, I don't record onto the camera these days. There are already so many cables running around the cameras and it's the last thing the camera department wants. I also don't have much time on set to continuously monitor recording levels on the camera.

Q - What is an SQN and how often do you use it?

Adrian - There are three or four manufacturers of four channel, battery operated location mixers. They are used for more portable situations. So if we have a lot of location moves or if we are in cramped conditions, say in a car, where we can't get our normal rig in, we would use a small SQN mixer. An advantage of using an SQN is that I can go straight into my hard drive recorder. The one that I used also had a good range of inputs and outputs on it, so if I want to send a feed to the director, or if I want to send power to certain microphones, I can do that. It is a really good workhorse tool. Most hard drive recorders these days have their own 2 or 4 or even 8 channel mixers built in to them. Try and minimise the pieces of equipment you need to do the job.

Q - If I were making a low budget feature would it be a wise to just record sound on the camera, via the SQN mixer?

Adrian - Yes. In fact that is probably the way I would do it. The lining up of your recording mixer to the camera line up is fundamental because you need to know what the camera is receiving. You do get a 'confidence feed' from the camera (so you can listen to what is recording on the camera), which is a secondary check. But fundamentally you need to check the meters and make sure they never get changed by the camera team.

Q - What is overlapping?

Adrian – It's when two or more actors are talking over each other. In a quickly spoken scene, they do tend to overlap each other. So you may be trying to splice these two pieces of sound together where they are overlapping each other's dialogue. That becomes very difficult to cut because where you want character A's dialogue clean, character B is speaking over it.

Q - Do you think it is fair to say that when most filmmakers start out they are obsessed with the image and oblivious to sound?

Adrian - I think it is very easy for a director to do that because they are so involved in the script and how they 'see it' in their head before shooting.

Q - What advice would you give to a new sound recordist?

Adrian - Try and visit as many film sets as possible. Try to talk to some sound recordists and see what is involved, what equipment is being used.

Q - Is it a good idea to apprentice yourself to a sound recordist for a while?

Adrian - I encourage that. I don't think there are many other ways to learn the industry as there is very little formal training now.

Q - What technology causes the most failures and problems?

Adrian - Headphones. It might be radio mics as well. But headphones on a day to day basis.

Q - How can filmmakers make your life easier?

Adrian - Get me on board earlier. Get me a script earlier. Show me the locations earlier. Get the main crew together so we can get to know each other earlier. Watch out for actors pulling wires out of their radio mics. They don't know how to unplug it so the cable just gets ripped out.

Q - What advice would you offer a new filmmaker?

Adrian - Watch more films. And be absolutely passionate about what you do.

Above all, get good clean dialogue tracks

Q – What is the role of the 1ˢᵗ AD?

Nic – It falls into two areas. The first is to breakdown a script, figure out the director's vision based on coordinating information between department heads and then create a schedule. If you have a decent game plan, then it makes your second duty, running the set, go as smoothly as possible. And with a 12-20 day schedule of low budget films that requires an immense amount of logistics, having a good game plan is essential.

Q – Is there a difference between US ADs and European ADs?

Nic – European ADs are like directors in training. They work with a director for a while and then go off and do their own film eventually. In the US on high budget shows, it is more of a production staff position because things are more controlled. But on low budget stuff in the US, it's closer to the European model.

Q – When does the AD come in to help on the set of a low budget film?

Nic - Many times you end up working with inexperienced directors, so an AD can become like a creative counselor. We have seen many different kinds of directors come and go, we know how it works and can provide input and advice. Often times when you're dealing with those kinds of budgets you may have to make creative decisions based on availability of equipment or something. And finding

When breaking down the screenplay, the First AD will give each scene a length or 'page count'. These figures are stated as fractions. Yes I too feel the shudder of my school teacher's cold clammy finger running down my spine... but fractions are the best way to do it, and it isn't that hard. All page lengths are calculated by the eighths... So a full page would be 8/8, a half page would be 4/8, a quarter would be 2/8, and one and a half pages would be 12/8...! Yes, a head screw. No matter how short the scene, the minimum length is 1/8, which reflects the fact that even the easiest of scenes to shoot will still take time to setup, shoot, wrap and move on.

Shooting a ninety page script over twenty one days means you need to shoot about four and a bit pages a day - or does it? Well that is the average, but there will be days when you will do less, and hopefully the occasional day when you will do more (yeah right!) It's a useful equation so that you can keep your eye on how much you are slipping behind (and you will be behind schedule by day two of your shoot) but it's not to be taken as gospel. What counts is the overall shoot, not the daily count.

creative compromises comes with experience. Otherwise you see the quality deteriorate. Other than that, creative scheduling can help. If you have a day where you are going to shoot 10 pages and you can't afford to move the film unit, you can make sure locations are very close together. Or even better find one location that can be used for many different scenes. And of course, you are the timekeeper. 10-12 page days with 35 setups... all the departments need someone on their ass to keep things moving.

Q – Do you make sure the director is getting the proper shot coverage?

Nic – Sometimes that's my responsibility. On low budgets, I tend to be with inexperienced directors and experienced DPs. There tends to be a lot of conversations with the DP to make sure we get as much coverage as possible.

Q – Do you watch the acting performance to make sure it's OK?

Nic – Rarely. If you're doing your job correctly, during the shot you're watching everything but what is on the monitor. You're making sure your PA's are locking off the set. You're getting ready for a cue. So unless you're in a very secure place, you are too busy. If you're doing a stunt or something dangerous that requires all your attention, you'll never notice the performance.

Q – Any tricks for keeping directors moving along smoothly?

Nic – Mostly it's just being a cop and making sure the director understands that due to the budget there won't be many pick up days or reshoots. So they may have to compromise a scene so they don't compromise the movie. You look at the schedule and see how many pages and scenes there are and do the time math. Then write it on your call sheet so you know by what time you want to move on. But, still, at the end of the day, all you can do is suggest. You give them the facts and they make the decision.

Q – Often these films won't have permits, but if they do, who makes sure it's being adhered to?

Nic – Me. One thing to know about permits is that the time limits are very real. On low budget shoots you can't afford to lose a day because you didn't adhere to the permit. Make sure you know what you want to shoot and get it on the permit.

Q – Do you take over location responsibilities?

Nic – Partially. On low budget films there usually isn't a location department or transportation department. The whole production staff, meaning the ADs and the PA as well as the office staff, end up sharing the responsibility. A good production manager will take over most of them because ADs are up against a lot on set. But if you're on a scout, the production manager might not be there so you end up taking down that information. When it becomes problematic is when you're shooting. You are so busy that if you add locations or transport to it, it slows everything down. That's when the office takes over and saves the day by talking to a homeowner or a cop.

Q – Do you oversee safety on the set?

Nic – For me, it's a shared responsibility between myself and the key grip (though it could just be the AD). I am generally the loudest voice on set as well as the focal point for information, so if someone sees an open manhole cover or whatever, they generally turn to me to make sure that problem is taken care of safety wise.

Q – Does digital filmmaking present any specific problems on the set?

Nic – It has made people lazy. It's so cheap that you can have a two- minute pre-roll before anyone calls action. Or you keep the camera rolling and get multiple takes in one series. The excuse is that it's just HD tape or if you're shooting on RED, hard drive space. But hard drives are expensive and you have to back up stuff three times. And if you are paying an editor, they have to spend more time logging footage. Plus if you just keep rolling, you slow things down and therefore you might lose setups. In a film environment, you can always say that you are burning film and we have to move fast.

Q – Do you handle the call sheet?

7. Ensure reverse shots match one another.

8. To reduce relighting time, get all your shots on one object or actor (master, medium shot, close up) at the same time.

9. If part of a take is good, but the rest is bad, you can 'pick up' from just before the mistake and continue through to the end.

10. Learn to work within your budget and schedule. Neither are limitless. Extra takes could mean you have to drop scenes later. Always be aware of the longer term impact of your choices.

12. Learn how to edit and work on other peoples films. You quickly learn what you need and don't need.

13. Know the rules before you break them. Oh and just to confuse you more, there are no rules!

If you had all the time in the world and the most perfect conditions, you would be able to plan every shot of your film down to the smallest detail. However, low budget filmmaking never gives you either of those conditions as you have limited time to shoot and those frequently occurring prop/location/actor/money/mother nature problems are always nagging at you. While you can plan for the best, you may find yourself winging it in order to get everything done. These five examples show you how much information you could offer in five different levels of planning for a scene.

Shot list - *A simple description of the shot that relates to the action. You can make these fast and they will work in any location under any circumstance. However, you have the least amount of visual information to convey to your crew.*

Overhead Plan - *If you are not good with drawings, you can sketch out an overhead camera plan (much like a blueprint) of where the camera, props and actors will go.*

Director's Storyboards - *Drawn by the director and limited by their artistic abilities. Often a storyboard artist will use these as a base for the actual storyboards.*

Full Storyboard - *A full illustrated picture of the shot drawn by a storyboard artist. If you have time and money to do this, it will give you the opportunity to easily convey the visual information to the crew.*

Previsualisation - *An animated film using a combination of your storyboards, actors voices, sound effects and music. Like making the movie without actually making it!*

Nic – Yes. My 2nd AD would create it and the production manager and I would check it for accuracy. If there's no 2nd then I do it. I like to have a draft of it done in the morning and then we give it to the department heads by lunch. They give their comments at lunch and we can have one distributed about a half hour before wrap. That discussion is important because we may be able make changes – for instance, take a daytime shot, shoot it night for day based on the logistics of the location and move the shot to the end of the shooting day.

Q – Do you check props and wardrobe?

Nic – I make sure those things get to set at the right time. And you make sure they are on the call sheet. With wardrobe, if you're doing water or blood effects, you want to make sure that you have doubles and figure out how much reset time you are going to need.

Q – If you have a problem with a crewmember, is it your job to deal with it?

Nic – That's a difficult question. On low budget films, many times people will be inexperienced and it will slow things down. We've all been there when we had to learn. If it's a real problem, you should talk to the producer about bringing people over to monitor them. If someone has a bad attitude and they're in your department, then definitely take them aside and speak with them. If the person is in another department, then you need to speak to the head of that department. But you should talk to a producer before you fire anyone because there may be logistical or political ramifications.

Q – What common mistakes do you see new filmmakers make?

Nic – Not every script can be made on a low budget. It may actually require a big budget because of the need to do lots of lighting rigging or use a multitude of locations. Do something that has minimal locations with a handful of actors so you have enough time to light properly and work with the actors.

Q – What advice would you give a new filmmaker?

Nic – Get out there and make it. No book, school or website can substitute for experience. Make your first film on your iPhone! And if you get a chance to work on a film set, do it as you can learn what every department does.

PRODUCTION DESIGN
MELANIE LIGHT

Q – What is the job of the production designer?

Melanie – Their job is to create the overall look and style of the film. Everything in front of the camera should be filtered through that creative and practical vision. The designer will work closely with the director, who on low budget films is usually the producer too. They will take the director's thoughts and ideas and then add their own to create the 'look'. The director will usually have lots of great ideas, but may not know exactly how to execute them, so they may not understand about colour matching or how to actually create a 'world' within a location. That's the job of the designer.

Q – What challenges do you face on low budget productions?

Melanie – With low budget films, especially with inexperienced directors, it can be frustrating to discover how little they respect the art department. They often spend a lot of money on cameras and actors, but very little on design. And it always shows in the final film. Even though audiences may not see it directly, they do pick up on a lack of design.

The art department is just as important as the costume, make-up and camera depts. You need each other and should work together in symphony. I recently

---

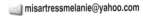 misartressmelanie@yahoo.com 　🏠 www.misartressmelanie.com

124

DESIGN FOR SUCCESS

The Production Design team is one of the least appreciated and understood departments on a film. When they are allowed to do their work well, we the audience rarely notice as we can get on with enjoying the story and the characters. But when it's done badly or not given proper resources, the foundations on which the actors and your story stand, begin to crumble.

Films are built on the ability of the audience to suspend their disbelief. This is a willing suspension, but it only takes one bad prop or an inappropriate location (that was not dressed correctly) to shatter the illusion. In a heartbeat you can lose your audience. Remember, stories are heightened reality, even complete fantasy, and the world behind the characters is the glue that seals the deal. And when it comes to sales, the first thing to flag up your film as being low budget, is going to be poor design.

The world in which your story is set must be credible. It's the design team who creates that world, the camera team who add the final gloss, and the actors who sell it as being completely authentic. Allow your design team the budget and time to get it right or pay the price at the premiere.

helped for a day on a low budget feature which had no real art department. When I arrived on set, I could see the car they were using had dirty windows that needed cleaning, and all the corporate logos needed covering up. So I just got on with it. If I had not been there, it would not have been done. It would not have ruined the scene, but these kind of small problems accumulate over the entire film, cheapening the work of all the film makers. There are lots of people out there who have an artistic eye, so in the worst case scenario, find someone who can just look at what is in front of the camera and be responsible for it.

So much time is wasted when there is no art department. Often the crew gets to a location and instead of setting up, they first have to make it look right for the story. With an art department, that team should have been on location ahead of time and will have everything ready for the crew to start work immediately.

Q – When do you get involved in production?

Melanie – Ideally I get the call ahead of time, so I can read the script and start forming ideas. The art department should be one of the first teams to be hired in pre production, especially if the budget is low as we will need time to get everything sorted out cost effectively. For instance, there are amazing props that you can buy very cheaply on eBay, but you need time to deal with the searching, bidding and delivery. I have done some jobs where the script is still being written in pre production, and that's just nuts!

Q – What drives your vision for the look?

Melanie – That will come from the script, from the discussions with the director and my own creative input. I also work with the cinematographer to find out how they will light the film as that impacts on my choice of colours etc. There are lots of very small things that pop out at you in the script or discussion, and when all of those things are combined, it creates an overall designed and considered look that is right for the story.

Q – Who is on your team on a micro budget feature?

Melanie – (laughs) If the budget is very low, it really can just be me and a couple of inexperienced workers who are not being paid. In return for them working for free I feel it's my duty to train them up as well as get the film made. That can be frustrating as when you are working with professionals, you know you can just leave a job with them and it will get done. But with inexperienced people, the workload can just go way up. That usually ends up with me not sleeping for a month and everyone gets a little crazy by the end of production.

During the shoot, if I am not on set because I am working on the next set or location, I need to leave someone on standby, to do any 'on the fly' design work and look after props. If that person is inexperienced, it can lead to serious problems. I can only ever be in one place at a time. So try and have at least two experienced people involved.

Q – Who deals with props?

Melanie – As soon as I get the script, I break it down and isolate the 'hero props'. I will usually source those hero props, either on eBay, by making them, buying things and working on them (spray painting for instance), or by using my existing network to source them. Recently I needed a severed head for a film - I was able to get that from an effects friend for no cost to the production.

So I get all the props and set dressings organised and ready before the shoot, so that when we are on set or location, we can just roll it out as needed. But do keep an eye on props as some actors have a habit of walking off with them and putting them down somewhere. Have someone retrieve props as soon as 'cut' is called.

You can hire props from props houses, but on low budgets, you simply can't afford it. So you need to trawl eBay, call friends, search charity and thrift stores, beg, borrow and steal.

Q – What about weapons?

Melanie - If you have weapons involved, you may need an armourer, and you must inform the police. You can use plastic guns and other lookalike

6. Watch out for wandering tools. Hammers, drills, nails etc., all just seem to go walkies on their own.

7. Buy from the trade suppliers and not big DIY stores. Get your production manager on the phone searching out the best deals for timber. Get them to deliver.

8. Make sure your set is 8 feet high or you might find tall cast member's heads popping over the top.

9. The secret is in the dressing. Make sure you fill your set with props, don't rely on the four walls to do it all for you.

10. Build as many flying walls as you can, it makes it easier to shoot and dress.

11. Try and reuse sets. Once one room has been shot, could it be repainted and dressed to be another location altogether overnight?

weapons which work very well, and for that you only need to inform the police, you won't need an armourer.

Q – What do you flag up as problems when reading a script?

Melanie – Animals are much more hassle and expensive than you would think. For low budgets, unless your script depends on an animal being present, or you have some unique and well thought out way of doing it, I suggest you cut it out. Other stuff would include remote locations where it's hard to get props and dressings to, vehicles, police units, firing weapons, explosions, stunts and special effects. Often it's quite obvious problems, and the production team have simply been in denial about the scale of what they are trying to achieve with no real budget.

Q – What key relationships do you need on set?

Melanie – Aside from the obvious, such as director and DP, it's with the production team and assistant directors. They produce the schedule and that is usually a source of many of our problems, due to an unrealistic shooting schedule and shot list. If there are problems with the schedule, by the end of the shoot, it can be complete chaos and extremely stressful. Many times I have been consulted about the schedule and flagged up problems, only to get to set to find that no-one listened, and now we all have a very big problem.

Having a good relationship with the cast is important too, as they need to feel comfortable with the props. A good actor will make your props look even better.

Q – Can you build sets for low budget films?

Melanie – You can't build massive and complex sets on a low budget, but you can build simple and effective sets, as long as you have a few people to help and a space big enough to accommodate it (and distance between the set and walls of the building you are inside, so that you can get lights into place). After doing your sums, it may be cheaper to build a set than it is to pay location fees. On the flipside, if you find the right location, much of the design work is already in place by virtue of it being a real space.

Q – What mistakes do you see over and over?

Melanie – Lack of experience, but there is nothing you can do about that as people have to learn. Sometimes I do wish they would listen to experience though (laughs). Unrealistic shot lists and poor schedules are a real problem. It's so frustrating when you have flagged these problems weeks in advance and yet no-one did anything. It's the result of inexperience and underfunding. A deadly combination (laughs).

Q – What advice would you offer a new film maker?

Melanie – Never think that you know everything because there is always something new to learn. Don't work with one set of people all the time, create relationships with other people by working on other productions. Above all, just go and do it.

COSTUME
SHANNA KNECHT

Q – Why is it a bad idea for actors to wear their own clothes when shooting?

Shanna – Most of the time an actor doesn't have what is needed to create the character the director envisions. So when they get to set, the director hates what they're wearing and wonders if they have anything else. And even if it is correct, it's doubtful that they are going to have multiples of their clothes should they end up getting wet or ruined during a scene. There are times when you can use stuff from the actor's closet and it works because it feels authentic. Usually in those cases, you use part of the actor's clothes and combine it with other things.

Q – Where do you go to get costumes when you're on a budget?

Shanna – Thrift or charity stores are always good, but again, it's rare that they will have multiples of a costume. There are also rental and hire houses that you can hire from. The great thing about those companies is that you can hire expensive looking garments, like a Dolce & Gabbana suit for a high powered woman, for a fraction of what they would normally cost to buy.

Q – Are there any things to know about color and texture?

Shanna – I tend never to use black unless it is for a character that is older and sophisticated. If you put a 20 year-old actor that is playing a 16 year-old in black, they are going to look 30 on camera. White is bad too, because it's so bright. It is all you look at in the frame. It's distracting. The clothes should never wear the person; the person should wear the clothes. Things need to be subtle. Don't use tight prints or stripes or else they will strobe. Bright colors work best especially in HD or digital because the camera tends to wash things out. Pale pink is going to look white and it's not going to bring out their features. Now, if the character is supposed to be monochromatic and non-descript, then that is OK. Another tip: if you have an overweight person, don't put them in light colors. They will look even heavier. Pants will do the same thing. Opt for skirts for women, as it will accentuate their waists. Also shoot them from an angle. Straight on looks awful.

Q – Is it helpful for you to get the script ahead of time?

Shanna – It's imperative. I need to know who the characters are. Is the girl a freak about animals, loves jewellery or obsessed with sex? Knowing that, I can tune the costume to the character and it will let the audience know more about who this person is. Otherwise, you can end up putting a non-descript, dorky girl who works at a computer in a mini-skirt and Ugg boots. That's distracting and would take the audience out of the movie. Also, I need to see how many changes there are. If someone gets shot, then I know I need to have multiples. On a big show, I would have 5-6 and on a smaller one I could get away with 3.

Q – For a film with no special effects that takes place in the present, how much pre-production time would you want?

Shanna – If the story takes place over one day, I can do it in 1-2 weeks. If there are a lot of days,

COSTUME TIPS

1. On a low budget, most likely you'll be working with actor's own clothes. Make sure you keep hold of the costumes for the duration of the shoot.

2. Directors may lose sight of the costume and only comment when it's entirely inappropriate. Have a second set of creative eyes looking out.

3. Consider making or buying seconds and thirds of the same costumes in case the originals are damaged either in the filming process (get wet, fake blood, ripped in a stunt) or the cleaning process (shrinking in the dryer).

4. Charity / Thrift stores are fantastic places to find cheap wardrobe - especially if you need something period or really worn looking. But you will never find doubles.

5. Big, bright and flamboyant costumes can look bold and exciting, thus adding to production value. But take care.

6. The costume department sees actors long before most everyone each day, and they can judge their mood. Always talk to your costumiers to see if there are any potential problems on the horizon that you can deal with early.

7. The Costume Department is the first to arrive and the last to leave (as they need to prep for the next day, wash clothes etc.) Be nice to them.

8. Keep your eye on the weather forecast. Have thermal underwear and blankets ready for your actors if it is cold, umbrellas and towels for rain and a cool spray if it is warm.

that means a lot of changes and I need at least a month. But that doesn't always work because many times actors aren't cast until the last minute. If you have to do that, then schedule those people's scenes later in the shoot so it gives me a chance to dress them properly.

Q – On set, how much time would you want with the actors before camera rolls?

Shanna – If the full cast were getting dressed, then I would want between 1-2 hours. Most of that time is steaming their clothes so there are no wrinkles and for little alterations. I generally don't like to work during make-up sessions because obviously it can get on the clothes, but if you have time constraints, then have a smock put on the actor so none of their clothes get ruined. Tissue around the collar is a good protector. But if you do get some make-up on the collar, don't use pre-wetted wipes – those just embed it. Use a white sponge instead, takes it right out. Don't steam them until afterwards or else it's useless.

Q – If you can't sew, what are some ways to alter clothes?

Shanna - Top Stick tape is great, especially for hems. It's double sided and I've made whole outfits out of it. Stitch-witchery is good, too. That's this stuff you iron on. If you need something very elaborate, the best thing to do is to take it to a professional tailor.

Q – Are there any tricks to making clothes looked worn or aged?

Shanna – Color fader is the best way to do that. But test it first. If you want things to look dirty, the best thing is to rub newspaper on it. That black print just comes right off and really works well. There is something called Smear that you can buy at costume houses, but that can sometimes look a little too dirty and fake. If you need to make a shoe's white sole look older then use dark wood polish. Works for purses and props, too.

Q – If you have a really ambitious costume in a script, how realistic is it that you can design it on a low budget?

Shanna – It's possible, but you need time. For example, if you are creating a Star Wars Stormtrooper like character, then with 4-5 days, you can go to rental houses and get helmets and the like to piece that together. You can spray paint things and add bells and whistles to make it look more authentic. I just did this thing where there were a lot of military costumes and the show had no budget. So I used gaffer's tape to look like armbands and cheap toy grenades that I attached to a leather string. At first, I thought it was going to look cheap and awful, but it looked pretty good. One time I used a 99-cent household strainer for an alien's helmet. We put silver paint on their faces and they looked great. You just need to be clever and use all the elements around you.

Q – Do you find that most directors know what they want?

Shanna – When it comes to sci-fi, yes, because directors of that kind are into that world heavily. But when they are not sure, that is when nightmares occur. That is when it can become expensive because they want changes at the last minute.

9. Try not to rush costume changes as actors want to feel right in the new 'skin' they are wearing.

10. Make sure actors have a space to change that is more than a toilet.

11. Continuity between takes should be carefully monitored. This means you may need someone on set from the costume department.

12. Make sure your actors do not take any of their costumes away with them.

13. Minimise costumes. As long as they are appropriate, costume changes wont add much to your film, and unnecessary changes will add to the budget and eat into shooting time.

14. Not all actors have the character in mind. Some will just want to look good, which may not be right for the character. Be aware.

Q – What do people need to know about cleaning or returning costumes?

Shanna – Everything has to be dry cleaned before you return it and that can add up. But a big thing to keep in mind is that anytime you rent a costume, you cannot ruin it. You cannot throw blood on them, light them on fire or throw them into a swimming pool. They will charge you 10 times the amount of the rental in order to replace them. So if you have a period costume where blood needs to get on someone, you have to build at least the top part. That can get expensive for low budget shoots.

Q – Are there any fabrics you should avoid?

Shanna – I don't like stretch cottons that are very matte. That tends to look uninteresting. Texture is always better. Shiny spandex especially for superhero costumes tends to look cheap.

Q – Does jewellery fall into your domain?

134

Shanna – Yes. Accessories are extremely important. You can have a plain outfit like a tank top and a pair of jeans and the right accessories can make it look like a million bucks. Belts, bracelets, necklaces, scarves, ear rings can make things pop. Don't over do it, but it can totally add an element.

Q – Do you ever discuss safety or other logistics with the director as far as wardrobe is concerned?

Shanna – Absolutely. If a scene calls for an actress to walk across a metal grating or a tightrope in high heels, then that raises a red flag and adjustments must be made to shoot around that. Sometimes it calls for a stuntman, which brings up other issues. For example, depending on the stunt they will perform, the may need to wear long sleeves or pants to hide padding. A good wardrobe person will have some of that in their arsenal just in case the stunt guys leave and there are still things that an actor needs to do like fall down.

Q – What common mistakes do you see that drive you crazy?

Shanna – The first one is when directors don't trust you to do your job. You give them suggestions and they turn you down and then they look at the dailies and realize that it looks terrible because they didn't listen. Respect me as a professional to help create your vision. The other one is when they cannot make-up their mind. You don't need to know every detail, but if you can at least have a reference from another show or movie in mind. It saves time and money.

Q – What advice would you give a new filmmaker?

Shanna – Have a good idea of the visual concept of your movie. Do your research from everything to costumes to set design to special effects. People will respect you a lot more.

Costumes are the skin of the character and essential to get right!

MAKE-UP
KAT BARDOT

Q – Why is it a bad idea to let actors do their own make-up?

Kat – Most actors don't know how to apply make-up properly so they end up looking all shiny. And if you are outside all day or under those hot lights, it's only going to get worse. Many actors don't use the right foundation so when they blend it in wrong you get things like really hard jaw lines, which looks terrible. Or their eye make-up might be all splotchy. If make-up is awful, it becomes distracting and then takes you out of the movie. Nothing drives me more insane than that.

Q – How does it affect continuity?

Kat – If in one shot an actress has cat's eye make-up and it goes to your eyebrow line and then in another shot it only goes halfway – that's distracting and amateurish. Unless you know what you are doing, it's really hard to do the same make-up on someone from day to day.

Q – When do you get involved in a production?

Kat – For web stuff and TV I usually get a call two days beforehand. If all I am doing is beauty make-up, I can just pick up my kit and go. But for a four-week

---

 katbardot@yahoo.com   www.katbardot.com

MICRO-BUDGET MAKE-UP

Make-up is often an invisible craft. When you watch a film, it's rare that you will notice the make-up, except when it's special make-up or really bad make-up. It can often be said of a film crew that they see make-up as unimportant and invisible too, which can of course cause friction. It's the primary job of the make-up artist to make sure everyone in front of the camera looks as good as possible, even when they are looking bad, and the production team MUST allow time for the make-up artist to do their job.

On ultra micro budget shoots, make-up is often little more than the obvious, foundation, blusher and lipstick for the girls and a powdering down for the boys (sometimes even done by the actors themselves). But as you get more serious, so will the make-up department, at which point workload kicks in . How do you cope with multiple make-ups for a single scene? The answer is a second make-up artist or assistant, ideally a multi-talented person who can be shared with the Costume department.

feature shoot that is heavy on make-up and effects, a month would be a good amount of time. That's because you have to make your own prosthetics – you can't just buy those at a store. And you can't really reuse them so you will have to make multiples, which is time consuming.

Q – How much time should be scheduled for hair and make-up each day?

Kat – If it is just beauty make-up and there's no rain or the like involved, I would want 30-40 minutes for each woman and 5 minutes for each man. I think a lot of make-up artists overcompensate for men, but really all they need is concealer for blemishes and anti-shine. Gel is best to start and then I go to powder for touch ups because it's faster. Then of course add a bit more time if it's humid or you start doing something more complicated like a bald cap. Those can take between 45 minutes to an hour depending on your skill level.

Q – Are all make-up products good for film and TV work?

Kat – No! Don't use the stuff that you buy from the local store. It's cheap and looks awful. Use the professional stuff. I sometimes use L'Oreal True Match Foundation because it's the best of the pharmacy lot if budgets are really tight. It's like $10 a color instead of $25 for MAC.

Q – How do you do common things like bruises?

Kat – I always carry a bruise wheel. I use it more than everything else in my kit. They're like $18 and they are easy to use. You lay down your lighter colors and work to your darkest.

Q – What if someone wanted something like a deformed ear?

Kat – Now you are into prosthetics. That can take some time because latex is slow to dry, you have to put it on, blend it, paint it to match the skin – it takes a while. Size matters too. A small bullet hole you can do in 20 minutes. But an arterial, gushing, neck wound? That's 45 minutes, easy.

Q – What about wigs?

Kat – I recently had to buy a $25 wig in a pinch and I put it on and it looked ridiculous. I had to trim it, cut it and spirit gum it in all the right places to make it look acceptable. It took about 25 minutes. It's really hard to overcome a bad wig or beard if it's not being done for comedy. It just kills a scene. One trick I do is to get a piece that is the same color as the person's hair and then pull it back on their head. Then some of their real hair comes through and you can blend it together.

A lot of wigs that don't have bangs on them look fake because the hairline looks fake. But a human hair wig is expensive – over $150 whereas a synthetic wig can be around $60. Also something to keep in mind is that there is some psychology at play here. If you don't see an actor pre-wig and then see them with it on, it's more likely to look real. Conversely, if you know what they looked like beforehand, it's harder to buy into the charade.

Q – Do you ever dye hair?

Kat – Almost never. It's best to pay for the actress to go to a professional salon and have it done. There are some sprays you can use that are cheap, awful and can get all over the make-up you just did if you're not careful. But if the shot and situation are right, it is a weapon in your arsenal.

Q – How has HD changed the way you do make-up?

Kat – HD is a make-up artists' nightmare because you can see everything! If you do someone who is 19, they still look good on HD. But when you get into older people – they may look good in the chair, but on HD? You can see every line and the make-up looks caked on. So one choice is to buy HD foundation, but it is ridiculously expensive.

So a tip I got was to take a wedge sponge, dip it in hot water, squeeze out 90% of the water and then dip it in your foundation. It thins it out and really works. Something else to try is HD powder which has no color to it at all. You can use it on anyone. Costs $40, but it lasts for a long time.

Q – What about tattoos?

Kat – Tattoos are tricky because directors usually want very specific designs so you can't buy generic ones from a store. Most of the time they will show you a picture of something and you either copy it or alter it to something that is similar. To put it on, you can buy tattoo markers, but they are stupidly expensive. So I just use a Sharpie and a bottle of acetone. I just draw what I want and then take it off. Acetone will not hurt your skin at all and it comes off so easily.

Q – What are the best conditions for you to apply make-up?

MAKE-UP TIPS

1. It takes special skills to know how to apply cosmetics and sculpt hair for film. If put in the hands of amateurs, what may look OK for a Saturday night out may look garish on a 40 foot screen.

2. On low budget movies, the Make-up designer and Hairstylist are usually the same person.

3. Don't assume your make-up artist can do all make-up such as special make-up FX like blood, cuts, bruises, prosthetics etc, as they require different skills. Ask first.

4. Some cosmetic companies will offer free or discounted make-up in exchange for a mention in the film itself.

5. If dealing with gore, special make-up or complicated wigs, it's a good idea to do camera and make-up tests. What you might consider looks realistic in real life can look really fake on screen and vice versa.

6. Make-up is where your actors start their day. If they're made up in a relaxing environment, they will leave ready for their shots.

7. A make-up artist can keep an eye on the actor's deeper feelings and fears and report back to the producer. You have a spy who is both on your side and the actors side.

8. Ensure you have enough time for make-up. There is always pressure to rush.

9. Consider hiring extra help on days when you have a lot of extras or principals in a scene. It may save you a lot of time.

10. Make sure your actors are out of make-up each day and their skin cleansed. You don't want to contribute to a bad complexion.

11. Ensure there is enough room for your make-up and hair to work freely.

Kat – I like working in natural light even though it might look different than it will under the movie set lights. This way you can see every single flaw, and when you are working in HD that really helps smooth things out. Ideally, it's great to have your own space with a table, chair and access to a bathroom.

I've been put in hallways with dozens of people going past and no table – that just makes things hard to do properly.

Q – Since it sounds like make-up is so costly, how can a production keep those expenses under control?

Kat – Samples are a really good way. You can write to make-up companies and state that you are hesitant to buy new product because you can't test it in a store. Sometimes they will send you samples or new products they want to get out into the market. I once got this pigment that can be used as different make-ups just by adding water. So I could put it around the eye as a dry power or add some water and it became eyeliner or mix it with petroleum jelly and it became lipstick! That saves you money right there.

Most of the time they want links to pictures of your work that they can use as advertisement. And something like that, I would totally buy their product again.

Q – Can a make-up artist pretty much handle any genre of film?

Kat – Some can, but many can't crossover. There are people who are great at beauty make-up, but get them to do some gory horror special effects and they suck. The best thing to do is look at their past work and see if it works for your project.

Q – Are there any common mistakes that drive you crazy?

Kat – It's not so much a mistake, but many times filmmakers can't tell you what they want an actor to look like, because they don't know fashion and aesthetics in that way. They don't know about products and pieces and how they all fit together.

Q – What advice would you give a new filmmaker?

Kat – Never take your crew for granted. You only have what you have on film because of what the crew does. And don't expect them to work for free all the time.

12. Schedule time during prep for your make-up and hair people to meet the actors to discuss any issues or ideas.

13. Make sure the 1st AD has make-up and hair check for imperfections just prior to the first take. This means you may need two make-up artists. One on set (on standby), the other making up actors for the next scene.

14. Photos of the actors should be taken from all angles at the end of each shot to ensure continuity.

14. Give them time and respect. Make-up artists are often pushed around by bossy crew members with big cameras because they are female (mostly) and their job can often be seen as not being as important. They will rarely ask for more time than is absolutely needed, so when they ask for it, give it.

Q – Why is it better to hire a stunt coordinator to do your gags instead of using your friends?

Nils – A well trained stunt coordinator and stuntmen will always make your action look better, but the biggest thing is that everyone will be safe.

Q – When do you like to be brought on in a production?

Nils – I like to have a bit of prep so I can read the script and see what needs to be done. Some of the bigger productions give you four to six weeks. I generally only need two weeks so I can see the locations to make sure nothing gets thrown at me last minute. That's when people get hurt.

Q – What things should you know when hiring stunt people?

Nils – You definitely want to take a look at their resumes and make sure they can honestly do what you need them to do. Otherwise people are going to get hurt – especially the stuntman.

Q – What should directors be thinking about when putting together a fight?

 poundground@aol.com

Nils – They are always the least expensive stunt and when done right look fantastic. Just give your stunt coordinator and two stuntmen a little bit of time and get the camera angles right and you are good to go. Camera angles are important because many times it's not the punch thrown, but the reaction to it that sells the punch.

Q – What if you add chairs or other items to the fight?

Nils – When you are dealing with props you have to either buy or create breakaways. Buying them creates expense. Making them takes a lot of time, which is expensive in another way.

Q – How do you handle high falls?

Nils – This is always a time when someone can get injured. And when actors frequently want to do the stunt themselves, it can get a bit hairy. You have to weigh the realistic look of the shot versus the potential for your actor getting hurt and shutting down production. That is why I am a fan of stunt doubles. And if you get over fifteen feet in height, you definitely want a stunt coordinator handling that.

Q – How do they usually do the fall? Do they use cables?

Nils – There are lots of ways to fall. You can fall into an air bag. You can fall into boxes. You can fall using a cable that connects to a machine called a Descender where the wire stops you just before you hit the ground. That's a scary thing for stuntmen. These days CG is used a lot and as the technology gets better, it will be used more.

STUNTS

1. Safety always comes first.

2. Ask for feedback on your script from a stunt coordinator. You might be surprised at hidden dangers.

3. Rewrite your script to remove all unnecessary stunts and action work.

4. Watch out for simple things like a character tripping up or playing with knives. These are often more complicated than they appear.

5. When shooting action, actors feel much more comfortable when there is a stunt coordinator around.

6. Plastic guns will appear real once muzzle flashes are added as a special effect in post, and gun shot sounds (as well as foley gun handling) are added.

7. Ask your stunt coordinator who all his friends are and see if you can get them involved too. These guys are all in an elite club, and might do it for free – like us, they love their work!

8. Where possible, avoid stunts involving water and/or fire. Especially fire. It never looks as good as when imagined, costs a huge amount and is VERY dangerous.

9. Work closely with costume and makeup – you may need doubles of clothing, extra size clothing and special makeup.

10. Stunts at night always look much cooler, but are obviously more time consuming and dangerous.

11. Remember. Safety first!

Q – What about if you want to use guns?

Nils – We all know about Brandon Lee and his accident. It's very dangerous. If your weapons need to actually fire, you will need an armourer, which can get expensive. But many film makers use plastic guns now and add muzzle flash later, and do bullet hits with compressed air. There are lots of very safe ways to do this. But if you need that very real effect that you only get with blank firing weapons, and explosive bullet squibs (hits) you will need a pro and it can get very expensive. Of course, if you use any kind of weapon in any public place, you must inform the police or you could find yourself getting arrested. All knives should be props too. Nothing bladed. That's a sure way for someone to get injured.

Q – Are horse stunts something that could be an option?

Nils – It depends. You can find people willing to bring out a horse for nothing as long as they get to work on the project themselves. But then you might end up getting what you pay for. If you do bring in a horse, it should be one that has been on set before so all the motion won't spook it. Otherwise people can get thrown and shoved around. The stunt person needs to know how to ride and generally be a good horse person.

Q – Any advice on dealing with glass?

Nils – Candy glass can be expensive and it's very delicate. I've seen panes break as they are being installed, so you need at least two pieces. If you have to do multiple takes, resetting glass takes a long time because you have to clean it up and put a new pane in. That can kill your day. Try to get it

STUNTS ON NO MONEY

By far the best way to deal with a stunt sequence in a low budget film is to cut it out of the script. That does not mean you lose that part of the story, but instead ask yourself, can it be done in a conversation, or an extreme close up flashback sequence, or with clever use of sound? Being forced to find creative ways to do what Hollywood would normally do with a huge team and a 'line item' in their budget can often result in stories that become far more interesting and compelling. Mother of ingenuity stuff.

Few people, aside from your close friends, will be impressed by low budget stunts and stunt sequences. Remember, once the lights in the theatre go down, it's a level playing field (which is good news, you just need a great story well told) and therefore you are competing with the likes of James Bond, Jason Bourne and James Cameron. You probably won't win.

If you really do need stunts and action in your film, then choose your battles wisely. If you can manage to pull off one extremely memorable sequence, that will go much further than endless average scenes of people hitting each other and running around with guns. And if you do need the services of a stunt coordinator, you will find it much easier asking the best in the business for help if they only need to give you a couple of days.

in one shot. Some people bring in an FX guy who will blow up tempered glass as the stunt performers goes through it. Also even candy glass can cut you so be mindful of having an actor go through it. If they get cut on the face, then you might have continuity errors.

Q – What about if you want to use fire on set?

Nils – Extremely dangerous. Usually expensive. You must always use trained professionals. You always have to have a Fire Marshal on set. You will have to pull special permits for it. Usually it is the pyro guy that does the stunt and the coordinator is there for safety. Make sure people keep their distance and wear the right clothes. If people do an actual burn, then there are gels you spread on

Stunts and practical effects go hand in hand. Blowing up cars, sugar glass windows, blank firing weapons, special gore effects, cobwebs, safe props (such as blunt knives), forced perspective models, fire, rain, mist... all are the domain of the practical effects team. For the most part, these kind of effects can be expensive and if possible are best avoided. For example, scenes set in the rain are a bad idea and setting a stunt man on fire is very very dangerous.

Most film makers are pretty good at figuring out basic practical effects – for instance, we have seen bullet hits in zombie films done safely with compressed air from a garden spray. But there will come a point when you know it's going to be dangerous, and that's when you bring in an effects team. On occasion, you may need an effects crew, or special make-up artist, especially with genre films.

Practical effects and stunts will be significantly improved in post production with clever editing, terrific sound, and perhaps even some digital enhancement.

the actors or they wear a hood to protect themselves from the flames. However, a burn on a hand or a leg with the right gel and an experienced coordinator can be pretty inexpensive and add a lot of wow to your film.

Q – How do you handle car wrecks?

Nils – Car stunts are probably the most expensive stunts to do. You need to buy a car and get it to set. You need to make sure the car works properly, such as making sure the brakes work. You need a trained stunt person for any car gag and if you get into flips or rolls, it's even more important. Some people do a car gag without professionals and they get away with it but then they do it again and disaster strikes.

Q – Is there anything a director can do to make your job easier?

Nils – Camera placement is so important to making everything look real. They should know that we use depth perception to make punches and kicks work. If they let us handle that portion of things, then we can make it look great in the shortest amount of time, using the least number of shots and save them a lot of money.

Q – What should a director know about padding?

Nils – When I break down a script and I see that a character is going to hit the ground, I immediately look to see what they are wearing. This is really important for women because they tend to be put in less clothes (by the costume designer). I will call the producer and then the wardrobe person to make sure that we can hide padding with long sleeves and pants if it is going to be needed. An actress or stuntwoman that shows up in a short skirt and a tank top is going to get bruised badly when she gets thrown around because I can't hide the pads.

Q – Are stunt people expensive?

Nils – We can be, but there are a lot of modified budget schemes through SAG that can make us really affordable. It's the same in the UK, and there are instances where a coordinator will either advise or help for free if they like the film makers and the project.

Q – What advice would you give a new filmmaker?

Nils – Be realistic. Everybody wants to emulate the big films, but you should work on a film that you can finish within your budget and resources. That way it won't look cheap and you will be proud to watch it.

Safety, safety and safety!

Ask a professional for help!

WORKING WITH ACTORS JAN DUNN

Q – How do you mange to get such great actors involved in lower budget films?

Jan – If you are asking a named actor, such as Bob Hoskins (who worked with Jan on *Ruby Blue*) to work with you they are more likely to say yes if it's a short and concise period of time. Also, try and work around their availability too, so you may need to reschedule. We did pay Bob reasonably from our microbudget.

Q – So you get involved in scheduling?

Jan – Yes. As the writer and director, especially on micro budgets, I believe it's essential to be hands on in both the schedule and the production. It's just easier for me to direct if I am scheduling too, and it's easier then to work around actor availability. We never go overschedule, and we don't shoot long days, but we are meticulously organized.

Q – How would you advise a film maker to approach casting a film?

Jan – Before going to experienced film actors, make sure you are experienced in directing. There are certain rules and phrases used that you must understand, and I have seen new film makers make crushingly basic mistakes, simply because they had not made a few short films to learn how to be professional and

---

jan@medbfilms.com   www.medbfilms.com

BLOCKING A SCENE

Blocking a scene refers to figuring out how the actors and camera will physically move through a scene, and it is done on set or location just before shooting it. Blocking allows the director and the heads of various departments, as well as the actors, to see where potential problems might arise. For instance, the camera team may realise that a light is in their shot during a tracking move, or an actor may not feel comfortable delivering a certain line at a specific spot on the set. Blocking also allows for the camera team to mark the floor with white camera tape, to give actors a specific point to stand on, so the camera team know the camera will be in focus (this is where the phrase 'hitting your mark' comes from). Resist the temptation to drop blocking. Five minutes blocking may save an hour trying to figure it out on the fly.

respectful. Often it's just as simple as checking out actors on IMDB so you know what they have done before.

I would also suggest you write a great part for an actor. You are not going to offer Bob Hoskins a small and uninspired part for instance. There are some actors who are visibly supportive of low budget and independent film, and if they like the script, and if their agent likes the project, you do have a chance.

Of course you always need to pass through the agent, they are like the testing ground. When Bob Hoskins agreed to do *Ruby Blue*, his agent liked the script which was very helpful, and we were clear that we wanted two weeks of his time, and we would work entirely around his schedule. Remember, this caliber of actor often has a tiny window of availability - we have always been willing to completely re-arrange our schedules to accommodate them – that's what I mean about being involved in the scheduling.

Q – So actors are very busy and often want to help but can't?

Jan – Yes, and they also get frustrated when they want to help but cannot because of clashes. If the film maker can then work around that problem, the actor may chose to do the film. The key is always to be respectful though.

Q – Why not cast your friends in a film?

Jan – I would always seek to work with experienced actors. I was an actor for 15 years and so know a lot of actors who have not had a film break yet – and so I would cast those actors, and count myself blessed to be able to get that kind of experience onto our set. Casting directors can help with this.

Q – How do you get a casting director?

Jan – You need to build relationships, and once more, that begins with a respect for the job of the casting director. If you are developing a feature film, there should be a portion of your budget set aside for casting and the casting director. Even in the early stages of development, you are going to want their advice, and it's their advice, knowledge and contacts that you are paying for. If you don't have contacts, it's essential you work with a casting director. It's a vital part of your budget. Even if you cast unknowns, you will need someone's judgment, someone who is aware of their skills.

Q – How do you approach the meeting with a named actor?

Jan – Personally, I am not starstruck, maybe because I was an actor. You cannot go into that meeting starstruck, you are offering a job - it is part of your job as a director to cast the film. You are, on a professional level, finding that person who is going to bring something extra, something important, perhaps the most important part, to your film, and it is key.

Q – How important are rehearsals?

Jan – On all the microbudget films I have done, we have had read throughs and one or two days rehearsal. So we end up doing most of the rehearsals on set on the day. But beforehand, I also have long and indepth conversations over the phone with the individual actors.

Q – What do you lose and gain with rehearsals?

Jan – That comes down to the screenplay and the individual actors. In reality though, rehearsals are so minimal for micro budget films because of the budget. If you can get two days, that would be very useful.

Q – Do actors need a place to relax when not being used on set?

Jan – That is essential. When looking for locations, the production manager should consider if there is also a place where we can put the actors without paying more money. They need that space. If you are lucky enough to get a name actor - then it is extremely important they have a quiet place to be away from everyone and that they do not have to queue for food etc., because actually they do need headspace enough to carry your film, after all. It's not a Diva thing but merely common sense that they should expect that they would have that. It doesn't cost anything extra. We borrowed caravans for Bob and Josy in *Ruby Blue*, they were hardly used, but an absolute necessity when they were used.

Q - How do you get the best out of an actor? The best performance?

6. Work with a casting director. They have contacts you don't and can add credibility.

7. Cast unusual actors. Look for faces that are interesting, not just pretty or charismatic. Part of what makes an actor stand out is their differences. Ugly can also be very beautiful.

8. Above all, respect what an actor can bring to the role. They may be neurotic and difficult, but that is part of the package. They are trained to deliver raw emotion. Your job is to channel that in the right direction and capture it on camera.

9. Great actors will bring gravitas to your set.

10. Cast your film well and it will almost make itself.

Jan – They have to feel completely safe, so they can explore. Providing emotional safety allows them to lose their inhibitions so they are free. Even on a tight shoot, you must try and do this. They must have total faith that you, the director, are in complete control, that you understand and comprehend the text fully. I feel the text and the acting are the two most important points for any film maker. Audiences don't care about the shooting format, they just care about following characters and a story. Always remember the audience.

Q – Should actors be allowed to rework dialogue?

Jan – Contrary to the myth that actors all want more dialogue, all most actors ever really want is the best out of any scene. Sometimes I have had dialogue reworked and it's been improved, or shortened, sometimes it's been reworked and we have later returned to the scripted dialogue. So there is no straight answer.

Q – What makes an actor's life hard?

Jan – Working with directors who don't know what they are doing (laughs). They want a director who is 'in the piece' with the cast. Actors don't like directors fussing about all the time, or losing their place in the script, or panicking, they want calm, organized leadership. I worked on one film where the director looked like he was about to have a heart attack all the time, and that was very stressful for everyone. If you are a new director, I suggest you work with a very experienced cinematographer, it will make everyone feel more secure.

Q – What makes a director's life hard?

Jan – When an actor attempts to take control of the set. The director needs to be in charge of the set. If that happens, I nip it in the bud.

Q – What mistakes do you see most often?

Jan – Bad casting. If you can, work with a casting director.

Q – What advice would you offer a new film maker?

Jan – Your first feature film is very important. So make sure you are completely ready for it, because if you mess it up, you won't get a second chance.

WHAT TO NEGOTIATE

Rate of pay and overtime - You don't want to agree to overtime, it's one fee to do the film.

Per diem - Are you going to give one and how much? The per diem is a tax free daily payment that is supposed to cover expenses. Often this is used by agents to get extra fees for their actors.

Credit billing - Who gets top billing? Whose name is biggest on the poster? Always go for alphabetical billing of your principal cast, unless of course you have a major actor whose status vastly overshadows the others.

Approval - Some agents may try to insist upon some kind of editorial approval. Flatly decline this. Others may argue for approval of stills, which you may want to give.

Points - Or to the rest of the world, percentages. What percentage will they get of the profits? They will want gross which you cannot give them, so they will have to settle for net. Never offer more than a couple of percent at the most and ideally, agree to none.

Nudity - Some actors are cautious about exploitation filmmaking. This may be a very serious make or break issue for some actors.

Now in your favour, you might want to add...

Re-shoots and ADR - If you need to re-shoot a scene or you need your actor to record some ADR (replacement or extra lines of dialogue) you need to know that they will be contractually obliged to do it even if they fall out with you during the shoot.

Movie release - Make sure they will support the release of the film by doing press interviews etc.

Q – To the outside world, the director looks like they 'make the film', but the producer is responsible for the business behind that PR face. What gets a producer through the heat of a film shoot?

Chris – Experience is the most important thing any producer can have, but of course that is a 'chicken and egg' kind of deal. So I would say, just go for it, throw yourself in. But with three caveats. First, learn as much as you can before your big project. Talk with other producers, work on other films, read books, take short courses. Get educated. Second, when you do get it wrong, learn from that mistake and don't do it again. Third, always, always think ahead. The ability to visualize multiple solutions to a single problem that has not even occurred is about the best skill any hands on producer could wish for.

Q – Why do so many film makers get into trouble on their first film?

Chris – It's the deadly combination of inexperience and underfunding. Throw in unrealistic expectations and ultra exuberant enthusiasm and it's a testament to

---

chris@guerillafilm.com

www.twitter.com/livingspiritpix

www.livingspirit.com

www.chrisjonesblog.com

Join our Facebook group 'Guerilla Film Maker'

the tenacity of film makers that so many films don't actually implode (laughs). So catastrophe on a daily basis is to be expected. It's something that is very hard to imagine when sat at your computer writing the script. In your head it's always sunny, the actors nail it in take 2, and all those cunning ideas the entrepreneur in you has had, well they all work out too. If only that were actually how it plays out.

When the film wraps, all that 'feel good' stuff of having a crew around you, the optimism and possibilities, can dissipate. You are left alone with the director, rushes, editor and a pile of bills that you may not have funds to pay. And sadly, no-one (outside of your film) really cares about your troubles. Not audiences, not investors. They just want a great story, well told. At the end of the day, it's the producer's job to make sure that the film is brought in on budget, on schedule and in accordance with the script. Of course things will change during the shoot, but anything that goes wrong either gets fixed on the day, or it ends up on your plate to fix later. The buck stops with you and no one is interested in hearing *'well we had problems with our lead actor'* or *'it rained...'* So expect unexpected and serious problems and deal with them promptly and efficiently.

Q – Who are the key people who can help keep things on track?

Chris – It always begins with the director. There are myths about directors who, in the pursuit of an artistic vision, pushed studios hard and got what they wanted. That is all well and good when you are in partnership with an entity with deep pockets. For most of us, that isn't the case. So you need a director who understands that the schedule and budget are tools to help get the most out of limited resources. They are not to be abused. I would even suggest that any new director should produce a film BEFORE they think of directing. This will give them a healthy respect for the problems you face. You can be sure that if they did this, they would be the first to suggest that aggressively cutting their script down to size before getting to set would be a good idea.

Q – What common problems will a producer face?

Chris – Without getting into the infinite list of smaller problems that will generally get fixed (without significant pain) there are a few key areas to keep an eye on. First is money. It's hard to get your head around how, if allowed, a film can easily spiral over budget as you lose track of the money. Have someone take on the job of dealing with receipts, invoices, tallying up and cross referencing with the

1. A film crew works better on a full stomach, especially if they are out in the cold. Tea, coffee and cold drinks should always be made available, with someone making sure that the key personnel (who are working harder than the others) have their drinks brought to them.

2. Feed a crew as much food as you can. Have energy snacks such as fruit, pastries, sweets/candy, crisps/chips, nuts and bread, all constantly available.

3. Film caterers / Craft Services are expensive, but they do provide a great service. Try negotiating them down to a price per head that you can afford.

4. If you can't afford a film caterer, find someone who is used to catering for large groups and employ them for the duration of the shoot. They may bring their own equipment and will certainly have good ideas.

5. On the whole, actors are fussier than crew, and often expect to be treated better than you can afford. Be aware of this very important factor.

6. Sweets/candy and beers after a hard week's shoot is good for morale.

7. Concentrate on foods that are easy to prepare, cheap to produce, and fast to distribute and clear. Draw up a list of meals and outline them in a schedule. This will allow certain meals to be rotated.

8. If cast and crew are away from home for a location shoot, you will need to cater for all their needs, breakfast, lunch, and dinner (more for night shoots). This quickly becomes VERY expensive.

9. Make sure that food is not left out too long in the sun or uncovered for insects to get at. You don't want your crew coming down with salmonella.

10. If you are shooting in a confined place, avoid farty foods for lunch!

budget every night. You cannot afford to run out of resources 75% of the way through shooting.

Generally, during the filming, a producer will wander around, trouble shooting on the spot. Do this as effectively as possible. Spot disgruntled crew members and listen to their concerns, take the actors a cup of tea, watch out for irate neighbours who may complain about noise... Develop a radar for problems. Of course this is all pretty thankless and exhausting, but it is in fact, the job on a low budget film. It can either be dealt with effectively in the moment, or left alone, in which case it may go away, or it may explode in your face.

All of this stress can also lead the producer and director to nervous exhaustion. Keep an eye on that and give yourself a break. If you 'lead' your crew from the front (as opposed to ruling with an iron fist) I have found that, if you do crash and burn, all those guys who you have previously been there for in the past, they all come to your aide. It's really quite an amazing feeling and it bonds everyone involved. This camaraderie under pressure, along with the elation of achieving the near impossible several times a day, acts like a drug for film makers and drives them to get back onto set as soon as they can.

Q – What happens if relationships become strained?

Chris – I have only ever had to fire one person and it was the right choice at the time. Mostly, cast and crew have good reason to complain. And even if they don't have a good reason, it's often better to let them blow off steam, after which they are usually happy to get on with it. Don't burn your bridges, you never know when you will need that relationship again. So get used to apologizing first. It's an effective strategy. It is not about being right, it's about listening, about keeping up momentum and raising spirits.

Not burning bridges is especially true of actors who you may need back for pickups and reshoots in post production. If the problem is severe, take them out for lunch after the shoot wraps. But keep the peace.

Q – As you shift from production to post production, what should the producer be doing aside from supporting the director and editor?

Chris – Post production is a long haul, so hunker down. If you have bills you can't pay, get on the phone and explain why and offer real solutions – maybe half now, the rest later down the line. People are much happier if there is healthy communication. I suggest the producer now leaves the editor and director and starts working on press materials, posters, a dedicated film website, and forming a festival strategy and pushing all their social networking.

After production, something will have changed in the producer. It's kind of an accelerated growth. The intense and focused experience gives everyone involved a new perspective on life. You may be exhausted and broke, but in a strange way, you are more alive than you have been for a long time. It's exhilarating.

Q – What mistakes do you see during production?

Chris – I have made all of these myself. Making promises I suspected I could not keep, and that would always come back, but with a vengeance. Trying to do too much, so I now delegate as much as I can to a few trusted production people around me, which leaves me free to deal with the critical stuff. I do see a lot of young producers misbehaving, trashing locations, lying to people, being disrespectful to actors and generally being idiots. I can understand how it happens, being inexperienced and under huge pressure is not a good place to be. So take a moment and compose yourself before you screw it up even more.

Q – What advice would you offer?

Chris – Go to the pub with the camera team at the end of the day and laugh about what happened! But leave early, you have plenty to do before tomorrow.

Deal with problems fast, be straight with everyone and lead from the front!

CHAPTER FOUR
POST PRODUCTION

THE GUERILLA FILM
MAKERS POCKETBOOK

Q - What is a Film Editor?

Eddie – The editor is the person who takes the footage shot by the crew and cuts the shots together to tell the story in the best way possible. Working shot by shot, one scene at a time, making sure the cuts flow smoothly and the audience understands the story and emotions being communicated by what they're watching. It's all about story, character and overall tone.

Editors have the responsibility to ensure that everyone's best work gets up on screen – a combination of the best performances, lighting, makeup, costumes, and sets. The editing process is also the last chance to correct any mistakes made during the shoot. If the script has problems, you have to fix them with re-structuring or ADR (lines recorded by the actor in a studio after the shoot). Similarly, if an actor's performance is disappointing, you have to cut around it.

George Lucas says that editing is the most important part of the film making process. You can radically change a film for the better in the cutting room. If there is life in the rushes and you have a good story to tell, taking the time to find the moments that work and then piecing them together to create a decent movie (even if it is totally different from the original script) is very rewarding.

So it's very creative, but it also requires an immense amount of organisation. Every single frame of film or video has to be carefully logged when it arrives in

---

 film@eddiehamilton.com 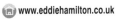 www.eddiehamilton.co.uk

THE MARATHON BEGINS

Whether you hire an editor or cut your project yourself, the cutting process can be both rewarding and frustrating. You will love seeing your film come to life, but may also cringe at shots or sequences that don't work, or at bad acting (that you let go on the day of shooting). You could blame the actors but now you suspect it's more to do with your script! Maybe you should have spent more time on that one final rewrite?

The key here is to keep on going through your first cut. Then have a few unbiased people watch it so that you can get feedback, make changes and schedule reshoots to fix problems that you could not see (as you are so close to it). Then repeat these steps over and over until you get the cut nice and tight. While the length of editing varies by budget and time constraints (one month to a year), a general rule of thumb for low budgets is 12-16 weeks for picture lock. Remember that the editor hasn't been on set and therefore isn't aware of how painstakingly long it took to set up your shots, or how difficult it was to get that perfect take. This is great news. They have perspective. Let them be brutal.

the cutting room so that it can be found at a moment's notice. Any inaccuracy can cause problems and if not spotted can cost a lot to put right.

The editor is also an ambassador of diplomacy. Sitting in the same room as the director working on their masterpiece for months takes its toll – emotions get charged, especially if there is a producer who disagrees with the director. The editor should serve the director's vision, but must speak up if he thinks the director is mistaken. It's important to try and stay objective and see the film fresh each time. Sometimes you have to be ruthless with the cut to improve the film. It's not personal. Everyone wants the best film at the end of the day.

Q – What should a film maker do BEFORE the shoot begins?

Eddie – Make sure you have your entire post production workflow mapped out in front of you, so that on day one of the shoot, you are not trying to problem solve unforeseen issues. As an example, I am advising on another film right now where

1. Label the tapes as they're returned from set. Organisation is your best friend.

2. If shooting to files, such as MP4 or RED, make backups of ALL media BEFORE taking into the edit system.

3. Digitise the material onto the editing system. Ensure that you correctly digitise timecode.

4. Break down the footage into the various shots and takes and sort them into bins for easy access. Make sure you can read and easily understand the labels.

5. Once digitised, store originals in a safe place.

6. For first assembly, order the scenes the same way as the screenplay had planned.

7. Don't worry about your first assembly being overly long, badly

they began the shoot using 'time of day' time code (to help sync sound between camera and sound), so every time they stopped the camera, they created gaps in the timecode on the tape. This creates all manner of problems in post production, and yet it was easy to avoid by either recording black on all the tapes in advance or by assemble editing each take one after another. If you can, find another film maker who has used the same technology and post route that you propose and see how they managed and what problems they encountered.

Q – What kind of space should you use for an edit suite?

Eddie – Normally as big a room as you can find, ideally with a window (and a great view doesn't hurt). It's great to have a large TV for the director, and a sofa too, as you will be spending many long days and months in this one room.

Q – What makes a 'good edit'?

Eddie – Well, there is no simple answer to this – whole books have been written on this very topic by people who've had a lifetime of experience editing films!

Q - OK, so what makes a cut between two shots work?

Eddie – The cut should be fluid (unless deliberately being obtuse). The flow, rhythm and emotion of the cut should not interrupt the audience's passage of concentration. It should feel natural. For me, it's a gut reaction, some kind of instinct. As you play through a take you feel the cut should be HERE, or you sense an edit needs a couple more frames on the outgoing shot. When you watch it back you just intuitively sense if a cut is working or not.

There are some grammatical rules to follow (though these should have been taken into account when shooting the film). When cutting between shots try not to cross the line (the imaginary eye line between the actors on screen). If you do, it will feel wrong. Just try it. You can sometimes get away with it if there's no option and you're careful but generally it's a bad idea (unless it's a deliberate directorial choice as in 'Moulin Rouge!', for example, where Baz Luhrmann crosses the line constantly).

When cutting dialogue I often find a natural place to cut to another character is on punctuation, where there's a natural pause in the delivery. I have read a theory that says it takes at least two frames for the audience's eyes to travel from one part of the screen to another between cuts. I would tentatively agree with this – if I'm editing a conversation I tend to trim the incoming shot back a couple of frames and find the cut feels smoother. Another tip, all subconscious emotion is shown through the actor's eyes. Even the subtlest movements give away a character's thoughts.

Lastly, make sure each cut is *motivated*. If the scene is playing well, don't cut for the sake of it.

Q - What makes an edited scene work?

Eddie – As you have no doubt discovered when writing or reading a script, most scenes have a beginning, middle and end and are designed to carry the plot forward, developing the characters along the way. This may seem obvious, but you

paced, or tonally off. These will be fixed in the next passes.

8. Re-edit, reorder, screen, then help with the reshoots. Do this until you truly have the best edit of the film (this stage could take many months)

9. Lock the edit.

10. Tidy the sound and co-ordinate with the sound editors. Or perform the sound mix yourself. Get good speakers!

11. Redigitise picture at full HD res, or recompile from orginal files at highest possible quality.

12. Take the edit to a facility for grading, or grade the film yourself. Make sure you have a true and accurate monitor if you are grading yourself.

13. Final lay off of sound and picture to broadcast videotape such as HDCam of DigiBeta.

14. Make DVD for screenings and festivals.

should take it into account when cutting a sequence together. How does the scene start? Where are we? Who's here? Has time passed? Subconsciously the audience will be asking these questions when the scene starts. Unless you're setting out to confuse them, you should try and set the scene as soon as possible so that they can get on with digesting the plot and characterisation.

Sometimes you can start with an exterior of where we are (e.g. a crowd outside the cinema for a premiere before cutting inside to show who's attending). Or maybe start on a detail and reveal the situation, (e.g. a digital counter counting down from 30 seconds, track out to reveal a small bomb under a table, track out to reveal two characters having dinner unaware of their predicament). These are obvious examples but the audience immediately knows what's what.

Now consider what the function of the scene is. Which character do you want the audience to identify with? Whose story is this? What plot details must the audience understand so that we don't lose them? For example, consider a scene where a woman is asking a man to marry her. She might beat around the bush a bit, nervous. At the start of the scene we might stay on a medium two shot showing both the actors. Then she plucks up courage – do we go in for a close up? Maybe. Do we want to show her extreme anxiousness? Or do we want to see the man getting intrigued about her emotional turmoil?

The answers are never clear cut, but if you know what the audience needs from the scene, it can certainly point you in the right direction. All the time you're listening to your gut feeling about whether the flow of the cuts feel right. At the last minute, the woman can't do it. She's trying to win a bet with a friend by getting engaged before the week is out but decides it's not worth it. The scene builds to this moment and without an explanation she leaves. The man is left standing wondering what he did wrong. Do we stay on a close up of his confusion, do we see his POV (point of view) of the woman walking away, or do we cut out to a wide shot of him standing alone and bemused? Any of these will work, depending on what you want to say. But for sure, the scene has drawn to a close. We've had a beginning, middle, and end. Very few, or even no words have been exchanged, but we've understood and the edited scene has done its job.

Q - What makes a movie work as a whole?

Eddie – When you've finished the first cut of a film, the fun really starts. Just cutting the scenes and putting them in script order is only 20% of the battle. If I'm cutting during a shoot I normally have a first assembly ready a couple of days after the wrap party. The editor and director will watch this and as a general rule it's very average and probably poor – it's too long, the pace is all over the place and there will probably be sections missing such as special effects or second unit shots. But this is to be expected – every editor I've spoken to says the first assembly always looks terrible. However, it's also exciting because it's the first indication that all the work so far has been worth it.

First you work through the film with the director getting the scenes how he or she wants them. You've been cutting alone so far; according to

5. If you're not sure about a scene, take it out and see if you miss it. You can always put it back in.

6. If you have to make major changes, note the scenes on index cards and stick them to the wall. This will keep you from getting lost.

7. Music and sound effects will enhance a scene that is tedious, but they will not fix the heart of the problem.

8. Dropping the end of a scene sometimes helps. It can create a question in the audience's mind - what's going to happen next?

9. Don't be afraid of inventing new scenes, or lines of dialogue, then getting the actors back and having a mini pickup shoot. If the audience doesn't understand something fundamental, you can fall back on the blunt instrument of explanatory dialogue.

10. Take a break before locking picture. When you come back to it, you will see the movie with new eyes and increased energy.

11. If you are faced with a long and dull scene or a shot that you can't cut away from, try hacking it with an unusual cut. It might work.

12. Listen to the people who view your rough cuts. While they might not know exactly what is wrong, they know what is working for them and what isn't. Don't fall into the mistaken position of believing you know better because you are the filmmaker.

13. Don't take anything personally. It isn't worth losing a friendship over.

14. Most Important! Sort out your entire planned post-production route before you shoot.

what you think works. Of course it's their film and they may have other ideas about how to approach a scene. It's a long process of going through the rushes re-working each scene according to the director's taste – but incorporating your input where necessary. Then you take a look at the film as a whole. Are the characters introduced correctly? Is the plot working? Is the tone of the film consistent? Does the pace lag anywhere? Is it too fast? As a rule, the film is probably too slow. How many people have seen a film that's too slow? Then ask yourself if you have ever complained about a film because it was too fast or too packed. Sometimes what worked well in the script seems redundant on screen. Sometimes the performances are lacking something. Maybe the relationship between the two lead characters is misfiring somewhere. Maybe a character is unnecessary now. Maybe some of the jokes just aren't funny.

What do you do? Well, work through the problems. Can I move some scenes around to get the pace more even? Can I intercut some scenes? Can I cut out this joke altogether? Can I shoot some pickups to act as clever cutaways or help with the plot? Slowly but surely you'll work out the answers over several weeks and months of cutting. Then screen your cut to a select audience of articulate people whose opinions you value and who aren't afraid of being brutally honest about the film. You want to fix problems, not have your ego stroked. Watching your movie with an audience is like watching it afresh. You suddenly sense when they begin to fidget. You sense when they're gripped. You know if a joke has hit the mark. Ask them questions afterwards. You'll soon find out what the problems are. There'll be comments like – But isn't he her brother? – when in fact the characters aren't related at all! The audience will come back with all kinds of comments that you hadn't even thought of because you're too close to the film.

Then it's back to the cutting room for more changes, more careful honing. You will probably have to cut some scenes you love because they just don't "play" to the audience or aren't needed in the film any more. Then screen the film again for a larger number of people. Get them to fill in a questionnaire. Read the forms and listen to what they're saying. Don't take them as gospel, but don't ignore them. Gradually you will get closer to the day when you lock picture.

There is a saying that films are never completed, just abandoned. This is partially true because you will never be 100% happy with the end result. The director will have had this vision for the film that can never be matched. You will always have to compromise. But with patience and creativity you will find the movie hiding in those rushes and it will take on a life of its own. The audience will watch it and forget that they're seeing dozens of cuts flickering across the screen – they will be engrossed in the story being told and then you'll know you've done a good job.

Q – What if the director is editing, maybe they can't afford an editor?

Eddie – There are directors who edit, but part of the fun of working with an editor is having someone to bounce ideas off, so you don't feel lonely while undertaking this monumental task. If you are editing alone, try to keep an open mind about changes that may need to be made. For many reasons, you may need to restructure the story. So when people give you feedback, be open to that feedback and don't try and constantly talk yourself round to your own point of view. Every audience opinion is valid and most of the time, if you get consensus in those opinions, you should listen to it and deal with it, no matter how hard it feels. It's tough when you end up cutting out entire days worth of work from the shoot, but that's the process and every film goes through it.

Q – What if an editor changes mid edit?

Eddie – It is possible that an editor leaves your film, especially if it's low budget, as they may get other paid work. Organisation is therefore very important, the new editor will need an organised project or they will spend a great deal of time just unpicking what has been done. Everything should be meticulously labelled and organised in the bins so it makes sense. Keep an archive of every version of

For the most part, it's best to get all your shots during principal photography. However, there might be some that you can't get due to time constraints, some that you realise after viewing your first assembly or a test screening that you now need, or some that were screwed up the first time around and need to be redone. Going back to "pick up" or "reshoot" shots is common and should be budgeted for both in cost and time.

Some pickups, such as close ups of fingers on a keyboard, a wide establishing shot of a location, a match igniting, or a coffee mug being placed down are very simple and can be done over a long weekend with a minimal crew. Even getting a certain look from an actor that resolves a loose end is fairly easy; only complicated by time schedules and continuity issues (making sure they are wearing the same shirt they wore the day of the original shoot). Larger reshoots of whole scenes or sequences can be more complex and more expensive (you'll need most of your full crew), but getting your film right is so much more important both creatively and psychologically.

the edit, organised by date, so that anyone can go back and watch previous versions of the edit.

Q- What is grading?

Eddie – Grading, or "color correction" as it's known in the US, is something that may appear unimportant, but it is crucial to your movie. Grading is when you choose a look for your film, and apply that throughout so that if feels like a unified artistic vision. At its most basic, it is making sure that all the shots in one scene match. Some exterior shots may be lighter than others because of the change in sunlight during shooting, and grading will even out all those differences to achieve a uniform look. Aside from that, you may want to give the whole film a visual feel, maybe darker and desaturated for a horror film, or a bright and colourful bubblegum feel for a romantic comedy. You can use the powerful image grading tools in Avid or FCP to do this (the "help" files in both Avid and FCP are very good). On bigger budget films, you would take the film to a post production company whose grading experts would do the picture grade for you.

Q – How should you master a film for sales?

Eddie – If you are just making a DVD or uploading your film to the internet, you can easily do that at home. But if you intend to enter the international sales market, sales agents and distributors have stringent technical specifications that must be adhered to. Unless you know exactly what you are doing, it would be expensive to do at home, and very easy to get wrong. In this situation, it's better to try and find a post production facility that will do it for you, ideally using your hard drives and opening your project on their machines. If you plan to do this, you must run short tests in advance to make sure everything works as expected. They will take your film and make sure all the sound and picture elements are 'broadcast legal', and make a tape for you, probably on HDCAM SR.

Q – Can you mix the sound at home?

Eddie – Yes both Avid and FCP offer very good sound mixing tools. When mixing the sound, make sure the sound meters never go into the red. With time and experience you can do a very effective job. I have done that myself on many projects. You will need very good speakers though, and even then, when you hear your film played in a cinema, everything you thought you could get away with when mixing at home, will be magnified.

The main stumbling block is that of cleaning up dialogue tracks. This is the removal of background noise and mixing it so that it sounds like it was recorded at the same time and in the same place. For instance, it may be windy on one shot and not windy on the other - cutting between the two will create an audio edit which audiences will hear. The people who do dialogue mixing like this are very skilled, and though doing this at home is possible, it would take time to get it right.

Q – What about music use?

Eddie – The bottom line is, don't use any music unless you know you can purchase all the rights you need. Audio Networks is a great place for cost effective music online. Or you could get a composer to record a score entirely on a piano – I cut a short film recently where the score was performed on a piano and it went on to win many awards.

HOLDING A TEST SCREENING

1. Showing your movie to an impartial audience is a vital way to tell if the mechanics of your story are working. Hold a test screening with a DVD-R, pair of speakers and video projector.

2. Have your editor copy the whole movie with all the sound, sound effects, temp music onto DVD-R. Where titles or scenes are missing, put up a card explaining what should be there. This is what you will screen.

3. Pure human emotion is always the best indicator of how things are going, so watch and listen to your audience during the film.

4. You may have several test screenings to check work as you keep refining and updating. Avoid family as viewers as they may not tell you the truth (they may lack objectivity).

Very often, film makers use too much music and rely on it as a crutch. I watch some films and wonder: "Why have they used music there?" Because it works perfectly well without it. And I am sure it's because the editor and director have lost sight of the power of the scene to play on it's own. Don't feel the need to use music if the scene already has strong dramatic drive.

Q – What mistakes do you see regularly?

Eddie – I think you never truly understand film making until you have experienced life in a cutting room. The understanding of how to structure a film and how to pace a story is so fundamental to film making that everyone should try editing at some point. It will give you a new respect for the art.

Don't rush into production without really working on the script and developing it until you know it's the best it can be. Many people don't plan post production properly and so end up in trouble very quickly. I can't emphasise enough how important that is.

If shooting and editing in Europe (PAL world) shoot at 25 progressive frames per second (aka 25P / 25PsF). If shooting and editing in the USA, shoot at 24 progressive frames per second (aka 24P / 24PsF), or 23.976 frames per second (because it downconverts to NTSC perfectly).

Editorial mistakes that I see often are that films are too long. They haven't screened the film enough times, or only screened to people who have an emotional connection to the project or the director, so they will never give honest feedback on what is and what isn't working. The director will be living in a fantasy world where they think that their film is better than it actually is.

It is very, very difficult to make good films. Out of the several hundred films released every year, there are only ever a handful of really good ones. Even the films nominated for best picture at the Oscars are hotly debated. So don't be under any illusion, making good popular successful films is very hard. If you have not been editing very long and you think you have created a masterpiece, you probably haven't. Keep working on it, keep screening it, keep thinking of ways to rework the movie and do pickup shoots to improve it.

Get out there and start shooting something. Shoot some video footage and start editing it together and try and tell a story. When you do that, you can call yourself a film maker.

5. Remember a test screening is all about finding the problems. Invite them to be as harsh as possible.

6. If you can't afford a video projection venue, then find someone with a huge TV and buy everyone pizza. Try to create as much of a theatrical experience as possible, so take the phone off the hook and switch off the mobile.

7. Draw up a questionnaire and ask them to fill it in. Do this before you get into a general discussion in order to reduce 'group think'. Have a big box of pens at the ready.

8. Hold a freeform discussion at the end of the screening, and ask questions about the things you suspect may be a problem.

9. This can be harsh for actors and directors. Don't let actors attend, and warn the director that it's going to be rough.

Q – What is your job?

Bernard – I am a Sound Designer. It used to be that everyone in Audio post production had separate jobs, so it would be a foley editor, a mixer, a dialogue editor etc., And that is still the case on big budget films, but on lower budget films, we are expected to do more and more. Right now I am doing the sound for a short film where I am responsible for all the audio, from first edit of the dialogue tracks, all the way through to the final mix. It's in complete contrast to what I was doing last week which was editing foley tracks on *Clash Of The Titans*.

Q – When do you get brought onto a film?

Bernard – Ideally before it's been shot as I might have some ideas about the sound that the film makers may not have considered. Most of the time that isn't the case though. The way you hear a film, changes the way you see it, so I would always recommend getting input from sound designers before shooting.

Q – What are the different kinds of sounds you work with? The different layers?

---

 bernardoreilly@mac.com   www.soundkitchenuk.com

TRACK LAYING AT HOME

Sound is an area where low budget films often fail, yet they need not. The technology is cheap and all a great soundtrack really requires is a little know how and a lot of work. Sound Effects CDs / online libraries are an excellent source of high quality stereo recordings of pretty much everything you could imagine. These are the same recordings as used by multi million dollar productions. And you can use them too! If you can't afford to buy the disks or buy downloads, try asking the studio where you plan to do your final mix and see if you can use their CD library.

Be creative with sound and try and fill your soundtrack. Work on cleaning your dialogue tracks or replacing them with clean ADR (getting actors back to revoice their lines), by adding thick stereo atmospheres from effects libraries, annotating everything on screen with a sound effect, filling out everything else with foley and finally placing music selectively for maximum impact. You can track lay the sound in your film with a number of semi-pro and domestic computer tools such as Adobe Premiere, Avid and Final Cut Pro. You will need a good computer with a big monitor, a large and quiet space in which to work, a good amplifier and speakers and a high quality microphone. Best of all, both Avid and FCP export OMF which you can take to a final mixing studio.

Bernard – You usually start off with sync sound, and that's mainly the dialogue tracks. It's crucial to get those tracks in as good a shape as possible. Computers can clean up sound a bit, but not as much as most people imagine. If the sound recordist is getting humms and buzzes on set, they may not sound too bad there and then, but when you get it in the cutting room or theatre, it can become very obvious. In that instance, if you can't clean it up, you may be forced to do ADR (where actors re-perform the lines later for sound only) and that's going to cost more money. You can fix some things in audio post, but it's always better to get it right on set. I think most film makers think we can do much more with problematic sound than the tools we have available allow. We often struggle with things like bad traffic sound in a period drama for instance. Then there are spot effects to drop in, that's close up hard sounds like doors and gun shots etc. There are also Atmos tracks (atmospheres), that's the background, non specific sounds, like skylines, room tones and bird song. An atmos track may not be that noticeable, but it helps the dialogue tracks and ADR (covering problems). They are also good

Dialogue Tracks (mono)
Keep dialogue tracks clean and bright, and where needed use ADR (dialogue replacement), but be mindful that ADR can sound pretty bad.

Sound Effects Tracks (mono and stereo)
Track lay an effect for as many things as you can. Differentiate between effects that will stay mono and are from the perspective of the characters (such as doors and switches), and effects that will be in stereo and add acoustic punch (such as police sirens and thunder claps).

Atmosphere Tracks (stereo)
Don't be afraid to lay several thick atmosphere tracks and mix them as they can provide a very attractive stereo image. Use atmospheres to help create continuity during a scene, and also to help illustrate that a scene has changed by switching to a different atmos track.

Foley Tracks (mono)
The movement of the actors in the scene needs to be brightened by a foley artist who will add these human sounds with expert precision and clarity. Don't be afraid of going a little over the top, very rarely do you make a loud swishing sound when turning your head, but you do in the movies.

Music (stereo and mono)
Always in stereo (except when it comes from a prop in a scene such as a TV) and sparingly placed. Avoid drowning out your sound mix with music and use it only when you really need it.

Tools
A sound mixer will have tools like echo and reverb (used for churches, canyons etc.), a noise gate (that can kill sound below a certain level, excellent if you have too much reverb), a notch filter (to help get rid of continuous sounds such as a fridge or the camera). Don't let these tools lull you into a false sense of security, get it right in the track laying.

for creating the feel of the world in which the story is set. Then there is Foley, which are the human noises such as footsteps and clothing, and that is crucial for the M&E (music and effects mix) track should you want to make any overseas sales. Finally there is music which is something that turns up at the last minute. I rarely have much involvement with the music, that's usually the composer and director.

Q – Have you ever worked with ADR that was recorded on location?

Bernard – Yes, if there is a problem with sound on set, on the same day, you can re-record the dialogue in a different place, where it is quiet and just ask the actors to reperform their lines. It doesn't always fit but it usually sounds better than re-recorded ADR in a theatre three months later, and it is cost effective as you can do it there and then.

Q – Where can you get sound effects and atmospheres?

Bernard – There are online libraries where you can buy effects. There are some free ones too, but they tend to be poor quality. Or you can record them yourself. Sound effects like thunder are often best purchased from a library.

Q – Can you do a sound mix at home?

Bernard – Yes. I would recommend Pro Tools, but there are other software tools, and you could even do a reasonable simple mix in Avid or FCP. I have heard temp mixes done by editors that were very good. The thing is, you need to make sure it sounds good on big speakers in a silent room, and editors don't always have either, so neither Avids nor FCP are good finishing tools for sound. The idea of sound in a film is to bring people into the film, into another world, and in a way, forget about the sound. As soon as you 'hear' or become aware of the sound, it breaks that connection. Even small things like being able to hear the cuts in the dialogue tracks are enough to take you out of the movie, so you need to get it right, and you need the right environment to do that work.

You will need very good speakers. But beware, how it will sound in your room may not be the same as how it will sound in a theatre. I would always recommend a final pass on any mix in a professional mixing theatre, where you can accurately hear the sound. I have just mixed this short film in that way, I did all the work at home and have checked the final pass in a film dubbing theatre.

RECORDING FOLEY AT HOME

When you record the dialogue for your film (on set) you don't record all the human sounds like clothes rustle, footsteps and jangling keys. That's all performed in post production by a person called a Foley Artist. Those sounds are later added to your films tracks and mixed into the final soundtrack later. You can record your own Foley too, and it's easier than you would think. You will need a very quiet place, a TV, a DV camera and a good microphone.

Set a DV camera up pointing at the TV, then position the microphone close to the Foley action – say you bring a paving stone into your home 'studio' so you can perform some footsteps (a little added sand will give it a nice extra crunch to the step). Play the DVD of your movie and shoot the screen on the DV camera. You then have picture to synchronize your movements to, and those sounds you make get recorded onto the audio tracks of the DV tape. Nice and crisp and clean. You can then digitize that into your computer and use the filmed TV screen as a visual reference so that you can sync your foley to your final movie. Cunning huh? The more foley you do, the better you will get at it. It's not too hard but it is time consuming. The difference it will make to your final soundtrack is incredible though, so it's well worth the effort.

You would also need a little four or eight track mixer with faders (mixing desk), something that would work with your software. You can mix using your mouse, doing levels and pans, but it takes much longer. You would need a microphone for Foley, ADR and spot effects too (with a mic preamp). I would recommend Rode condenser mics, they are inexpensive and good all round workhorses.

Q – Dialogue mixing seems to me to be the most important and most difficult part to get right. Why is that?

Bernard – Dialogue mixing is the most technical part of the mix. Everyone, film makers and audiences, know how dialogue is supposed to sound, and even if people cannot articulate what is wrong with a bad mix, they know it's a problem when they hear it. In order to make dialogue match, line after line, you do need good EQ and reverb tools (to make the sync cound consistent), and you need the experience to know how to do that.

Q – As a low budget strategy, would it be a good idea to get an expert in for the dialogue premix, then you add and premix all the other tracks, then get the expert to do the final mix in a professional dubbing theatre?

Bernard – Yes. If the dialogue mix is not done correctly, it will just sound amateurish. Again, audiences will pickup on that.

Q - What software tools do you use for the dialogue mixes?

Bernard – Compression, EQ and Reverb – a combination of those tools. The key with the dialogue tracks is that the quiet bits need to be made louder, and the louder bits need to be pulled down, so there is less dynamic range. Effectively, the dialogue tracks are squeezed into a narrower dynamic range. Once that is done, all other sound effects and music are mixed to match those levels. They form the spine of the sound mix.

Q – What is the M and E mix?

Bernard – It's a mix of the film with everything except the sync dialogue. You need that for sales abroad. If you think you will need an M&E, it's best to build it into your full mix, so Foley everything and spot effect things where live sound may also work. Typically, when you complete the mix, you do the M&E mix and remove the sync dialogue tracks, and that takes everything like live footsteps and effects with it, so you need to foley over all of that too.

Q – How do you deliver these final mixes?

Bernard – As separate WAV files on a DVD. Ideally you should do two mixes, a 5.1 mix for DVD and theatres and a stereo version for TV. The stereo version should also be remixed to be less dynamic as broadcasters don't want theatrical mixes that are very loud in the loud bits and very quite in the quieter bits. Also for Broadcast, you need to meet strict technical specifications.

Q – What common mistakes do you see?

Bernard – Sync dialogue that is poorly recorded, badly edited and badly mixed. Audiences can hear this and they pick up on it. Another big problem are film makers recutting the film after they think they have locked the picture. That causes us endless headaches, increases time and costs money (or good will).

MUSIC
JERMAINE STEGALL

Q - When do you like to be brought on to a project?

Jermaine – As soon as possible. As soon as a filmmaker knows they want to use original music is ideal.

Q – What should a filmmaker give you at your first meeting in order to give you a better idea of what they want?

Jermaine – I love to see footage so I know how it was shot. Storyboards are helpful because they convey something visual and composers who work specifically in film are inspired by visual media.

Q – What kind of score could a filmmaker get for ultra low budgets?

Jermaine – It depends. If you have a friend who has access to a recording studio or knows players who want to work on your project, then you could be in a good position to get something really cheap. But if you are going to go into it blindly and ask for favors, then it will be difficult to do it on a low budget. I have seen it done before where if music is really important they will spend a fourth of the budget on music.

Q – How much time do you need to prepare a score?

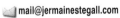 mail@jermainestegall.com　　 www.jermainestegall.com

SPOTTING AND TIMING

After the temp track has been cut, the director and composer figure out where and how the real score will be placed in the film. The first part of this process is called spotting and second part is called timing.

Spotting - The 'spots' where you want the score to be. Written down as spotting notes which contain very general 'in' and 'out' cues as well as any specific instructions about the score such as when certain themes are to come in, or if there is to be an absence of score. The final version of these notes is called the master cue list.

Timing - A precise (to the 1/100 of a second) list of the music cues that is given to the composer to execute. In addition, this 'cue sheet' contains descriptions of each shot, which includes it's cuts and lines of dialogue. This is rarely done for low budget films.

Jermaine – It depends on how much music you need and how long the film is. Short films tend to take less time than features. Still I hope to get as much time as possible so we can collaborate and get better results. It also depends on the style of the music. For a small score with a few instruments I would like a month or two. In any case, rushing a score is not something you want to do because it won't come out great.

Q – What is cheap and what is expensive when recording?

Jermaine – When recording live music, one of the most expensive things is the space in which you are going to record. Renting scoring stages is expensive. Then you need someone to record that sound – an engineer. Their fees can be pricey. Then you need to pay the players, who are generally found through a contractor if it's a union gig. So you can see how this can add up if you go this route. For a low budget feature film, it's best to find a friend who has a small recording studio that is manageable pricewise. Then keep the size of your score small so that you don't need a big orchestra with live players.

While you are editing, and before your original score has been written, you will want to put some music tracks down to help set a tone and find the pace of scenes and your overall movie. You will find yourself browsing the soundtrack section in music shops and plundering the collections of music score collectors, in search of the appropriate feeling score to use as a guide. Music editors sometimes call this 'tracking'. At this point ANY music is fair game as you do not have to pay royalties (as the film will never be screened publicly in this unfinished form). Many film festivals will accept temp music in your submission for entry, with the stipulation that you will have a permanent score in place should you get into their event.

However, beware when it comes to temp music. On one hand, it can be very helpful to your composer to have famous music tracks as temp music in order to give them an example of what you want from the score. On the other hand, you may grow too attached to that style of music and not open yourself up to alternative ideas. All too often, new filmmakers lay in some temporary John Williams or Jerry Goldsmith, and not surprisingly, it improves their film. BUT, neither John Williams or Jerry Goldsmith, nor the London Symphony Orchestra, are likely to do a low budget indie film.

Q – What would be a minimal kit that you would want to see a composer have?

Jermaine – It's at the point where people can do most of their score in their studio with samples. So for low budgets you want to make sure that the composer has enough samples in his studio to replicate as many instruments or sounds as possible. Then do the mixing and editing in ProTools.

Q – What do certain instruments convey emotionally?

Jermaine – One of the interesting beauties and mysteries of music is that all instruments can create any kind of mood. Brass instruments don't just do one thing and strings another. They can conjure up emotions equally. It comes down to the orchestration and filmmakers shouldn't be too pressured to learn what instruments do what. Rather they should learn how to convey to a composer what kind of emotion they are looking for. If you say you're looking for a warm feeling then a composer with generally know how to give you that. And that comes from developing a good working relationship with a composer.

Q – What happens once you have completed the score?

Jermaine – Well, you are missing a step where I first have to mix the final score in my studio. Then if it's a larger scale thing like a feature or a TV show, I will have to supply stems, which are the different groups of instruments on separate tracks – brass, percussion, etc. For smaller projects, I might just give a stereo mix. Then I hand that off to the filmmaker and they take it to a music editor that the composer has hired at an audio facility and they marry it to the picture using ProTools. Then they do a final mix where they put together the other sound elements with the score.

MUSIC RIGHTS

To use music in your film, there are three distinct legal rights you MUST acquire before locking and mixing the sound. Failing to do this could result in a film that no one will sell, buy or even screen in a festival.

PUBLISHING RIGHTS - Copyright owned by the author or composer of the work, literally the notes on the page. These become public domain 50-75 years after the death of the composer dependent on the country. These rights are controlled by a music publisher on behalf of the composer or author. Where there is more than one writer, then two or more publishing companies may own a share of the work.

RECORD / MASTER RIGHTS - Copyright in the recording of a song or composition owned by either a record company or the entity that has paid for the recording and thus owns the master tape. Different record companies may hold the copyright to a recording in each separate country.

SYNCHRONISATION RIGHTS - Rights granted to a filmmaker to 'synchronise' the copyrighted music in conjunction with the film. Publishing rights are granted for the composition or song by a music publisher on behalf of the composer or author. Record / Master rights are granted by the record company to use a recording of that song or composition.

181

ONLINE MUSIC

There are ever expanding sources of music for films on the internet and also with software tools like Magix Music Maker. There is some good stuff. And lots of bad stuff. Our favourite web site is www.audionetworkplc.com where you can buy a blanket licence for £200 ($300) – you can then use as much music as you like, as long as it's for a single production or film. We plundered this on our Oscars® shortlisted short film Gone Fishing, and the results were exceptional.

One thing to be aware of with downloaded music is consistency. Just like your script, photography and performances, you want the music to feel like it all comes from the same place, a unified artist with a uniform feel. Using lots of music from different composers and sources can end up making your film feel patchy and inconsistent. So look for music from one composer and within a single theme (audionetworkplc.com does this very well with many tracks offering multiple arrangements).

Keep an eye on the theme to your music too. We believe it should be memorable, in the same way that a great performance from your lead actor is memorable. So wherever you source your music from, try and work a consistent and memorable theme into the acoustic landscape of your story.

Q – Do you oversee the final mix?

Jermaine – I do. But as I advance up the food chain, as my projects become larger, I think I will become less effective, as there will be less I can do. A music editor at the studio level is the person who makes most of the decisions and is the advocate for volume levels. Most of my decisions will have been made already.

Q – What should filmmakers be aware of as far as temp score is considered?

Jermaine – One of the biggest issues out there is the temp music process. Some people don't like it at all. It helps to show someone what the final movie will look like with some music that approximates the correct emotion. But when working with a composer one of the most stifling things you can do is to be completely married to the temp score and not see other possibilities. To hire someone to do a knock off of someone else's work is not a great part of the collaborative process. Temp music can help me communicate with directors, but you have to know its role. You need to let the composer have their original voice come through in the music.

Q – Do you get to keep your royalties or is it a straight work made for hire?

Jermaine – For independent projects that are lower budget, it is standard for the producer to allow the composer to keep the writer's share and the publishing rights. It's a way for us to use the music any way we want later. If I am working for a studio, the music is being published by someone else, be it 20th Century Fox or whatever. And if the music is aired anywhere then there are royalties that can be collected by ASCAP or BMI (in the UK the PRS).

Q – What are the common mistakes that you see a filmmaker make?

Jermaine – I don't know if I would call it a mistake, but many filmmakers can't convey what they want clearly. Then it can get very frustrating when you do many different versions and they say it still isn't right but they can't tell you in what direction it should go.

Q – What advice would you give a new filmmaker?

Jermaine – Keep an open mind. Putting sound and music to picture is the other half of what a movie is and there are many things that can work. It's great to have a vision but when you bring someone on you should collaborate.

DO NOT OVERUSE MUSIC

DO NOT MIX MUSIC TOO LOUDLY IN THE SOUND-TRACK

MAKE SURE ALL MUSIC RIGHTS ARE CLEARED

DOCUMENTARY EDIT
AMAYA CERVINO

Q - How different is editing a documentary to editing a narrative?

Amaya - With narrative films, the editing is a lot more structured because you have a script to follow and usually a director with a very clear vision. Non-fiction films are generally more unstructured as you're finding the story in both the production and post production process. A doc filmmaker may have a general idea and clear vision of what they want to do, but its only when they get into the footage itself, that they can really see what's what. However you should approach a documentary film much the same way you approach a narrative film. Determine your logline, make sure the film has a beginning, middle and end as in a standard narrative three act structure, and make sure that every scene, character revelation or twist will move you one step closer to that overarching theme.

Q - For documentaries, how much of an editor's job is also really the job of the director and what is that relationship like?

Amaya - Obviously, if you're editing your own footage, you're one and the same. But if you've been hired, it really depends on the director and the project. I've worked with some directors who might as well have edited the film themselves as they've had a very defined visual of the final film before they've even started

---

shooting. And then I've worked with others where I've taken some directorial attributes, because it was like digging for gold, trying to find the hidden story in 80 hours plus of footage. Cracking the story like that is the most rewarding for me. As for the relationship between an editor and director, you need to be flexible and respectful of the director's creative vision. Depending on your relationship and the director's ego or humility, it can be the best or the worst of times!

Q – Should you edit your own film?

Amaya – You could, but the advantage of bringing in a separate editor is that you're bringing in another point of view from someone who's hopefully on the same creative page. If the filmmaker is editing themselves, then they might be too close to the material, lose perspective and need a second eye. As in most creative processes, there's an ongoing creative dialogue in which you question your choices. If you are on your own, then you're holding this dialogue with yourself and if you reach an impasse, you might stall. With an editor, you can bounce around ideas, try different things and get back on track.

Q - So much footage can be shot for a documentary, how is the best way to organize this as an editor?

Amaya - Ideally, the director will bring you on board BEFORE they begin shooting. Together you can go over essential questions that need to be asked during an interview, crucial and supporting b-roll or stock footage to be obtained, and work out the best system to mark different takes, label, number and store tapes as well as the timecode system to be implemented. This will make your job so much easier when you're in post.

Once you begin importing the footage, you want to be as methodical as possible. Label your bins clearly with character names, location or by date, and make sure you stick to that system. Always backup the project file before you resume editing. This will ensure that you only lose the most recent cutting if something goes wrong.

Draw workflow chart and pin to cutting room wall

BACKUP EVERY NIGHT

BE ORGANIZED AND STAY SANE!

Q - How do you know where to start when faced with all that footage and possibly an unpredictable storyline?

EDITING DOCS

1. Docs will shoot MUCH more footage than drama, so be VERY organized. Label everything. Log everything. You won't remember what it is after three months so be clear in your description. Keep a log book too.

2. Work out your complete post workflow so you don't need to change technologies half way through. Stay on Mac or PC.

3. Backup your project and media regularly. Buy a bunch of USB hard drives and store one copy offsite in case of catastrophe.

4. Commit to the long haul. It could take months. It could take years. Do not rush.

5. Beware of overshooting. It's one thing dealing with 50 hours of material. It's another dealing with 200 hours.

Amaya – I bring up the question, "How do you eat an elephant?" The answer: "One bite at a time"! The director will have a gut idea of what his or her most powerful footage is. Go with your gut to find your starting point and then chew your way through the mountains of footage. Scene by scene, bite by bite. Sooner or later you will have worked your way through all of it. One way you could start is by distilling the essence of each character down to 3 act stories, asking questions such as: What does this person want? Where are our turning points? What is this person feeling in this scene? Once the individual storylines are figured out they need to be weaved together, always with your logline in mind.

Q - How long should your doc be? Pacing is an important issue for any film, but for a documentary, how do you get this right?

Amaya - You probably have an idea of how long you want the final piece to be when you begin shooting, but make sure that the footage you obtain is as compelling as you hoped it would be. Just because a piece is longer doesn't mean it's better. You may find that your story works best as a 10 minute non-fiction short than an hour long broadcast piece. As for pace, rent and watch as many documentary films as possible. Study those that are closer not only in theme, but in structure and pacing, to the story you are trying to tell. How is the story structured? What are the most dynamic moments? Where does the filmmaker give us a break to process what we're watching? How is sound, silence or music used to underline particular story elements? Don't be afraid to study and try out these techniques. Every story has its inner pacing. Trust your gut when you first edit it.

Q - Some docs may be wall to wall interviews; how in editing can you make the interviews not boring or monotonous? And how can you instill emotion into this?

Amaya - Try to underline whatever important information is being conveyed with compelling b-roll. Don't be afraid to cut back and hold on an interviewee when they are being particularly eloquent or uncomfortable. Pregnant pauses can be extremely powerful.

Q - Many docs can be full of a variety of different formats - different camera formats, stills, historical documents, archival footage, home video, voice over, music etc. What are the problems with this in post, if any?

Amaya – There are no problems apart from the usual making sure you get the correct permissions, rights etc. However, what you must do, within the first 10 to 20 minutes of your film is to inform your viewer about what to expect from your stylistic story-telling devices: use of archival footage, different camera formats, innovative use of stills such as the technique used in *Dogtown and Z-Boys*... If you spring a new format on them two thirds of the way through it will seem jarring and out of the blue.

Don't be afraid to experiment with fancy and stylistic choices, but make sure they support the story you're trying to tell. Just because a story-telling device looks good or you've figured out it's cool, it doesn't mean it's the right choice to tell your story.

Q - Does it matter what editing system you use?

6. Pre-edit material to weed out useless footage so editing is less painful.

7. Ask the camera team to think like editors. Get establishing shots, close up cutaways, reverse reactions. Shoot to edit.

8. Shoot PAL or NTSC HDV progressive. You can shoot 24P - BUT your prime markets will be DVD and TV and you may well integrate footage from other sources, like libraries, home movies, TV news etc. And you want that to slot in easily.

9. Check out online library footage like Artbeats or iStockphoto for extra sizzle shots that are cheap to buy.

10. Don't let the project on your computer get messy. Become a little OCD.

11. Downconvert HDV to DV for offline, and reconform to HD at the end. Don't underestimate the strain on your computer even at DV res.

Amaya - Some software such as FCP will only work on a Mac computer so the kind of computer you own will determine the best system for you. Price is also a factor. Otherwise, they all perform the same basic editing tasks. Keep an eye on the forums if you're looking for particular bells and whistles.

Q - What problems do you encounter on low budget docs?

Amaya - Filmmakers are so eager to get started with shooting that they do not think the project through properly. Make the film on paper first. Then shoot it. Dailies will probably come back different than expected but you will be ready to roll with the punches. Also, on a no budget film, the crew tend to double up and perform several roles. This can lead to problems such as forgetting to get release forms signed because you're too busy performing another task. Make sure that you budget enough money for post-production. Often, people underestimate how expensive stock footage or music rights can be. They also forget to get universal rights in perpetuity of a particular photograph or music clip, which stops them from being able to distribute or broadcast their doc. Lastly, try to bring on board competent people to help you make the project. If you don't have money to pay them, offer to barter services. Just stick to whatever promises you make.

Q - What technical problems might you come across on a low budget or a no budget doc, that could be avoided beforehand?

Amaya - Never skimp on sound. Sound will make or break your film. Always get room tone. If shooting outdoors, stop to get enough ambient sound. I cannot stress enough how important it is to record good sound.

Q - What advice can you offer a filmmaker making a no budget doc?

Amaya - Make sure you are as clear as possible about the story you want to tell. Paper is cheaper than having to rent extra equipment, setting pick-ups or hiring crew and having to buy extra hard drives etc. Then choose your crew carefully. Just because someone is available doesn't mean they are the right person to bring on board. Always draft and sign a contract, especially if you're working with close friends and wish to keep them! You don't have to hire a lawyer. There are standard contracts in a number of entertainment books at your local bookstore or Amazon (and www.guerillafilm.com). Think about time commitments and your creative vision. Making a low budget film, documentary or not, is like embarking on an adventurous road trip.

Q – What is it really like in post production on a low budget film?

Chris – It's a rollercoaster of highs and lows. High because you did it, you shot a movie. Low because there are so many problems you didn't see coming. High because you can fix them in the edit. Low because it takes a long time and it's hard work to do it. High because it's so much fun. Low because you have run out of money... and so on. What's important is a commitment to getting the very best film out of the shots you have available. It's true that a film is made three times. Once in the script, once on set, and finally in the edit. In some ways, you need to abandon the script and find the best story in the footage, and for any film maker, that is hard.

Taking time out to get perspective is vital too. A producer's head is filled with all sorts of nonsense when you see the film – that actress was hard work, that location cost too much, it rained that day, we lost the light that day... All of that stuff kills perspective on a great story well told. So take a short

---

 chris@guerillafilm.com   www.twitter.com/livingspiritpix

🏠 www.livingspirit.com   🅱 www.chrisjonesblog.com

📘 Join our Facebook group 'Guerilla Film Maker'

holiday to try and ditch those negative connections that audience members will never feel.

Q – If the director and editor are working on the edit, what role does a producer play in post production?

Chris – Assuming that the director is not the producer, which is often the case, there is all manner of stuff to keep the producer occupied in post. From social media updates, poster design, meeting sales agents, trawling for information on new ways to distribute etc.

The producer should be making inroads and laying the groundwork for sales and distribution. Above all, the producer should be fighting for the best cut of the film. Often the director will be reluctant to cut their film hard, and more often than not, a good hard trimming is exactly what the film will need. So I urge any producer to take a long hard look at their film, and if it's slow and dull at any moment, fight hard to fix it. There is nothing worse than watching that buyer from a company like Lionsgate walk out of a screening because the film is just too long. You really don't want that experience.

Q – What if the director does not want to test the film?

Chris – I would be concerned if that were the case as I would always be anxious to see how audiences respond to the work. These screenings offer rare and powerful insights into the mechanics of your story, and as such, are extremely valuable. If a director is twitchy about it, don't let them attend. Certainly don't let them ask questions at the end as they will get defensive, and you need to remain open, you need to invite criticism from the audience.

Q – What about mastering the film?

Chris – We all know you can edit at home, and that is a wonderful tool to have. But the ability to master your film for commercial release on that same equipment, while possible, is not advisable (unless you are very technologically experienced). You can make DVDs and BluRay disks though, as well as Quicktimes, and I suspect in due course, even JPEG2000 Digital Cinema Packages may be possible (aka DCPs – these are versions of your film in HD on a hard drive for theatrical presentation).

KIT AND SETUP FOR POST

We don't recommend heavy investment in technology, better to borrow someone else's camera, but one area where we do feel you should make an investment is in post production - an edit suite. For a feature project this should really be a dedicated computer that is not connected to the internet – it is isolated to reduce the possibility of gremlins getting into the system or editors doing some late night surfing. Everyone has a laptop now, so insist they use that for any Facebooking, emails, uploading of video clips etc.

The room you setup in is also important as you will spend many months in there. You will work late and make noise, so don't back onto the baby's bedroom!

Whether you go for PC or Mac, it does not need to be the latest and greatest computer, though if you are inheriting an older computer, we would suggest you wipe the drive and reinstall Mac OSX or Windows. This alone will make the computer run much faster. Equally, don't install any unnecessary software to slow things down. You will also need a stack of several terabytes of external hard drives, good monitors and very good speakers (on a budget, good quality old HiFi speakers and an amplifier are best). Your editor can help you here.

Get used to backing up your project every night, and saving it to a USB thumb drive that never ever leaves your pocket. You want a backup regime in place whereby if your computer fails to boot the next day, or your house is burgled, you can rebuild your edit on another computer in less than 24 hours. So you will also need access to the backups of your footage, either tapes or data drives, which you stored someplace else (you have made backups haven't you?) Under you mum's bed is usually a good place.

But for TV sales and sales to foreign territories, via a sales agent, you will need to pass rigorous technical standards, and it's often best to get your film mastered at a top facility for this. It's not cheap, but it will mean that your film will pass these quality controls. Most film makers skip this, do the work at home or on the cheap, and hope that their film passes quality control - but it rarely does and you waste time and money in the process. You don't really want the headache of figuring out how to connect an HDCam deck to your Final Cut Pro!

Q – What mistakes do you see over and over?

Chris – For me there is only one unforgivable mistake any film maker can commit. That is allowing your film to be too long and therefore boring the audience. We all know problems occur on set, that maybe your script could have been better, maybe some actors were a bit poor, maybe some of your film is out of focus, or the sound is bad. I can forgive all of that. What I cannot forgive is self indulgence in the cutting room.

There is an implicit agreement between film maker and audience. The audience will keep watching if what they are watching keeps them interested. The surest way to break that agreement is to allow your film to dawdle along. Whenever the director says *'Yes, but let it breathe…'*, unless it's a director with several Oscars under their belt I would say *'No, don't let it breathe, in fact cut it hard and move on…'*

Q – What advice would you offer a new film maker with regard to post production?

Chris – Make sure there is nothing more you could have done in the edit before you proclaim it's complete. If you can, take a break after locking picture, as long a break as you can, then come back to the edit. You may be surprised at what you find and realize you are not finished at all.

EDIT...
RE-EDIT...
TEST SCREEN...
RESHOOT...
EDIT...
RE-EDIT...
TEST SCREEN...
AND SO ON...

CHAPTER FIVE
FESTIVALS, SALES & DISTRIBUTION

THE GUERILLA FILM MAKERS POCKETBOOK

FESTIVAL ORGANISER PATRICK SCHWIESS

Q – What kind of film attracts your attention?

Patrick – When we are programming the festival, our demographic is first and foremost. Our festival patrons want films that make them think and yet entertain. They want to go away from a film feeling inspired or wanting to do something. And that usually means the film has to strike an emotional chord whether it's happiness, sadness, grief or shock. So that means we don't tend to program horror, sci-fi or very cutting edge, over the top stuff.

Q – How important is it that the film looks professionally made?

Patrick – We only take that into consideration when we're down to the very end of selection and there are several films contending for the final few spots. We know that a lot of filmmakers are working on a budget, especially short filmmakers, so we don't want to turn a film away if that's the only strike against it.

Q – What is the process after a film maker submits?

 director@sedonafilmfestival.com www.sedonafilmfestival.com

FESTIVAL BLISS

When it comes to screening your film, there is no better place on earth than a film festival. Not every festival of course, but the ONE where the audience really gets who you are and what your film is about. Festivals feed the soul of the creative inside every film maker, providing an important and affirming ritual after the battle of production.

Festivals are great places to get feedback too. Just being in a theatre with 200 strangers watching your film is a truly amazing experience. And when it's 2,000 people, (and it could happen), well that's mind blowing! Festivals are also a great place to see other films, ones that you would never catch on TV or at Blockbuster. You can meet the film makers too, people just like you. It's a great chance to travel the world, explore new cultures, and relax after the hectic experience that was the making of your film.

But beware. Becoming a festival junkie takes its toll too. You will suffer from jetlag as you zoom from one country to the other, you will rack up a bill on your credit card, and all this time you cannot work as you are on the road. Unless you have funds, which most of us don't, you will return broke. Plus, you should be working on the next project, writing scripts, taking meetings, and if you are always on the road, this may never happen. So it's about balance, and only you can figure that out.

Patrick – We take a very personal approach with all the filmmakers – even those that don't get in. As soon as we receive their submission packet, they get a personal e-mail from us stating that they have met the requirements and their film is now in the hands of the screeners. I always thought that was a festival standard, but apparently it isn't. At that point, filmmakers can expect to be treated fairly in the judging process, as each film has to be seen by three separate screeners and the two heads of our selection committee. Once decisions have been made, every film will hear from us whether they are in or out. If they do get selected, they can expect a very personal film festival that is all about the film maker. We don't focus on celebrity. We have some, but that's not why we are here. A filmmaker can be guaranteed to be accomodated for up to six nights and they are fed too. They get passes to go to all the events and screenings.

Q – What can a filmmaker do to make their screenings successful?

1. There are thousands of festivals. It's a bewildering choice. Use the web to research.

2. In general European festivals are more art driven, US festivals are more story driven.

3. If you have actually heard of a festival, that's a good sign (and not one that just sounds vaguely familiar)

4. By all means, submit to the top tier festivals. Don't hold your breath!

5. If you find feedback from film makers that the festival was good, that's a good sign.

6. If the festival has been running for five years or more, that's a good sign. Over ten years is a very good sign.

7. Don't judge by the website. Some great festivals have terrible websites and vice versa.

Patrick – Self-promotion. Not all films are created equal here. There are some that have high profile cast and the media will latch onto that aspect. For the others, you have to be more aggressive. You should arrive a few days before your screening so you can pass out postcards and make contacts in order to get a buzz going about your film by hitting the pavement. You should use social networking to get word of mouth spreading. If there's a novelty angle to your film like fortune cookies, you can use that to your advantage. Some filmmakers have luck bringing their props and costumes and leave them in the lobby. We had *Shadowlands* here, which is odd because vampire films are not our thing. But the filmmakers brought along a lot of their set decorations and they created such a buzz that got people in that wouldn't normally be our demographic.

Q – Do you help connect the filmmaker to the press?

Patrick – We do our best to help, but we have 140 films a festival and we just don't have the bodies to give each film the attention they deserve. Therefore if a filmmaker wants to take the time to do additional press, then they contact me and I connect them with our publicist. He then will help set up those meetings and can be very helpful if the film has some special angle that can be used to sell editors or specialized publications or TV programs.

Q – What format should a filmmaker prepare to screen?

Patrick – If you can get us a 35mm print, then we drool. But we realize that's not always possible, so we are shifting to HDcam and Digibeta. And Digibeta can play Beta SP so we can still do that. We only do DVD or Blu-Ray as an emergency back up because we've had too many problems with freezing and pixilation.

Q – Film festivals can tire you out if you aren't careful. Are there any traps filmmakers should avoid in this respect?

Patrick – That is very true. Especially when you have to market your own film, do press and then try to go to as many screenings and panels as possible. My advice would be to pick the brains of the hosts of the festival to see what they can do to help promote your screening. You should also take the time to enjoy the area where the festival is. Don't get bogged down constantly watching films in theaters. So if you come to Sedona, go on a hike. Go on a jeep tour. Have a good time! Don't always be in the filmmaker lounge. Come early so you can have a tech check so that you know your film won't end up in the wrong aspect ratio.

Q – Do film festivals ever offer feedback as to why films don't get in?

Patrick – We do if we get asked. I feel it's our responsibility. We may not be able to do it right away if we are in the throes of the festival, but we will always give the filmmakers the screeners' feedback. In fact, there was a time when our comments made a huge difference in the life of a film. A documentary came through and the subject matter and concept were very good. But it needed to be cut down by forty minutes. It was two hours and if it were an hour, twenty, it would have been brilliant. We told the filmmakers that, they went off

8. Check the rules before submitting. You may find you don't agree with everything they are asking for (they may ask for TV rights or DVD rights for instance).

9. Withoutabox.com is the easiest way to submit to a lot of festivals, but it costs.

10. We suspect that because Withoutabox.com is so easy, most film makers use it, driving up the competition numbers. Use it but also look elsewhere.

11. Submit to places that you would actually enjoy going to. Hong Kong? Australia? California? Get over to Google Earth and start imagining the possibilities...

12. Submit to Sedona, it was our favourite festival on our last film!

and made the cut, they sent it back and we loved it! We put them into our next festival and now they are getting into lots of festivals and may have even got distribution.

Q – What kind of entry fee should one expect to pay to enter a festival?

Patrick – Generally speaking, film festivals charge between $40-$80 dollars to enter. You can get early bird rates that are really cheap and then there are late deadlines where the price goes up. We charge $25 if you apply to us by an early date and $85 for the late people. Sometimes features are more than shorts – for example our late entry for a short is $60.

Q – What are some of the common mistakes that filmmakers make?

Patrick – I realize economics are an issue, but try to enter as many film festivals as you can. Get your film, especially a short film, in front of as many people as possible because it's your calling card as an emerging filmmaker. We scout other festivals looking for great films, as do other regional festivals. So if you make yourself available, you could have a really long festival run as more and more programmers watch your work. The other major mistake is not following up with people. Always return phone calls and e-mails because you never know when your big break is going to happen. And don't think that you are going to hurt our feelings if you can't show it here for whatever reason. We are all big kids. We can handle rejection too.

Q – What advice would you give a new filmmaker?

Patrick – Learn how to handle rejection and know that it's not personal. Many times the rejection letters that we send don't accurately convey that sentiment, but it's the truth. Don't let it kill your enthusiasm, stifle your creativity or change your career path. Most of the time the reason you didn't get in has nothing to do with the quality of the film, but rather how it fits into what the film festival demographic and how many spots we have.

NOTE - You can watch our adventures in Sedona on the video blog at...
www.chrisjonesblog.com/2009/03/sedona-the-complete-webisode.html

OUR FAVOURITE FESTIVALS

Sundance (January) www.sundance.org
Toronto (September) www.tiff.net
Cannes (May) www.festival-cannes.fr
Slamdance (January) www.slamdance.com
Tribeca (April) www.tribecafilm.com/festival
South by Southwest (SXSW) (March) www.sxsw.com
Edinburgh (September) - www.edfilmfest.org.uk
London (October) - www.bfi.org.uk/lff
Berlin (February) - http://www.berlinale.de
Venice (September) - www.labiennale.org/en/cinema
Telluride (September) - http://telluridefilmfestival.org
Palm Springs ShortFest (June) - www.psfilmfest.org/festival
Oberhausen Short Film Festival (April) - www.kurzfilmtage.de
Karlovy Vary (July) - www.kviff.com/en
San Sebastian (Sept) - www.sansebastianfestival.com
Sydney (June) - www.sydneyfilmfestival.org
Pusan (October) - www.piff.org
Sao Paulo (October) - www.mostra.org
Santa Barbara (February) - http://sbiff.org/main
Vancouver (September) - www.viff.org/home.html
Montreal (August) - www.ffm-montreal.org
Hot Docs Toronto (April) - www.hotdocs.ca
IDFA (November) - www.idfa.nl
Silverdocs (June) - http://silverdocs.com
Yamagata Doc Festival (October) - www.yidff.jp

And of course our favourite, **Sedona** (February) - www.sedonafilm.org

FESTIVAL VETERAN
SUSAN COHEN

Q – Who are you and what have you made?

Susan – Like most people in the independent film world, I am a professional beggar. I have made a number of short films that have had incredible festival runs.

Q – When you made those films, what were your hopes for the festival circuit?

Susan – For the first short film I don't think I had any expectations, and it did very well, playing many big festivals around the world. That really opened my eyes to the experience and possibilities. But that was 2003 and it's a very different landscape now. Digital film making hadn't really broken out, and now with HD and digital projection, there are many, many, more submissions to festivals, and also more festivals too. I heard this year, Sundance received 6,000 submissions for short films alone.

Q – How competitive is it out on the festivals circuit?

---

 susan@6ft1productions.com   www.6ft1productions.com

 www.openyoureyesmovie.com

200

Susan – It's incredibly competitive. You have people who have made films for say, $500, who have done very well because they have randomly hit on a subject that is suddenly very relevant to the time, or a genre film that has caught everyone's attention. And then at the other end of the spectrum, you have films that cost tens of thousands of dollars that also do very well. It comes down to your story. Does your film connect with the audience? If it does, it could have been made for $25 or £250,000, it doesn't matter.

Q – What types of festivals are there?

Susan – There are thousands of festivals and there is one for almost every film type and genre. A film maker should have a plan, they should do their research so they understand where their film is going to fit. If you have a 'coming of age' story, there is no point submitting to horror festivals, unless someone gets slaughtered – it's a waste of money as your film is not going to get selected. I would advise any new film maker to attend festivals before they submit to festivals, so they know what they are getting into before they invest a huge amount of time, money and energy into the process.

Q – Why does your film get accepted at one festival and not another - sometimes it can feel a bit random?

Susan – Yes. There could be a bunch of reasons why your film does not get into festivals. Of course you have to accept that your film could suck (laughs). There could be a film that is like your film that has a different spin, so they may choose that one. It could be that your film does not fit into a program of films - shorts tend to get bunched together into a two hour or so program, and if your film doesn't find the right home, it may get rejected. It does not mean your film is good or bad, it just means it does not fit into the program they are trying to create. Sometimes, festivals create themes for each year's program. So there are lots or reasons why your film might not get accepted.

Q – Should you submit to the bigger festivals?

Susan – Yes. But when it comes to the very top tier festivals like Berlin, Toronto, Cannes, Venice… it is much harder to get in, and if you don't get in, don't be discouraged.

Q – What does it mean to win an award?

Susan – It's wonderful to be recognised, both for yourself and for your team. Some awards can really help get other festivals interested in your film. A few years ago, winning an award was probably more prestigious than it is today, unless it is one of the A list festivals such as Sundance, Berlin, Venice. There are several others, of course. Also winning at a festival like Cannes or Palm Springs ShortFest or AFI Fest or Cleveland can qualify your film for Academy consideration (a complete list of qualifying festivals and awards can be found on the Academy's website).

Q – There are so many festivals out there, how do you choose which to submit to?

Susan – For me, a recommendation from a film maker is very important. You want to attend festivals where the organisers embrace the film makers, where there is no line between short, feature and documentary film makers. Sometimes there is that dividing line, and I understand why, it's just frustrating when it happens. There are some festivals that help promote you and your film, irrespective of what type of film you have made – short or feature – and so talking to other film makers is a great way to get that information. Some of the better festivals I have been to are often quite intimate, like the Bend Film Festival. It's a great festival where they got everyone in the community excited about the films and festival, and when you walk into a theatre and it's packed with an excited audience, it makes such a difference. I experienced the same thing at Palm Springs ShortFest. It's a larger festival, but has really excited audiences who want to see shorts and meet the film makers.

Q – To get that information though, you just have to throw yourself into the festival circuit and start networking?

Susan – Yes. It's really the only way to meet lots of other film makers and share information. Everyone talks about how film makers are very competitive, but my experience has been completely the opposite, and I have formed new relationships which may lead to opportunities in the future too.

Q – Are there good festivals and bad festivals? Have you ever walked into a screening and there are just three men and a dog?

Susan – (laughs) Oh yeah! There are some festivals where the projection is so bad, your heart just breaks. Overall, my experience has been very good though. You just don't know until you go. If you do hear from a film maker that it's not a good festival, it may not be worth submitting or attending (if you have been accepted). Again, reach out to your new film maker friends and share knowledge.

Q – What online resources are available? We all know of www.withoutabox.com, but what else is there?

Susan – I would recommend Chris Gore's book, *The Ultimate Film Festival Survival Guide*. Online resources I use would be www.britfilms.com, www.filmitalia.org and www.filmfestivalworld.com. Using these sites, and others, you can research festivals and form a plan.

Q – So this is a lot of work?

7. Posters. Send them in advance too.

8. Press packs, both hard copies and on USB thumb drives.

9. Your next project. Ideally a script and proposal document on a USB thumb drive. You never know who you will meet.

10. An up to date website, with downloads of press materials available.

11. A phone that will work abroad so you can send Tweets from screenings.

12. Camera for shots of you at the festival. Upload to Facebook for your ongoing campaign.

13. Of course, your toothbrush and all the other stuff you would normally take.

14. Space in your bag, just in case you win a big award!

DON'T FORGET YOUR TOOTHBRUSH

What you'll need to take with you to a festival...The usual stuff...
- ☐ Clothes, suitable for the climate.
- ☐ Toothbrush and toiletries (although you'll probably come home with more than you took, care of your hotel).
- ☐ Passport - check two months before going, it might have expired.
- ☐ Local cash and credit cards.
- ☐ Local translation book or iPhone app.
- ☐ Travel itinerary. Call hotel to make sure they have WiFi.
- ☐ All the other stuff you take on a normal holiday.

The not so usual stuff...
- ☐ Backpack - you spend a lot of time walking around with 'stuff'.
- ☐ Tux or posh frock and shoes for that gala premiere.
- ☐ Flyers and postcards.
- ☐ Laptop - keep working on that new project while looking out at the inspiring mountains / sea / ghetto etc.
- ☐ Cellphone for calls, Skype, email and Twitter. Make sure it will work abroad.
- ☐ Posters - ideally ten in a cardboard roll to keep them in good condition.
- ☐ Press packs on USB thumb drives
- ☐ Camera - so someone can click away when you go up to collect an award (hopefully!)
- ☐ DVDs for journalists / distributors who didn't make the screening.
- ☐ Business cards.

Susan – It's a ton of work, and I recommend you find people to help you. Sometimes you just want to get a straightjacket! Every festival seems to want stuff in a slightly different way, hand written forms, different synopsis, different formats. Not all festivals have an automated submission system like withoutabox.com and it creates a huge amount of legwork. And once you get into a festival, that's a whole other can of worms! So yes, it's more work than you expect.

Q – How many festivals should you enter in order to get into a few?

Susan – Of course there is no straight answer to that. I would start by working on submitting to about 50 or 60 festivals in order to get a handful of acceptances. Even the smaller festivals are getting submissions in the hundreds, even thousands, and you are up against so many film makers. If you get rejected, don't take it as a sign that your film is bad, it just means your film has not found a home on the festival circuit yet.

Q – How much should you budget?

Susan – Assuming you already have DVDs mastered (region free NTSC) and you have posters, a website and marketing materials in place, I would suggest a minimum of $1,000 for submission fees and sending out packages. That would be a minimum. Through withoutabox, festival submission fees can average between $40 to $50 per film. For some people, especially those who may have only spent $1,000 making their film, that may seem like a huge amount of money to invest. You can contact festivals and ask if they can waive the fee, and sometimes they may help.

Q – How do you track all these submissions and acceptances?

Susan – I have an Excel spreadsheet with all the data in it – submission deadlines, notification dates, festival dates etc. I tracked it all so I could figure out my success rate. A short film has around an 18 month window, and you don't want to submit twice because you forgot you submitted last year! Again, it's more data than you would expect, so start logging it all in a spreadsheet as early as you can.

Q – If you get into a festival, should you attend?

Susan – It would depend on the festival as very few will cover travel expenses. Some may accommodate you and feed you, but almost always, it's going to cost money to attend. I would recommend you set some funds aside to help with expenses should you get into a major festival, but if you don't, hopefully you will get into a lesser, but still well regarded festival instead. It's important to attend festivals as you get to see an audience react to your film, and you get that feedback, which as a film maker you need.

You always want to have spare DVDs, posters, postcards, everything you use to promote the film at the festival. Of course a festival is also a place where you

When your film is screened at the festival, it's expected that you'll introduce it and hold a Q&A session afterwards.

1. Audiences love film makers who are nervous. So enjoy the nerves.

2. Thank the audience for coming to see your movie, and remind them that this a very special screening for you.

3. If you are really bold, as you climb onto the stage to introduce the film, trip up and stumble ;-)

4. When doing the Q&A session, kick off as soon as you can. Ask the organisers to start as soon as the credits roll by dipping the music and bringing the house lights up. You don't want to let any of the audience leave as the credits are rolling.

6. Don't be an artist. There's no greater way to bore an audience stupid than to reflect on the naval-staring you performed during the 'conceptualisation of your allegorical story of the inner child's journey from the womb to the grave... blah blah blah', BORING! Tell them a funny story.

7. If an audience doesn't start asking questions, launch yourself into some entertaining anecdotal but relevant story.

8. Have a list of questions and give it to an organiser in the audience. They can then ask questions to which you have amazing answers.

9. Keep answers short and sweet. If you have inexperienced actors with you, beware, they may ramble.

10. Ask audiences to tell their friends about the next screening, remembering to give them times, dates and venues.

might meet a potential collaborator, agent or investor, so you want to have a script for the next project too, and have it on a USB thumb drive as no-one wants to carry a heavy script around with them and an added benefit is you can add other marketing materials to enhance your project. Also, watching other films that you might not ordinarily be exposed to is one amazing and important bonus of a film festival.

Q – What advice would you offer a new film maker?

Susan – Have a plan. Don't just apply to the top tier festivals, submit to various tiers as you never know where your film will find its home. One of the key goals is to network, to meet other film makers and see other films. If you are not good at 'working the room', stay away from the alcohol! I have seen some film makers blow it because they just don't know how to work a room. I have also seen some film makers be very ungracious when they don't get the response they expect from an audience. Don't be offended if someone does not like your film.

Film making is collaborative. But, that being said, there are a lot of naysayers out there and a lot of us wouldn't be doing what we love if we listened to those folks – there is a great book by Hugh Macleod called *Ignore Everybody and 39 Other Keys to Creativity*. I highly recommend it.

Finally, remember that you are always on a job interview, so be on your best behaviour. You don't know who people are at a festival and you don't want to be closing doors, you want to be forming relationships.

Winning awards will boost my career...
Enter loads of festivals...
Budget time and money to do this...
Research, research and research!
See films and have fun!

MARKETING
SHERI CANDLER

Q - Film marketing.
Isn't that just a website, trailer and poster?

Sheri - Marketing encompasses more than just advertising tools like websites and posters. There is a whole strategy that needs to be addressed, starting at the birth of the idea at the scriptwriting stage. Ask yourself 'who is my audience?', 'who is my target?' If you skip over this or decide that the film is for 'everyone', you will be unable to make decisions about the strategy and marketing plan. Independent filmmakers cannot afford to focus on a broad audience. You must decide on your primary target audience and expand out after you conquer that. Reaching a broad audience takes a lot of money to advertise (radio, TV, bill boards etc.), and too much time if you were to do it from a word of mouth perspective. Create a niche film or find an element in your film that is a good hook for one type of audience and put all of your efforts into capturing it.

Mostly it is about building a "tribe" of fans and influencing them to see and / or buy your film. This 'influence' takes the form of convincing your potential audience to identify with you and your film at an early stage, so that they align themselves with your mission to the extent that they will be interested in seeing the film and buying it when it is completed.

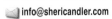 info@shericandler.com    www.twitter.com/shericand

www.shericandler.com

www.facebook.com/SheriCandlerMarketingandPublicity

In its basic form, a marketing plan has 4 components that must be well thought out to be successful. Product (the film), Place (where and how you are going to sell it, also known as Distribution), Price (pricing strategy based on the distribution method) and Promotion (these are the tools you use to advertise and get people to be aware of its existence!). Don't just address the Promotion.

Q - What elements should I have in place when I complete my film?

Sheri - Again, the strategy and plan are foremost from the START of the process, not an afterthought once completed. In the plan, you develop your tactics, the ways you will reach your audience. Assuming that you have a limited budget, I recommend that indie filmmakers take the grassroots approach to reach their audience. For this you will need a web presence of some sort, a production blog where you can upload pictures and videos, add pages for press and upcoming screenings when you need to, and provide a sharing toolbar so that viewers can

START EARLY

All the tools to create amazing marketing materials, to build a professional web presence and to reach consumers, fans, followers and potential collaborators are now freely available. It's not expensive and it's not rocket science. There is no excuse for a shoddy or poorly thought out campaign. Most people who fail to create an amazing marketing campaign do so because they don't start early enough. When they need it, it's just too little too late.

Thinking of your key artwork and creating something in Photoshop, building a website and starting a blog, starting a Facebook page and twittering – these are all things you should be doing at the same time as developing your script. You need to be an expert in all of these technologies and skills because when you get into production, or close to the release of your film, there just isn't time to get creative. All you can hope to do is add and maintain what you have already begun to build. Plus by then, it's way, way too late to begin to build a social network around your film.

Remember, it's what all your competitors are doing, and they are doing a damn fine job of it too. Audiences won't be interested in your film if they don't know it even exists.

1. Get a publicist on board. If you cannot afford one, go ask for advice and do it yourself. It's not too hard, but you have to be quite charming, persistent and put in the hours.

2. Doing press for a film is pretty much a full time job, especially in the run up to the release - don't try and take on too much.

3. A press pack is vital. It should contain a synopsis, cast and crew bios, production notes and four or five good stills, including one of the director.

4. Setup the Facebook page and Twitter accounts as soon as you can, so you can start early.

5. Work out the unique selling angle of your film and play on that. If the film is controversial, stir it up even more.

6. Network with other film makers and bloggers to raise awareness.

pass your content around easily. Don't be afraid of allowing comments to be posted too, as this allows you to see what the viewers are really thinking and address it. If you are worried about people posting off topic comments, moderate them. It is a valuable tool to see what your audience is thinking and how they are responding to your film.

The reason I don't say make a website is that this entails hiring a web designer which is great for a real professional touch, but if you don't know how to do updates on the site with the software they use, it is a pain to keep it current because you always have to go back to them, and pay them. I like the ease of a blog platform. You can still have it customized for the film by a professional, but you can do the regular updates (that you MUST do) yourself.

Next, you need a good trailer. Even if your film is only four minutes long, make a clip at least. Your trailer is the face of your marketing campaign. It should be the essence of your film, told in no more than 90 seconds, in a highly compelling way. I recommend using a professional trailer editor to do this work as the filmmaker is often too close to the project to look at it from an advertising perspective. If you have only a little money to spend, spend it on the trailer! Then, post the trailer everywhere your audience will be found online. Every film festival you screen at should have access to your trailer on their event site and on their social media sites.

Then, you will need some printed material (key artwork) for festivals or other public screenings. Using a graphic designer is a wise decision because people make their viewing choices based on how a film is presented. You want that material to have a professional look to showcase your quality film. The posters and postcards should have the same basic theme so that there is a definite brand identity for the film. Do not have two different people design two different looks and use both. Your film's identity is very important and it shouldn't get confusing.

Since social media pages are so prevalent and free, so you should definitely have some set up for the film. I like Facebook best because it allows you to search for people who are likely to be your audience more easily than MySpace. But MySpace does have a Film page feature that is useful. Whatever platform you use, be sure to keep it updated frequently.

Q - What grass roots stuff should I be doing?

Sheri - When we talk about "grassroots," we really mean word of mouth and community building. Your best low cost bet for doing this is online. Be aware that this is a time consuming and labor intensive process though. You cannot wait to start after your film is completed or it will take that much longer to build your audience. Better to start at the beginning of preproduction.

Use the social media pages I talked about (Facebook, MySpace etc.) and I like Twitter too. Be careful with Twitter though. It works best if you are not constantly "advertising" to your followers. Twitter is more about being part of a community, building a community. Who wants to hear from a community member that only talks about themselves and their product? No one! Join in the conversations, post relevant information to your community whether it is about music, indie filmmaking, art, interesting news articles, whatever

7. An electronic press kit (EPK) is helpful - loosely edited interviews with cast and crew with long clips from the film and shots during production. Usually supplied on DigiBeta or DVCam.

8. Journalists will almost always hunt out the story. If you don't want it to be printed, don't tell them - EVER.

9. Magazines will work with long deadlines, contact them as early as possible.

10. Your story will probably only break once, so try and time it for maximum effect i.e. the weeks leading up to your release.

11. Local press, TV and radio are easy to involve which can help solve local pre production problems.

12. Avoid talking about the budget and focus on the film and its unique selling point.

your community is interested in. Solicit their opinions on topics, some related to your film, some just related to what they care about. You can't force participation on Twitter, by that I mean you can't pretend to relate. For Twitter to work for you and your film, you really have to know your community and what they like to talk about. If you aren't willing to do this, don't use Twitter.

Going back to the blog platform, keeping a blog filled with regular content is a good way to attract and keep your audience interested in you as a filmmaker and your films. So a filmmaker has to be a bit of a writer too. Blogs are like an online diary / OpEd article in a newspaper. In building your fan base, tell them about your experiences and the experiences of others working on your production and in your field. Interviews are a great way to provide content and cross promote with someone else, preferably a person with their own following that you can now have access to.

Online publications and bloggers are my favorite way to get the word out about a film. There are tons of them for every genre of film and they are all hungry for content. Yeah, a review or article in the New York Times or The Guardian is wonderful, but often you just don't have the leverage to get that kind of coverage, plus does your fan base even read these publications? If not, then what do you care what The Guardian reviewer has to say? Pitch bloggers and writers of publications online that your target audience reads and get as much coverage as you can. You can also write your own articles and distribute them on EzineArticles.com or other article distribution sites. It raises your online presence in the search engines and helps to drive traffic to your sites.

Of course, you should be writing and distributing press releases whenever something big happens. These would be things like notable cast involved, a local angle involving where production is taking place, festival acceptance, festival wins etc.

Using film forums, chat rooms, and industry networking sites are additional places for you to build your community. I like Linkedin, Tribe Hollywood, IndieProducer, MySpace forums, Filmmaker Magazine forums. You can keep up on the latest topics in filmmaking and communicate with like-minded filmmakers. Plus, filmmakers like to champion their colleagues' films. More word of mouth for you and you should reciprocate as well. As far as audiences go, find chat rooms and sites where your audience hangs out and participate. Again, do not always advertise to them or you will turn them off.

HANDLING INTERVIEWS

You will at some point get asked to do interviews for video or audio (usually web channels and podcasts). Often, the folks interviewing you have not had a lot of time to research you, so have a list of good questions in your pocket ready to go. They will thank you for it. Before recording, ask how long they are expecting you to talk so you can pace your answers – they might expect one minute or one hour. Big difference. Give a beat before answering questions, and attempt to repeat the question at the start of your answer. This makes editors lives much easier. Also, try and end each chunk on some king of pithy statement.

Always refer to your film by name, not just as 'the film' and try and mention websites and blog URL's too. Of course, if you are wearing a T shirt or a baseball cap with your logo, you are a walking advertisement too. Have a DVD screener, as well as photos, your PDF press pack, QT film clips and music clips on a USB thumb drive and business cards (so they know how to spell you name and reach you) at the ready to hand over as soon as you have done the interview. Finally, ask them to notify you when the interview goes live so you can link back to your blog, Facebook etc.

And always be gracious, especially about other film makers and their films.

Q - Why should I get someone like you involved?

Sheri - The advantage of having a professional film marketer involved from the start is to help you formulate that strategy and plan at the beginning. Marketing takes a particular skill set and working with someone who has expert knowledge about the film industry and how to market a film will be invaluable to your film's success.

I spend my days researching and exploring the latest methods for marketing indie films and working on campaigns. This is knowledge anyone can gain, but it takes full time dedication to that one subject. Unless you want to spend your full attention gathering this information instead of working on your projects, it is best to work with someone to take that burden off of you. Marketing a film by grassroots methods is a full time job!

213

Q - What do you think makes a film punch through where others don't?

Sheri - Probably you will think I have a one track mind, but marketing makes all the difference because so few filmmakers think to do it until it is too late in the process. Of course, having a stellar product helps a lot, but even those can slip through the cracks if no one knows about them. Building a committed fan base who want you to succeed and who want to be affiliated with a successful film will make your film stand out from all the rest that have no community behind them.

Q - Is what you do the same as what companies with big budgets do? Just on a smaller scale? Or do you have different strategies?

Sheri - I guess it depends on the company. I don't think that companies with big budgets depend as much on grassroots methods. Big budgets buy wider audiences with mass advertising and if you have a big budget, you can use this to great effect. They also consider you to be an account and treat you as such.

I work with the smaller budget filmmaker and the methods I use are slower and more labor intensive, but they get results. The advantage to using me is that I get intimately involved with your production. I will be your greatest champion. I get to know all about you, your film, what you want to accomplish with this film and your future films. I use my network of personal contacts to promote you and your film. I want to see you succeed as a filmmaker.

Q - Should I be promoting at film festivals and if so, how?

Sheri - YES! Film festivals are the best marketing tool you can have as an independent filmmaker, especially as a low budget, independent filmmaker. Don't think of them as free screenings of your film. Think of them as almost free publicity for your film. Don't even go into them with the thought of winning. Winning is great of course, but your mission is bigger than that.

First, just getting into a festival gives you credibility as a filmmaker and recognition from someone with film critique experience who liked your film enough to program it. Milk that! Put official selection laurels on your site and promotional materials. You instantly rise above the thousands of films who are not participating in festivals. When you win, put those laurels up too.

Next, gear up your publicity machine ahead of the event. Contact the publicity officer in charge of the festival and ask to be included in media coverage they are soliciting. Festival staff vary. Some will be very helpful, some couldn't care less about you especially if you aren't a 'name' or have 'named' cast. If they aren't accommodating, find out who the media sponsors are and go to them directly. Tell them you want to be included in their coverage and have your press materials ready. These are cast and crew bios, synopsis, jpg format production stills (not behind the scenes stills), and a quote from you about why you are thrilled to be at this festival in this great town.

Access the festival's social media pages and post your trailer and a synopsis about your film and when it is screening. If you have an EPK, post it or post a link to where it is being hosted. These pages are viewable to attendees of the festival as well as the other filmmakers participating. You want to put as many people in the seats of your screening as possible and the only way to do that is to get in front of them early.

Big festivals have press rooms and you will want some sort of press kit there. I wouldn't spend a lot of time on this or make it very fancy. Mostly the press will just be covering films with name talent attached or ones that have won prestigious festivals previously. A lot of smaller festivals don't even have press rooms so you have to reach out to them directly. All towns have newspapers and they want to cover local events. Make sure your film is the one that gets the coverage!

When the festival starts, bring your poster and have some postcards for the lobby. Make sure that all contact details are listed on both and have your

MAXIMISING LOCAL PRESS

1. Invite local newspaper, TV and radio reporters to the set for a first hand look. Local reporters are always short on stories.

2. Do interviews now, which means using your cast while you have them. It is much easier than trying to get them back later when they are on another project.

3. A constant flow of press coverage will keep investors happy. It makes blogging easier too.

4. Build a well maintained website for delivering press materials efficiently.

5. Collect and archive your press articles. It will come in handy to add credibility to your next project. Get into the habit of recording your TV and radio appearances as rarely will you be able to get copies out of them AFTER transmission.

Film Marketing & Distribution Plan (how most people do it)	Film Marketing & Distribution Plan (how it should be done)
Idea for a film	Idea for a film
↓	↓
Write the script	Research the viability of the idea
↓	↓
Get some cash (usually self funded)	Target audience identified – how they can be reached?
↓	↓
Make the film	Write the script with target in mind
↓	↓
Search for a Distributor	Build a business plan (including marketing and distribution strategy and budgets)
↓	↓
If none found, begin to think about marketing	Get some cash (through investors or self funded)
↓	↓
Film either unsuccessfully self distributed or shelved	Early marketing plan put into action
	↓
	Make the film (start building the audience with various marketing tools)
	↓
	Build awareness through festivals (continue building audience)
	↓
	Distributor interested because audience is attached and film has a proven market
	↓
	Film is mass distributed

Dont just focus on the film, remember to start marketing early...

Think backwards from the market to the story idea, not the other way round. Who is my audience?

Start building that group BEFORE making the film.

screening date and time on the postcards. You can just put a sticker on your preprinted postcard and use them at many different festivals. Also, don't waste the opportunity for sales. If you have a DVD for sale, tell everyone where they can buy it while you have them in front of you. If the festival will let you, sell onsite. If not, offer a special discount code to festival attendees and give them a website they can go to. If you decide to advertise in the program, this would be the place to promote the sale of your DVD.

Participate in any opportunity to showcase yourself and your film. If you are asked or able to wrangle a spot on a panel, do it. Go to those seminars and workshops. Meet as many people as you can and introduce your film. Definitely do the Q&A with the audience.

Festivals are totally exhausting, but they are one of the best ways to build your community and get your film out there in a theater. Especially a theater you don't have to pay for yourself. Also, have fun. Soak up that attention you get as a legitimate filmmaker.

Q - What is the biggest mistake you see over and over?

Sheri - Not having a marketing strategy at all because you thought the distributor you would inevitably find would do this for you. After not getting a distributor to take on your film, you decide to try and do a bit of low cost marketing. At this point, you cannot take advantage of the months of production time that you could have used to build your audience, so now it will take even longer. So you are floundering. Also, you do not know who your audience is, what genre of film you have, or where you can go to promote it.

Q - What advice would you offer an emerging film maker on their first film?

Sheri - Learn all you can about filmmaking and the business process of distribution. If the business part is not your thing, get a producing partner who will take care of this. For a film to be successful, you have to have the best film you can make and the business acumen to get it to a paying audience.

Q – What is the job of a sales agent?

Julian – Sales agents represent films in a global market and sell those films to distributors in individual territories.

Q – How do you sell a film?

Julian - The sales agent will take the film to all the major sales markets around the world, such as The Marché du Film in Cannes, the European Film Market in Berlin, Filmart in Hong Kong, The American Film Market in LA, TV markets like MIPcom and MIP TV which are also in Cannes and Eastern European markets like DISCOP in Hungary. While at the market, they will take a stall, put up posters, show trailers, publish adverts in the trades and screen completed films. They will meet with and attempt to sell the film to distributors who they either know and have an existing relationship with, or any new distributor who may show a passing interest.

The sales agent will then negotiate a deal with a distributor, say one in Germany. Once that deal is in place and signed, they will receive the first payment from the distributor, or the 'minimum guarantee' (often abbreviated to MG) and then the sales agent will arrange for delivery of the film to the distributor. Further down the

 jr@jingafilms.com 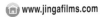 www.jingafilms.com

WHY NOT SELL YOURSELF?

It's a good question. Why not sell the film yourself? You have spent so much time and energy making it. The truth is, if you feel like you are equipped to sell it, and you have a strong desire, maybe you should. There are no rules. And it isn't rocket science. We know film makers who have both succeeded and failed to sell their own films.

Sales Agents are professional negotiators though, they know market trends, they know buyers (the good and the bad), they understand the markets, they know how to draft contracts and they have existing relationships with buyers. Ultimately they will never care about your film like you do. This is a double edged sword. On one side it will mean that if they find it very hard to sell your film, they will only go so far before moving onto the next film they pick up. On the other side, they are not emotionally connected to your film, so they will aggressively represent it in the market place in a way that might make many film makers blush. I have heard directors throw hissy fits when they see the poster the sales agent is using, but then, they are not selling the film. We filmmakers tend to have skewed perspective on these things.

Probably the biggest reason why you shouldn't sell the film yourself is that you are tired of it, and in your heart, you know it's time to move onto the next film. It shouldn't be this way, but it usually is.

line, if there are any royalties, they will manage those monies too. From those payments, the sales agent will take a commission and recoup any expenses. The remaining balance (the residue) should then be paid to the producer.

The sales agent should report to the producer after each market and every quarter, explaining what deals have been made and what gross receipts have come into the account, and if there is any residue, make payments.

A big part of what we do at Jinga Films is marketing. That would involve creating a film festival strategy, and we have relationships with many good festival programmers and directors. There are thousands of film festivals and that can be daunting for a film maker. A sales agent can help plan which festivals are suitable or worthwhile.

SALES AGENTS TIPS

1. Consider the viability of your film as a salesman - would I want this film and if not, why?

2. Sales agents are tough to deal with - they are professional hardcore negotiators.

3. Alongside your film, you will have to supply a huge amount of delivery items (see the Delivery List). Without these items, no sales agent will touch the film or they will fulfill the delivery list and charge you top dollar for doing so.

4. Attending one of the big film markets like Cannes or the AFM will broaden your outlook of sales agents and of how films are marketed and sold. Go to the next one.

5. Get a performance clause in your contract. If they don't do a certain amount of sales in a certain amount of time, you can void the deal.

Other marketing duties are the creation of key artwork (posters) and a trailer to play in the market stall. Some buyers acquire films on artwork and trailers alone, so it's vital to get these elements right. They might not have time to watch the film itself - so as long as the trailer and key art hit the right notes (remember that distributors have to sell the film to exhibitors who also have to sell it to the public). You may sell your film on those two elements alone. We can create, or help create those two vital elements.

Q - What kind of percentages do you charge and how much will be spent on expenses?

Julian – The normal amount of expenses is between $50,000 and $100,000. However, a producer can work with a sales agent to reduce that by helping with things like the key art, trailer and other sales deliverables. So by coming up with some stuff yourself you can get this figure lower. You may have produced a micro budget film, so why not apply those skills to help the sales agent keep marketing costs down.

At Jinga, we represent a number of films that are not going to make very much in the market, but by working with the film makers we have kept costs down so that when money does come in, they see it sooner. So when we ask, *'do you know a designer who might help with the poster for free or a nominal fee?'*, it's a way for us to save your money. And I think that is a better way for a sales agent to work, because other agents can accumulate so many expenses that the film maker never sees any money from gross receipts because it has all been spent on marketing.

Q – You are a film maker. Why become a sales agent?

Julian - A film is really only of value in the market for the first three years, after which it becomes a library title. If for any reason, those three years are interrupted, it can destroy your film. With my first film, the sales agent liquidated halfway through that period and the film did not quite realize its full potential. With the second film, which was a $5m film, something similar happened. The producer had a disagreement with the first sales agent, and went to a second sales agent, who then liquidated. The creditors of that liquidated agent then sold all of their titles to another agent who just added them to its library. So after 12 months it became a library title, no longer selling as a new film. That's very frustrating. And it reflected badly on me too, as people ask 'What happened to that film? It never appeared...' and it ends up sounding like you are making excuses.

For my third film, *The Last Horror Movie*, I decided to get involved in sales myself. I worked with sales agent Bill Gavin, and he had a good run, before he himself liquidated. But this time I had a clause in the contract so that the rights would revert back to me in the event of liquidation. That's when I set up Jinga Films and used what I had learnt, working with Bill, to start selling *The Last Horror Movie*. I also had the benefit of Rosana, my partner in both life and work, joining me – and Rosana also had a great deal of experience in film sales working with Bill Gavin and Jane Barclay at Capital Films. We did well with *Last Horror Movie* and attracted other film makers, and now we are selling over 30 films, and doing business with the big distributors.

6. Cap their expenses so that they have to get written permission to spend more than you agreed initially.

7. Be tough from day one. Insist on reports as agreed, prompt payment and accurate information. Make them understand that you will not tolerate complacency.

8. Don't sign with the first agent who shows interest, but move quickly as you don't want to appear as though you are on the fence.

9. Ask other film makers who their sales agents are, and what experiences they have had.

10. Remember, when you sign and hand over the film, it's now their film and not yours.

11. Insist on a clause that states the rights revert back to you should the sales agent cease trading, FOR ANY REASON.

10 THINGS TO SPOT IN A CONTRACT

1. Ask yourself first what interests you need to protect and are they sufficiently protected.

2. Do you have any existing contractual obligations to other people and if you enter into this agreement are you going to be in breach of those existing contractual obligations?

3. What are your liabilities in this agreement and if things go wrong, what are you liable for? Look out for clauses which make you personally liable even though you may be contracting through a company i.e. are you being asked to give a personal guarantee for a loan which is being made to your company?

4. What is the agreement asking you to do and is it reasonable and within your power to deliver or achieve?

5. What sort of controls do you have over the conduct of the other party? Are the promises they are making under the agreement sufficient to cover your interests? What happens if they are in default of their promises?

6. If you are providing your own original work or any intellectual property owned by you under the terms of the agreement, what

happens if the project does not go ahead? Do you have the chance to regain or repurchase your property?

7. If you are due to receive any royalties or profit share under the agreement, make sure the other party has an obligation to collect any revenue derived from the film, that they must show you their books and you have the right to audit those books. Check that your share of Net Profits (as defined in the agreement) is as agreed i.e. are you receiving a share of the Producer's net profits or a share of all net profits?

8. What are the possible sources of income to you from the film or project? Are all those sources being exploited and if so are you getting a fair share of that income?

9. If you are required under the agreement to do something, ask to change any reference to your using your "best endeavours" to "reasonable endeavours".

10. Remember that if the agreement is being provided by the other side, the terms will be very much in their favour. This does not mean that they are necessarily trying to stitch you up, this is just business.

Q – What type of films sell?

Julian – There are certain genres that sell well, and others that are very hard to sell – for example, art house films, or drama, are very hard to sell, even if they win very big festivals – it helps of course, but it is still a hard sell. If you do choose to make a drama, you need to find a way to make it marketable. With a drama you are not going to be able to do that with the story and concept alone, you need cast. You will need a face that a distributor can sell to the public. Cast is essential at every level, all the way through to a sale to TV. The other thing you need is a marketing hook, and that could be anything. For instance, with *Colin* the zombie film, the hook was *'Colin cost £45...'* I would not recommend you copy that hook as the success of *Colin* was largely about the 'right time and right place'.

Q – How many films are there out there?

Julian – Too many films. Distributors don't have time to watch them. I spoke to a buyer from Canal+ last year who told me that the most films he had watched in a day is forty. I asked how he could do that as each film is roughly ninety minutes, and he said... *'I watch the first ten minutes and based my decision on that...'*

In reality, the promo, the key art, the cast and finally, the sales agents that he has a relationship with, will all play an important role too. There are thousands of films out there and only a few can find distribution. It's a buyers market, which is also why the price is being driven down.

Q – How do you find films to sell?

Julian – Film festivals are important for us at Jinga. For instance, we just picked up 2 films from a film festival in Italy, one Italian, one American. If film makers want to get sales agents interested in their film, they should set up a screening in Soho in central London and invite all the sales agents to come and watch. Don't send a DVD as that's the worst way for a sales agent to see your film, it sends a signal that this film is not very serious. If you must come in on DVD, flag up any awards you have won, or get a godfather 'referral' from someone whose opinion we trust..

Q – So once you have seen it and like it, what happens next?

Every sales agent has different delivery requirements, but here is what we think would be the bare minimum needed. Unless you can deliver ALL of this stuff to world class professional levels, you will be unable to sell your film.

Video Master - Either 16:9, Full Height Anamorphic (FHA) PAL DigiBeta with stereo mix on tracks one and two, and M&E mix on tracks three and four. AND / OR an HDCamSR 24P master with the full mix and M&E. The video tape MUST pass highest quality control standards.

Textless Clips - Any clips where there are titles over picture, should be added to the end of the film WITHOUT the titles. AKA Textless backgrounds.

Sound Master - If you mixed in 5.1, supply the full mix and the M&E mix as separate WAV files on a DVD.

Trailer - Should be added to the end of the movie, with stereo and M&E mixes.

Stills - They will ask for more than you have, but make sure you have at least ten really great images from the film.

Transcript - This isn't your shooting script, but an accurate and detailed transcription of all the dialogue and action. You will need to sit down with your PC and a DVD and do it from scratch. Do not rewrite your shooting script, it will take longer.

Press Kit and reviews - Copies of the press kit, on paper and disk, and copies of all press and reviews.

EPK- Electronic Press Kit - DVCam tape of interviews with actors and principal crew. Shots of crew at work, plus clips from film and trailer.

Music Cue Sheet - An accurate list of all the music cues, rights etc. (example on www.guerillafilm.com) Used by collection agencies to distribute music royalties.

US Copyright Notice - Available from The Registrar of Copyright, Library of Congress, Washington DC, 20559, USA.

Chain of Title - Information and copies of contracts with all parties involved with production and distribution of the film. This is needed to prove that you have the right to sell the film to another party. Usually this includes the writer, director, producer, musician, cast and release forms from all other parties involved.

Credit List - A complete cast and crew list, plus any other credits.

Julian – We then negotiate the deal with the producer and enter into an agreement. We will negotiate the term, that's how many years, and that's usually fifteen years. Then we negotiate territories. Which countries do we cover? Sometimes the producer will say, *'We will handle our own country, you sell the rest of the world'*. That's OK if you have experience, but I would not recommend producers deal with distributors unless they know what they are doing. Then we work out an expenses budget, say $50k capped. Then we discuss the commission, which is usually 20%. All of those things are negotiable and dependent on the film, its quality, what agents are competing, its marketability, its value in the market, etc.

Then the producer has to make delivery of their film to the sales agent, and once they have done that, the sales agent is now in control. This is often when most mistakes are made as the producer underestimates how much it will cost to make that 'full delivery of a feature film'. The sales agent won't start selling the film until the film has been fully delivered by the producer.

Q – When you say delivering a film, do you mean a DVD copy? Is there more?

Julian – Yes, much more. There is a comprehensive list of items, or 'deliverables', that US distributors will request. It's eighteen pages long and could cost $50,000 or more to fulfill. For instance, an Errors and Omissions insurance policy could cost $15,000. The question is, do you need it? Well you only need it if you sell to a North American distributor, so the chances are, that could be struck off the list and procured if and when you do a deal in North America. As for 35mm elements, again you only need to deliver that if a distributor intends to release the film theatrically..

Essentially, what we would need would be a PAL or NTSC, 16:9, full height anamorphic fully finished and graded copy of the film on DigiBeta . It should have the full stereo mix on tracks one and two, and the M&E (Music and Effects mix) on three and four. If you mixed in 5:1 Dolby Digital, you can supply that mix as separate WAV files on a DVD.

We are moving into an HD future, but many countries are still resisting the shift to HD. We may well start requesting HDCam masters too, and also masters of the film on a hard drive.

We will also need the key artwork, supplied as a multi layer PSD file, so further work can be undertaken by other designers.

One common problematic area is stills – you will need up to 300 excellent stills, great shots of the cast in action – you should hire a professional for this during your shoot. If you shot HD, it's possible you could do some frame grabs from FCP, but they must be very high resolution and colour graded. We have lost sales of films because the film maker could not supply good quality stills. Don't underestimate the value of getting the right key art, it's the first thing we do at Jinga. Sometimes the film makers don't like what we do, but our job is to sell the film, not create posters that the film makers feel are aesthetically pleasing.

Q – What makes you pass on a film?

Julian – We see a lot of social realist dramas. Unless they are directed by Ken Loach or Mike Leigh, it's a tough sell. I would only be looking to represent films that I can recoup my investment.

Q – That sounds very corporate. But there is a practical reality to being a film maker for life?

Julian – If you are independently wealthy, or if you are subsidized, or if for any other reason you are not concerned about the film failing to sell, by all means, go for it. But for me, part of my agenda as a film maker is to create a sustainable industry and career. If you are going to make a drama, get the casting right, get the marketing hook right, as well as the editing, the cinematography etc. Other problems are often as simple as poor editing, cinematography, storytelling, being shot badly on a domestic digital format. One common problem is the film being too long - even big budget films we have seen have been ten minutes too long. It's almost always all in the first act. And that's the crucial part where buyers make their decisions. It happened to me on my first film, and only years later did I go back and trim several minutes out.

The experience of screening a film that is too long is horrible. You can see it within five minutes. If the buyers are not hooked, they are gone. From a sales point, that's a disaster. That screening for five buyers could cost $1,000, and if they all leave in the first five or ten minutes, we have just lost $1,000! The first ten minutes of the film are so critical. You could argue that there is a creative conflict there, how can market forces dictate that there is an inciting incident in the first ten minutes? There are many films that are ponderous, but that may be a festival film that is championed, but even with festival wins, those films may not make money.

Q – Do film makers sometimes lose sight of what they have made? Thinking it's a horror when it's a drama?

Julian – The big thing to avoid in sales is what we call an 'inbetweener'. It's neither one genre or another, but a fusion of both, and fails to deliver in both camps.

Q – Where do most film makers run into problems with sales agents?

Julian – Making sure you get the money you are owed. So I would suggest you get a Collection Agent as part of the deal – it's the only sure fire way of guaranteeing you get your money. This is fine for films where there are a lot of sales, as the cost of a collection agent could be $25,000. But if your film is small, it's another enormous cost to pay before you start to recoup.

What we do at Jinga is setup a bank account for a film, and that account has to be countersigned by both Jinga and the producer. That way, no-one has access to the sales money without consent from the other. I would avoid allowing a sales agent to just put the sales money into their own bank account as you may find that they use it to cashflow their own company and eventually liquidate and you end up with nothing. That neutral countersigned bank account is the way to go.

Q – What are your thoughts on film makers expectations?

Julian – Everyone thinks their film has more value in the market than it really has. It's good to be ambitious and push a sales agent to realize the true potential of the film, but don't be too pushy or egocentric, becomes sometimes, selling a film can be a thankless task. If the film sells for much less than the film makers expectations, the sales agent usually gets blamed. Producers rarely look to the failings of their own work or examine if their expectations are in any way realistic.

Q – What fuels those unrealistic expectations?

Julian – I hear it all the time, a film like *Paranormal Activity* took $100m and ours is like that, so even if it does a tenth of that, we are going to be rich. It does not

The delivery list is full of stuff that most new film makers wouldn't even dream of! Here's a breakdown of the biggies.

Music and Effects Mix (M&E) – This is a mix of the sound with everything present EXCEPT for the actors dialogue. It is used to re-voice the film in foreign territories. This means you will need to fully track lay and foley the sound as when you pull out the dialogue tracks, there will be very little sound left and it will feel empty (foley is all the human movement sounds and is performed by a foley artist). Buyers will reject a film if the M&E is not done properly.

Errors and Omissions Insurance (E&O) – An insurance policy that indemnifies buyers against all manner of crazy and unforeseen problems. It's a kind of catch all policy that US buyers will want. It costs around $10k to $15k, but can be maneuvered around and bought ONLY when you actually do a deal with US buyers.

Paperwork – There is endless paperwork, contracts, certificates, transcripts to supply. Get it all together as a series of scans and PDFs and supply it on disk. Do not underestimate how much time this will take to get organized.

DCP aka Digital Cinema Package – Not yet on sales agents lists, but is bound to appear soon. This is a cinema version of your film, but on a hard drive. This will replace the need for 35mm prints in the near future.

Clear genre, great artwork, great title, great cast, great photography, great sound, edited nice and tight, delivered to full professional standards, full delivery list...

Then I have a shot at SUCCESS!

work like that. For every *Paranormal Activity*, there are a hundred similar films that did no business at all.

Q – What common problems do you see with films technically?

Julian – Failing Quality Control because the film maker did not master the film professionally. You really do need a professional picture grade and conform. Unless you have experience, you can't do this at home.

Make sure you also do an M&E mix – music and effects – and do it at the same time as the full mix (the M&E mix is a version of the sound mix without the dialogue, and is used by distributors to create a foreign language dub).

It's probably worth having the film put through your own Quality Control at a laboratory so that when you do deliver it, you know it's technically acceptable. You don't want your sales agent to make copies, ship them out and have them fail with the distributor who bought it (most distributors will put the film through quality control at their end too). You end up wasting a lot of time and money by doing that. And every time a film fails QC, you will get billed.

Q – What mistakes can sales agents make?

Julian – I have seen some sales agents overvalue a film and spend too much selling it by throwing a party in Cannes or funding a publicity stunt. And then they struggle to recoup. It may make the sales agent look important in the market, it may boost the ego of the film maker, but it's at the expense of the film in the long run. So keep an eye on it.

Q – What is the biggest mistake you see film makers making?

Julian – Unless you have experience, don't do a deal with a distributor who approaches you directly as they will see you as naive, eager and easy to exploit.

Q – What advice would you offer a new film maker?

Julian – Think of the market as well as the creative side of the film making. It's not something to tack on the end, but something to start with. It's what 50% of the success of your film will come from.

DOMESTIC DISTRIBUTION DAVID WILKINSON

Q – What does a distributor do?

David – A distributor will acquire a film for release in a territory (country). Once they have the rights, they will create a strategy and campaign to release the film. They probably won't consult with the film makers, unless it's for some kind of promotion. The campaign will involve designing posters, booking cinemas, working out a PR strategy etc. They will then run similar campaigns for the DVD release and VOD release. Finally they will sell it to television – and with TV, the greater promotion, the greater the profile, the greater the price a broadcaster will pay for the film.

Q – How does a distributor differ from a sales agent?

David – A sales agent will sell the film to distributors like me, but across the globe into potentially 144 separate territories. In every territory in the world there are a number of distributors.

Q – If I had made a $20,000 film, what am I facing with distribution?

 info@guerilla-films.com    www.guerilla-films.com

David – The reality is that one or two in a hundred of those micro budget films will actually be of interest to distributors for cinema release. A dozen or so more might be interest in other rights. For a distributor to get involved there would have to be something that was unique and exciting, and it's hard to say what that is, but you know it when you see it. For most micro budget films, the distributor is not going to offer you any money at all.

Q – What is the minimum you could release a film in theatres for?

David – In the UK, I would say $15,000 and that is of course if you can get your film in. If I show a film booker a micro budget film, they are comparing it to *Avatar*. Audiences pay the same price for a ticket for *Avatar* as they do for a micro budget film, and for film bookers and theatre owners, it quickly becomes just about the number of tickets sold. They want to know that if they take that micro budget film, that I am going to do an awful lot to promote it. So the reality is they will release on one or two screens, and then they will go for the ancillary markets like DVD, VOD, TV. The UK does not generally operate 'four walling' like they do in the US, where a film maker can hire the theatre for their own release.

Q – So it's going to be tough to get any money back unless you are that one in a hundred?

David – Yes. I pay a larger royalty than most, and I have films that have done well and sold, but the costs are such that the film maker sees nothing at the end. I recoup first, that is my business, I can't afford to subsidise films. Many films I have taken have not even recouped my costs after ten years and so I have lost money on them.

Q – Do you think that as film makers are taking more control over their marketing, through social media and the internet, it makes sense for them to bypass the distributor altogether?

David – Yes. I am a film maker who became a distributor because I was frustrated with how distributors were handling my films. The film makers love their own films more than I do, and with that inherent passion, I sometimes wonder why they just don't do it themselves. I think you have to ask, if a distributor is not going to give you an advance, what are they really going to do for you?

If you are going to enter into a deal with a distributor, there should be a clause whereby if they fail to get it into theatres, all the rights should revert back to you. DVD is dying and I believe that the internet is going to be the way forward. I don't think traditional broadcasters are going to take many micro budget films, but I do think new channels that seamlessly integrate the web will emerge. So my question stands, why do you need a distributor?

I think many film makers are lazy and say *'I just want to get on and make my next film...'* But they need to understand that unless their first film is successful, they are going to find it hard to raise money for the next. The hardest film to make is often your second one. I think many also believe there is some mystique to distribution, but there really isn't. And who better to sell the film than the passionate film maker themselves?

Q – The old model would be you just hand the film to the distributor and move onto the next film. The new model states you make the film AND sell the film. You now have to be responsible for both aspects. We used to hope the distributor would pay us a lot of money and we could just move on.

David – That's not going to happen to the majority of people reading this book, but it will happen to a very lucky few. If a distributor hasn't picked up your film in the fist six months of it being in the market, it probably isn't going to get picked up. If you want success I believe you are going to have to distribute it yourself. I can't see away around it.

Q – So if I decided to release myself, how should I do it?

David – It's all about persuading people and with a film maker, that passion will shine through. I really question the choice to go into cinemas because that is going to cost a lot of money and you will almost certainly lose money. Sure there is the kudos, but you pay for that kudos. If you really want to do it, then go to your local cinema, persuade them to screen your film and promise to promote it very hard. Then build from that single screen theatrical release. You can tour around other cinemas once you have proven it worked on that first screen. It's the cheapest way to do it and you still get the kudos of a theatrical release, and you don't need a distributor.

Q – So it's moving into an area where films are screened in theatres for a short period of time – very focused releases?

DISTRIBUTION POINTERS

1. Cash Advance / Minimum Guarantee: Rarely given, usually only if the film needs completion money, in which case the distributor/agent might take a higher commission.

2. Number of Years for the rights to be licensed to the Distributor / Sales Agent: From 5 - 35, standard is 5-10 years. NOT in perpetuity. Try to have the initial term be relatively short (say 2 years) with automatic rollovers should the distributor deliver a certain amount of revenue in that time and / or deliver a specified release (so they can't just sit on the film). If those performance requirements are not met, rights would return to the film maker.

3. Extent of Rights requested by Distributor / Sales Agent: i.e worldwide, worldwide excluding domestic to be negotiated between the parties.

4. Fees / rate of commission: Usually between 15-30%.

5.Ownership: Make sure you, the producer, will still own the copyright to the Film. If you are licensing the rights to certain territories you will remain the copyright owner.

6. CAP on expenses: Make sure there is a maximum limit (a ceiling) on expenses and that you are notified in writing of any large expenses i.e. over a specified amount, that you are able to refute if necessary.

7. Direct Expenses: Make sure that overhead of the Distributor and the staff expenses are not included in Distribution expenses.

8. Sub Distributor Fees: Make sure that these fees are paid by the Distrib. / Sales Agent out of it's fees and not in addition to Distribution expenses.

9. Consider your position on Net Receipts: i.e. Monies after Distributor has deducted their commission and fees subject to any sales agreements you enter into with a Distributor. Make sure this is clearly delineated in the contract with no loopholes.

10. Errors and Omissions Policy: *See if this is to be included in the delivery requirements as this could be an added expense. Distributors are often willing to absorb this cost and recoup from gross profits. It is important that you as the film maker are added as an additional named insured on the policy.*

11. Cross Collaterisation: *Where the Distributor will offset expenses and losses on their other films against yours. You don't want this.*

12. P&A (Prints and Advertising) commitment from the Distributor: *Negotiate total expenses that will be used on P&A in the contract i.e. a fixed sum. Include a floor and a ceiling.*

13. Domestic Theatrical Release: *Negotiate what print run is expected, and in what locations.*

14. Distribution Editing Rights: *Limit ONLY for censorship requirements although if you are dealing with a major Distributor this will not be acceptable.*

15. Producer's Input: *Request involvement in the marketing campaign.*

16. Trailer commitment: *Will this be another hidden additional cost? Make sure theatres have this in plenty of time.*

17. Release Window: *Get Distributor to commit to release the film within a time frame after delivery of film to Distributor.*

18. Audit Rights: *The Producer has the rights to inspect the books with a ten day notice re: the distribution of the film. The Film maker should receive statements (either quarterly or monthly) from the distributor with any payment due to the film maker.*

19. Limitation On Action: *Make sure that you have enough time to act on any accounting irregularity that you may discover. Fight to have at least a three year period from receipt of a questionable financial statement in which to file a demand for arbitration.*

David – Yes. But that is if you want to release theatrically and I am not convinced that is the right way to go for many film makers. I hope that the internet will provide a new platform for low budget film makers. If a low budget film maker can get $2 each from 200,000 internet viewers around the world, that makes sense and is viable. No distributor is needed, as long as you do your own promotion.

Q – If you wanted to do your own DVD release, how would you do that? Is it possible to get it into a large store?

David – You will need to hire a 'sales force' to handle that for you. There are about six in the UK who handle the sales for the majority of distributors, and you can work with them too (assuming they agree). The supermarkets and larger retailers do take massive discounts though, so you sell at a very low price.

There is one thing you can do which is great. Recently, a film maker approached me, a very nice charming man, and he wanted me to take on his film. He thought it was going to be very successful so I asked him why he thought that and he said 'I have been selling it at petrol stations and convenience stores where I live in North London, just by going in and asking if they would like to sell it, and I have sold 5,000 units in six months.' He was burning the disks himself and selling them to the shops for something like £1 and the shops were selling it at £3.99. He had made back his money doing that. Whether it was worth all his time and effort I don't know, but he did sell 5,000 units which is extraordinary. It was a film with very poor production values and I doubt any national chain would take the DVD. Film makers are returning to small, specialised and localised production and distribution. People like to watch films with some kind of local aspect.

Q – What kind of materials are you going to need to do deals?

David – At the moment you are going to need a decent quality DigiBeta. I am amazed at what people are getting out of very cheap cameras, they are far better quality than a lot of feature films that were shot on film that I was selling ten years ago. I do see a day when films are supplied on disks to broadcasters etc.

Q – What advice would you offer a new film maker?

David – Go to the sales markets and listen to what sales agents and distributors tell you. On a practical level, you need lots of great stills. Make sure you have copyrighted all your music and make sure you have proper contracts with the actors. I have lost sales in the past because those contracts were not in place, so make sure you have them. That film remains on the shelf to this day.

You do need to stand back from your film and compare it with five other films that are like it, films that have done reasonably well, and ask *'How does mine compare?'*

Make the film you want to make. But it's a double edged sword. If you do that, don't blame anyone else if it fails to perform. There is a lot to be said for self distributing, because if it fails, you know you did your best and it didn't work out. There is no-one to blame. If it does work, all of the money you make comes back to you.

And if a distributor does show interest, and does offer money, don't blow them out of the water. I distributed one film where the film makers had been offered £800,000 for the UK rights, and the distributor needed an acceptance by the end of Cannes. The film makers thought, this is the first offer we have had, we will get more money if we wait. Even though they were advised to take the deal, they didn't. It eventually came to me and I picked it up for nothing. And it's sold very well for me, but it's nowhere near £800,000.

I see a lot of people giving up because they have made a film, it fails, and they take it to heart. There are people out there who have made bad first films, but who have gone on to make good second films and create a career. So don't be disheartened. But also be realistic. There are so many people chasing so few opportunities, you have to make that film the best it can possibly be. Don't rush into it. It's a mistake we have all made, where we have taken a script, fallen in love with it, and made it before it is ready. Work on that script until it is perfect.

Show movie to
distributors...
Take deal if offered
cash...
otherwise self
distribute...

SHORT FILM SALES
LINDA 'O' OLSZEWSKI

Q – What kind of films do you look for?

Linda – Films with heart and a well-executed, original story with interesting characters. Nothing turns me off more than seeing a copycat of a film that was already successful or worse yet, a replica of a bad film. Oh my – I've seen that too. I also look for high production value. The audience is not forgiving in this aspect as they are used to seeing professional acting, directing, editing and lighting at the theaters, on TV and on their iPhones... Also if a short film has won major festivals or has recognizable actors, this also helps to sell the film.

Q – Are there any genres that sell better than others?

Linda – Comedy and CGI animation. People like shorts films that are fun. The best selling shorts are the Pixar shorts or those that look Pixar-produced. For example, *Gopher Broke* by Blur Studio has been very successful on iTunes and other platforms. Parents buy these types of shorts for their kids, and tweens and teens buy them on iTunes too. Also global buyers that we work with always ask for comedy before any other genre, but they buy good dramas, Sci Fi, horror and docs as well.

Q – What technical specs does a filmmaker need to adhere to?

---

 linda@shortsinternational.com   www.shortsinternational.com

SHORTS - WHAT ARE THEY WORTH?

The hard truth is, not very much. Even the best shorts, the Oscar winners, the ones with huge stars, amazing production value, don't make much. So in some ways, busting a gut to do a deal with a sales agent may not get the results you had hoped for, especially if you are going to spend a lot of money just delivering the film. It's hard to put a specific figure on what a film is worth as that is dependent on length, genre, awards, production value etc. But we can tell you that most short films, even really amazing ones, will struggle to get back $5k. In truth even $500 would be a good result.

We successfully managed to sell 1,000 copies of our short film Gone Fishing on DVD though, via our website and at festivals and events. So always have a few signed copies in your bag. For online sales, we set up a dedicated URL, www.buygonefishing.com, which made it easy for people to find us. If we could do it again, we would also put that URL in big bold words on the end credits of the film. You will need extras on your DVD to flesh out the package too. Finally, keep your sales web page VERY simple, with a one click to buy button.

Linda – Filmmakers need to shoot in true HD – 1080p or better. Forget about SD. It just limits where we can sell the film in the current digital age. Even iTunes wants HD now. And of course, your audio and lighting must be top notch. When you master to HDcam. Also separate your music and FX tracks from your dialogue. This will help for dubbing purposes for sales in other languages, like Italy or Germany.

While the tech specs have changed, I would also recommend studying cinematic classics like *Lawrence Of Arabia* for craftsmanship, studying the early directors like Fellini and Satyajit Ray, looking at the cinematography work of Caleb Deschanel and Dion Beebe, as well as becoming aware of composers such as Hans Zimmer and Rachel Portman. Also consider looking beyond film to still photography by James Nachtwey and Steve McCurry, and look at the lighting and tone in art by painters like Johannes Vermeer. Do your film justice by learning this visual craft and all its layers that should be fully utilized to drive your story forward.

Q – Should a filmmaker be thinking about the universality of their story?

Linda – If you tell a story in your own personal voice, then it will become universal naturally. It's a mistake to approach a short film by hitting demographic audiences. That's what the studios do for feature films and it doesn't always serve them. In this medium, with equipment costs being affordable, you can make the film you want or need to make, so why not truly go for it and say something fresh and inspiring, since you have the freedom to do so?

Q – What can a filmmaker expect if you sign their film?

Linda – First they must complete our submission form, which is at www.shortsinternational.com which asks for basic information such as contact details, tech specs, and story information. In addition we require two DVD screeners for myself, our Head of Sales and our ShortsTV programmers to review. ShortsTV has several zones (Animate, Stars in Shorts, Editor's pick, Best of Fest, Midnight, Comedy, Romance, etc.) so the ShortsTV programmers check to see if it fits into any zone. In addition, our sales department reviews all shorts for more traditional distribution like TV broadcasters such as Sundance Channel, and I look at it for iTunes. After the review process, we get a sense of where we can sell it, and what kind of deal would make sense for the particular film. Sometimes I can just tell from a festival screening if a film is going to sell, so I start working on a deal on the spot.

After we pick up a film for distribution our sales team puts it on a showreel for various buyers. Every 6 months a statement is generated detailing all sales for the film at which time the filmmaker then invoices Shorts International for the amount due. Filmmaker payments via wire transfer or PayPal follow shortly thereafter.

Q – What kind of distribution could they expect?

Linda – While under an overall deal with Shorts International a film will go out to broadcasters, airlines, DVD compilations, iTunes, inDEMAND, VOD, education institutions and our SHORTS-TV channels. We've done limited theatrical runs with the Oscar nominees which have recently opened up theatrical interest for short films. Hopefully each film will be embraced onto a wide variety of platforms which will translate into revenue for the filmmaker (and Shorts International) as well as visibility for the film and the filmmaker.

Q – What is the length of license?

Linda – Seven years. If it is an older film, we will do five years because it's harder to sell to premium buyers who are looking for fresher films. iTunes deals are ten years. Some filmmakers get concerned about the lengths of a deal, but feature films are 10 years into perpetuity. As a filmmaker I'd rather have someone trying to sell my film who believes in it and has reach to buyers that I probably do not have access to.

Q – What commission do you take?

Linda – 50/50 split on all sales. This also covers all films in our library with our Errors & Omissions insurance, which saves a filmmaker money, trouble and stress. Other sales agents take 30%-50%, but they don't offer E&O. And we also split all costs to sell the film with the filmmaker, however we try to keep costs low.

Q – Are advances ever given?

Linda – For Academy nominated films, we give advances. They deserve it and we can because we have presales in place, but it's not the norm for most short films.

Q – Is it difficult to get short films on iTunes?

Linda – Yes. There's limited real estate on the iTunes stores so only specific types of films are selected. And iTunes has some strict requirements they ask us to adhere to, such as no frontal nudity, no porn, etc. We have been providing shorts on iTunes for four years and are currently selling shorts on iTunes USA, UK, Canada and Germany.

DELIVERING THE SHORT
Making delivery of a short film to your sales agent is easier than a feature. Shorts are usually only screened to audiences who are cinephiles who tolerate subtitles, widescreen formats and esoteric images.

1. DigiBeta or HDCam (24P) copy, fully graded, PAL or / and NTSC.

2. A Quicktime of your film, with stereo soundtrack.

3. A trailer (uncompressed QT file - 60 seconds).

4. A transcript of the film, with timings.

5. Ten great photos and your key artwork. One shot of the director too.

6. A music cue sheet (see www.guerillafilm.com for more information)

7. They may push for an M&E sound mix.

7. They may ask for more, so prepare to negotiate.

Q – What time lengths work best?

Linda – For iTunes, we prefer live-action to be a minimum of 10 minutes. Animation can be slightly shorter. But they do make some exceptions if a film deserves it. For example the Academy nominated film *Octopodi* (which was only three minutes) made it through because it was so fantastic and because it was an Academy nominee. And it quickly became one of the most downloaded shorts on iTunes. For other types of distribution such as ShortsTV we generally ask films to be under 30 minutes. The ideal length is generally 10-15 minutes.

Q – Do you distribute documentaries and do they have any issues?

Linda – Yes and yes. We rep a wonderful documentary *God Sleeps In Rwanda* by Kimberlee Acquaro which was Academy nominated and also won an Emmy and tells inspiring stories of several female survivors of the Rwandan Genocide. It's been on HBO, but some broadcasters want short docs and some don't - even though it's an amazing film.

The short film world is a very niche, difficult market. In America, audiences are just becoming aware of shorts because bandwidth is now good enough to view on the web on YouTube and the like. Before that, shorts were really film festival pieces and docs were an even smaller subset of that.

Q – Do you handle the press?

Linda – During the Academy Awards we have publicists in LA, NY, London and Paris who work in conjunction with each nominee's publicist. So yes, we are active in that regard. We generate press releases for iTunes releases and other films if they have a specific angle that would be attractive to press like the recent Spike Jonze / Kanye West collaboration, *We Were Once a Fairytale*.

This is actually something I always tell our filmmakers – to think about your marketing strategy to sell your project, and also your film festival strategy. If you get into Sundance or Tribeca, immediately hire a publicist to work for you and your film.

Filmmakers should also shoot great stills while in production and produce postcards/posters to let audiences know when their film is screening during a festival. Also collect business cards and start an e-mail fan list. Send your fans newsletters or Tweets with updates on a regular basis. A large fan-base is important for films going onto iTunes. Any filmmaker that just parties at a festival, but does not work to build a fan-base, is really missing a huge opportunity.

Q – What do you see as the future of online sales?

Linda – iTunes. They have their pulse on the global public. There are other players out there, but they aren't as professional and dynamic.

Q – What do you see as up and coming distribution platforms?

Linda – Pay-per view, inDEMAND, IPTV and Apple TV are a great way to get shorts to the public. Also I believe the iPhone will continue to improve and dominate the mobile market. And of course ShortsTV which is currently in the USA, UK, France and Turkey.

Q – What are the common mistakes you see filmmakers make?

Linda – Consider NOT showing a pan of photos in the very beginning of your film to introduce your characters. Also hire a composer or get free music off the web instead of using music from your favorite Top 40 band. It's too expensive to get the rights for distribution. If you use SAG actors, get the paperwork sorted two months before you begin production with SAG.

Most importantly keep in mind that people working in the short film industry - the crew, actors, the distributors - are in it because it's a labor of love. Nobody is getting rich, so be truly kind to everyone. It's a small world and everyone in this world knows everyone else. And have fun. It will show in your work, and this will attract good situations for you as a talent. I was Roy Scheider's assistant a while back and I learned something very important from him – "It's only a movie."

Q – What advice would you give an emerging filmmaker?

Linda – Follow your heart and make the film you are supposed to make - for you. You will know if it is working. The rest will fall into place if you're willing to work hard, stay centered and accept collaboration with grace while on this wonderful creative journey. And blog about the experience on your website.

BEYOND TRADITIONAL DISTRIBUTION JON REISS

Q – How does an ultra low budget filmmaker get their film out there?

Jon – The first thing a filmmaker should figure out is what their goals are with their film. Do you want a long-term fan base? Do you want money? Do you want to launch your next project? Then I would recommend they figure out who their audience is. It's essential. And you must be very specific as to whom they are. 18-35 men isn't deep enough. Next you have to figure out where that audience congregates and further, how they consume media. Recently I did a consult at Slamdance with some filmmakers who made a college comedy. They figured out that their audience consumes media through BitTorrent, so they promoted heavily there.

Q – When should you start reaching out to potential viewers?

---

jon@jonreiss.com

www.twitter.com/Jon_Reiss

www.jonreiss.com

jonreiss.com/blog

facebook.com/ThinkOutsidetheBoxOffice

Jon – As soon as possible, and by that I mean way before you finish your film. It takes a long time to build an audience, so the earlier you start using Facebook, Twitter and maybe MySpace, the better.

Q – Is crowd funding a legitimate way to raise funds for your project?

Jon – Yes. Not only that but it's a way to engage your audience. That might be more important. Kickstarter or Indie Go Go are great for that. Now you're opening it up to the world instead of just your friends in your city.

Q – Are those places becoming too saturated?

Jon – A bit, but it depends on how you're targeting your audience. There's a lot of noise in the media landscape, and how you penetrate it is what it's all about. So for example, if you blog, your posts must be unique and engage your viewers in a way specific to them.

Q – How much time should you devote to marketing your film this way?

Jon – I believe in the new 50/50 rule. 50% of your time should be spent making your film and the other 50% should be spent to marketing it. Now I realize it's a huge burden just to make a film, so that's when I came up with the idea of a new crewmember called the producer of marketing and distribution. These tasks will be assigned to that person. It might even be a good idea to get an intern to start working on this while you prep your film. Get them Twittering and get clips on Youtube. And remember if you're making a small drama with no stars you have to do something on your end to get people to notice you.

Q – This seems a lot like how documentaries are marketed.

Jon – Yes. The doc world has definitely figured this out. It's easier for them because there's usually a cause or issue at the center of a documentary, which means there is a built-in audience congregated at the center of it. For fiction, genre tends to help. Horror tends to do well. Sci-fi has an edge. Fantasy has a community online. It's harder to be a filmmaker who wants to go out and make a small drama. But if it's a drama about an autistic child for example, then you can tie into an organization or NGO (non-governmental organization) who might want to use it as a teaching tool or as the centerpiece of a rallying event.

Q – How can Bit Torrent be monetized? Isn't it a "free" download?

Jon – There is a guy called James King who has set up an organization called Vodo, which is specifically designed to work with Bit Torrent agencies and sites and have them promote their films. It provides a way for the users to donate to the films. One filmmaker had 5 million downloads and raised $30,000 so not that many people donate, but at least it's something. It's all about how to monetize piracy. There is a movement to stop fighting piracy. A comedy that I'm working with right now, the producers want to give the film to the Bit Torrent community a week before it gets released on DVD as a way to acknowledge the fan base out there. If you can't beat them – join them.

Q – Can you give any tips on how to connect to the audience?

Jon - The best way is to give the audience a way to connect with the filmmaker. So if there is a way on your site to give a sense of who you are and how and why you made the film – that can make a big difference. Your audience wants to know that you are not part of some faceless corporation who is making money on this film off the backs of some starving artists. This is called transmedia or multiplatform. It's how to get the experience of the making of the film out there beyond just the EPK or the behind the scenes part of the DVD. Start to think about these things as more robust avenues for creating new form of content, connection with your audience and creating a brand for yourself in the media landscape. The world wide audience consumes media in different ways and they experiment with media in different ways. So if you can then provide different ways to connect with you, then that is a way for you to organically connect with people.

Q – So this is where blogging, your website, webisodes and Facebook would come in?

Jon – That's a good start. Make it personal. I would go for Facebook pages over groups, but that's a grey area. And when you're starting out it might be a good idea to keep it as a group so it doesn't overwhelm your personal page because then you may have people who are fans of your work but then you have thousands of people on your Facebook. And I would also have your own personal website for the project because the problem with Facebook and Twitter is that you don't own your fan data. They do. And if you get kicked off Facebook, then you lose that data. You can collect email addresses with your own website. And you can make it dynamic via blogging, which then helps your Search Engine Optimization due to your activity. I also would recommend your own website rather than a blogging site because it is your own site and you own the data.

Q – Do you think that in this environment a low budget filmmaker can make any money?

Jon – It's hard. It depends on how good your film is. Do people want to see it? Is your goal is to make money? If so, you should think about staying in tried and tested genres. Think about what would work in the marketplace. In any event, keep the budget as low as possible because the monetization is so sketchy. The good news is that there are so many more avenues to getting your film out there. Distribution is actually the easiest part of it all. You can get it up on Youtube and become a partner then share ad revenue. You can find an aggregator and get it on iTunes. Marketing is the hard part.

Q – What are the different models of distribution these days?

Jon – I break it down in my book into three categories. First is live events and theatrical, which is the conventional way of thinking. That's when a film opens in a theater on a Friday and closes on a Thursday and is played in a building with a screen, projector, sound system and popcorn is sold. I think that filmmakers need to redefine theatrical as *any screening* in front of a live audience in the way that the filmmaker intended. This can be living rooms, parking lots, clubs, museums and cultural centers, conventional theaters and film festivals. The key here is to create community. Creating a one night special event is better than a long run sometimes because more people come together to see and talk about your film in a shared space.

Then the second area is merchandise for which DVDs are only one component. I think you have to understand what your audience likes to buy, whether it be t-shirts or posters. The comedy people said they had a lot of pot smokers so now they are researching putting their brand on bongs. And maybe it should have a design or be a prop from your film that you replicate and now sell via your website.

And then the third area is digital rights. Youtube, Hulu, iTunes - all are part of that - it's any internet, cable VOD or, TV, anything where it is sold digitally.

Q – Is video on demand becoming bigger?

Jon – Yes and I hope it will continue. The issue there is the user interface and how people find out about the different films that are on there. There are new channels popping up all the time and that's great. For me the next movement will be curation. So for $20 a month you get a whole bunch of channels showing content that is catered specifically to your likes. There is so much content on the internet it can get confusing and this is a way to hone that down. You will know you will like that content when you buy it.

Q – What are the percentages that filmmakers can expect money wise on video on demand?

Jon – It varies. Cable companies take half and then your aggregator takes a chunk. And if you have to go through an intermediary, they will take a chunk. So out of a $10 sale you might see $2-$3. There's a good website called New American Vision and they have a list of the many digital outlets and how they function.

Q – So can you get rid of sales agents?

Jon – It's hard because as an up and coming filmmaker, who do you know? A reputable sales agent will be introducing you to people that you wouldn't know otherwise. After you have been around for a while, a certain amount of the stuff you can do on your own. I like them because I might be too busy to deal with a sale or don't want to get into the legal aspects of things and they can handle that.

Q – Have sales agents caught up to this new model?

Jon – I think many of them have, especially in the US. They have to because that's where the market is. If you are going to go with one, then you should talk to other filmmakers who have used them and see if they have been served well. We have a distribution and marketing website coming out called www.ultimatefilmguides.com and the idea of that is that it is a Yelp.com (real people real reviews site) for indie filmmakers. You can look at services and see how filmmakers have rated them. All of this is in my book called *Think Outside The Box Office*. You can buy it from us or as a PDF off our website. If they download the PDF, we can give you chapter updates.

Q – What is affiliate marketing?

Jon – That's when you get like-minded people to market or talk about your projects and then you give them a percentage or fee for it. You can create alliances so when your film is ready to go, you have all these people ready to help you promote it.

Q – What common mistakes do you see?

Jon – First, not having a strategy or a plan. Many filmmakers release their films haphazardly, not coordinating the rights and allowing them to work together and benefit each other. Second, not preparing for distribution and marketing and not preparing soon enough. This work needs to start as early as prep/conception. No later than production. It is harder to engage the process if you are just starting when you have finished your film.

Q - What advice would you offer a new film maker?

Jon - Understand that making a film is only half the battle. Sales and distribution is equally important as making the film, and takes just as much work getting it out into the marketplace. And as I said above, this work needs to be integrated into the filmmaking process. It will be more pleasant and even creative if you do so. If you don't like doing this work yourself, get someone who does. In my book I created a new crew position - the Producer of Marketing and Distribution or PMD. This person is as important as your DP or AD.

For a larger perspective, see how your work fits into your overall career. What is your role, your unique position in the media landscape? How are you going to make your mark. Think strategically.

WHAT NEXT?
CHRIS JONES

Q – So the film is complete. What next?

Chris – Let's take a step back. First off, I believe that if you have slogged your guts out to make a film, you deserve to give yourself one big indulgence. A premiere that you will remember for the rest of your life. Hire as big and swanky a venue as you can find, invite everyone you know, get dressed up and make an evening of it. You will be amazed at the reaction you get. I believe that the premiere is very important to mark your achievement, and while it's clear that your premiere is a great PR opportunity, it's actually more in alignment with ancient rituals to mark milestones in our lives such as birthdays, anniversaries, weddings, funerals etc. It's a time to sit back and celebrate, to enjoy your achievement among your loved ones, for the old film maker to die and the new one to be reborn. It's a truly amazing and inspiring event. Enjoy it.

Q – What's it like the day after the premiere?

Chris – Very quickly, the glow fades as we begin to wonder about what we should do next? Which project? And ironically, the current job (film) is nowhere near completed, even though emotionally, we feel it is. Managing sales, distribution and festivals may well take many years.

✉ chris@guerillafilm.com   🐦 www.twitter.com/livingspiritpix

🏠 www.livingspirit.com   📧 www.chrisjonesblog.com

📘 Join our Facebook group 'Guerilla Film Maker'

AGENT OR MANAGER?

An agent is really more the businessman of the two. Agents will negotiate the deal, send your screenplays out to 'the town', set up meetings for open writing/ open directing assignments (unassigned writing and directing gigs looking for writers and/or directors) and set up meetings with studios and producers for your own projects/or projects for hire. If you're a writer, you want to give your agent your script in its best possible state as they only look at it from the perspective of whether it's ready to go 'out to the town' or not (i.e. will people buy it now?) There are big agencies and boutique agencies. The downside of a big agency is that you may get paired with a newer younger agent (who won't have as much clout) and also that big agencies have numerous clients, meaning they won't (and can't) focus so much on you. However, the good side is they have a lot of power, can get your script out to anyone and can also help package your film with their own talent (actors). Boutique agencies are smaller and can afford to pay you more attention. An agent takes 10% commission.

A manager is much more focused on you and your career. They're thinking about the 'now' and the future. The best managers are those who are willing to work with you on draft after draft of your script, to make sure your screenplay is as strong as it can be. Some managers are also producers (agents legally are not able to do both). A manager can work without an agent, by sending out your scripts, get you meetings etc., but if you're looking at working with studios and the big production companies, they will want to work closely with an agent. A manager takes 10% commission.

Why have both? Because the more ground you can cover, the more contacts you have – the more likely it is that you'll get that job. But you will have to pay 20% commission (10% to each). We would suggest you find a manager first, and then, when ready, find an agent. In addition to an agent and manager, there's the lawyer who will do the actual nitty gritty of the deal. Once you're ready to go out to the town with a pitch, screenplay etc., it may be a good idea to get your lawyer in place. Your team will tell you when the best time is to look for and appoint a lawyer. The lawyer takes 5%. None of these guys take any fees unless you get the job. They work entirely on commission, which is refreshing!

The way that distribution is going now and how film makers are taking control away from sales agent and distributors – all of that is great. But the down side is that there is a new and huge workload to manage. Completing your film is only half the journey.

At the same time, you really do need to start work on the next film, because your current film always raises the question from everyone you meet… 'so what are you doing next?' You want a great answer for that question. Of course most of the time it will just be interested people, but sometimes it will be an agent, an actor, a manager, a studio executive, a famous director… You don't want to say 'Ummmm, I don't know?'

Q – So why not just get on with it?

Chris – There are many difficulties. First you are exhausted from the emotional experience. It can be really draining. Second you may be jet setting around the world, going to festivals and having a great time, which we recommend. Third, you may be broke. Making a film is financially draining. More so than you can ever know unless you have done it. I know many film makers who have ended up back in that Pizza delivery job because their film nearly bankrupted them. Finally, the actual act of making the film will have changed you, and for many, these changes can send ripples out through their personal lives too, leading to broken relationships, quitting of day jobs - all manner of unpredictable personal stuff. So a combination of some of those factors will cause many of us to falter and choose to take a rest - EXACTLY when we should be ramping up for the next big one. Emotionally, it's very much like breaking up a relationship. That thing that was there in your life, every day, all day. Well it's kind of gone now. And it leaves a void. And looking at a blank sheet of paper, waiting for inspiration for your new film, well that's just daunting. Personally, I tend to watch loads of movies for a few weeks. That seems to reboot my mojo.

Q – What about agents and managers?

Chris – If your film is good enough, yes you might find yourself being courted for representation, but your film really does need to be exceptional. Agents and managers are in the business of making money by marketing and selling talent. You need to be able to deliver on that talent and your film must show that you are a film maker of exceptional - and I mean <u>exceptional</u> - talent and ability. No one will open the door for you. The phone will not ring. You must proactively seek these new relationships. And if you can't make it work on this film, follow up again after the next film. Commit to the marathon that is a life and career in film making. And if you aren't getting the results you think you should be getting, try something different. Just keep going. And make sure you keep making movies along the way.

Q – Should a film maker go to Hollywood?

Chris – If you have any aspiration to work in commercial film, you need to go to Hollywood, at the very least, visit so you have a feel for it. Who knows, contrary to any preconception you may have, you may love it, you may hate it, but you should try. At the end of the day, it's just a flight, a cheap hotel and couple of weeks of your life. Again, no one will call you or open doors, you need to be proactive and create your own opportunities. Just don't fear Hollywood. These

7. When you get to LA, rent a car, and buy a pay as you go cell phone.

8. Stay in Santa Monica. It's by the beach and is a big British ex-pat spot. If you want a more central location, stay in West LA / Beverly Hills / Hollywood / Studio City.

9. Valet parking is everywhere. Don't worry, they won't steal your car!

10. Remember sales tax is added onto the price tag at check out. Currently CA sales tax is at 9.25%.

11. Tipping. 15% is standard.

12. Everyone in LA is in the movie business, so network with everyone you meet. Go to parties, bars, dinner, coffee shops, AA meetings and sell sell sell!

13. Watch 'Entourage'.

guys really only have one question, *'How much money can you make me?'* There is nothing wrong with that. Personally I find that clarity and honesty refreshing. Of course, no one wants to make a bad movie, they want it to be great art too. But first and foremost they want it to make money.

Q – What common mistakes do you see in film makers careers?

Chris – The biggest mistake I see from people is that they just give up. I know it's hard, but nothing in life worth doing is ever easy. And we only get one shot at life, so make it a good one. Other common mistakes I see are film makers believing so passionately in their own talent that they cannot take any advice, in particular, feedback on their script, feedback on their final edit and guidance about their film in the marketplace. I guess everyone has to make their own mistakes, it just causes me pain to see people make the same errors over and over. So learn from others if you can, but you must learn from your own mistakes. If you cannot, you are doomed. And develop the ability to listen. You don't need to agree with what is said, but if you do listen, you might find something worth hearing.

Distribution is changing, which is great news. But I still see many film makers abandoning their films after they played a few festivals, have been to a market or two and finally realised just how much work sales and distribution can be. It's almost like they lose interest. I can understand that, because many of us love story telling, being on set, working in the edit and planning new films. But this is a business and if you need to make your money back, you really do need to manage the sales and distribution of your film. You cannot hand it over and just hope the money comes back to you.

Q – What advice would you offer a new film maker?

Chris – Remember that the worst day of being a film maker is better than the best day of many other peoples lives who have 'normal jobs'. So I am always grateful that I am lucky enough to do this crazy thing called film making, and knowing this helps me when things seems insurmountable. Commit to the long haul. This is not something you can just have a go at, it requires focus, determination, tenacity but most of all, staying power. Create your own destiny by taking action, and inspire others around you to follow on your journey. You will be amazed at what happens if you do this. **Above all, MAKE ANOTHER FILM AFTER THIS ONE.** Finally, remember, there is no end point to your journey. You will never get 'there'. The journey is so much more important than the destination.

CHAPTER SIX
CASE STUDIES

THE GUERILLA FILM MAKERS POCKETBOOOK

'COLIN'
MARC PRICE

Q – What is Colin?

Marc – It's a zero budget horror movie, shot with an old domestic camcorder, made with my friends, and edited at home on an old PC. The camera really was a home video camcorder.

Q – Why not make a short film, or go to film school?

Marc – I just wanted to make a movie really. I was inspired by other film makers who had just gone out and done it on domestic formats such as DV, like the guys who made *Open Water*. So I had confidence that the audience would look at the story and not the technology we had used.

Q – Why make a genre film and not a drama, set in one room? Surely that would have been an easier film to make?

Marc – I tried making a drama but it was not a very interesting film, visually at least, and I got stuck in post production. When I moved to London, one of the guys who lived in our house was an FX expert. So I said, 'let's make a zombie short for our showreels…' and astonishingly, he agreed. We got a load of people I barely knew to come round to the house. We then made them up into zombies,

---

✉ marc@nowherefast.tv   🐦 twitter.com/colinmovie

🏠 www.colinmovie.com   🅱 colinmovie.wordpress.com

 www.facebook.com/COLINzombiemovie

256

and shot a couple of action sequences. I knew it was possible to create big and dynamic sequences with no resources, we'd done it before on some of my shorts. But that was the genesis of *Colin*. I liked the idea of zombies, but wanted to do something different, and I had never heard of a film told from the zombie's perspective, and so that's what I chose to do.

One film that inspired us was a film called *Infestation*, which was also in your book (GFHB UK 3rd Ed). Their case study really showed us that it could be done.

Q – Did you think making a genre film would be easier to sell?

Marc – It was just a story I wanted to tell. I knew the 'zombie' perspective would be an interesting twist, but I didn't really consider sales and distribution.

Q – How did you make the film? Was the budget really £45?

Marc – (laughs) It's probably my fault! I think I said to a journalist it cost 'about £45', which is pretty much all we spent... certainly not much more. The "£45" thing was a platform that I could use to talk about the story and characters. In reality we made it for nothing. The only thing that would have cost money was the make-up. What I noticed with the make-up guy I knew was that he acquired make-up and equipment as 'left overs' from films that did have budgets. The effects team for *Colin* were asked to bring their own equipment, most of which were their 'left overs'. In return, they had total creative freedom to do any zombies they liked, so they were happy to be involved and use their own stuff.

Q – Did you pay for expenses and catering?

Marc – I explained to everyone involved, about 100 in all, that there were no expenses. One actress did want expenses, which I understand, but I didn't have any money, and if I set a precedent with her, it would not have been fair to everyone else, and so she was not involved in the film. Even if all I covered was a travel card, just one day shooting in London with everyone would have added up to over £500. That was impossible for me. Everyone who was involved, paid their own expenses and for their own food, and were happy to do so. We were very courteous and respectful to everyone who helped out and because of the way we made the film, everyone just got involved, even pitching ideas in.

It's not like we kept people waiting around too – people would turn up in the morning, get made up as zombies, and we'd film them. Then at lunch we'd clean them up and they would be filmed as humans. In some scenes, some people are seen as zombies, chasing themselves as humans! We'd often get people to play two parts to increase the appearance of people in front of the camera.

Q – So instead of crowd sourcing your movie, you 'actor-sourced' – instead of donating £10, you got people to buy lunch and buy a train ticket?

Marc – Yes, though I hadn't thought of it that way (laughs)! The main point is that we were able to make the film with the cheap, basic technology we had available to us, friends, friends of friends, and anyone else happy to join in.

Q – Did you have any special kit, permits, insurance – the usual film stuff?

Marc – No insurance, we just went for it. No permits. Again, we just went for it. In the street fight sequence, one policeman did turn up in response to a call about a riot. I think they sent one guy as they didn't believe there would be a riot on a Sunday morning in a cul-de-sac in London. When he turned up to see smoke billowing, people everywhere, blood and body parts in the street, for a moment he thought... 'WTF!' but then I went up to him and told him we were students. He was so relieved he just took some photos on his phone and left us alone. We shot all day in London without being stopped.

We used the microphone on the camcorder and we had no lighting, aside from a lamp usually used to light gardens at night. We knew we would do work on the colour grading, and being a zombie film we knew we would drain a lot of the colour, so I didn't worry too much about colour correction when shooting.

Q – How did you approach the edit?

Marc – I used Adobe Premiere, and having made a couple of shorts, I had a good idea of what we could do. I was pretty well versed in what needed to be done. I also knew how important sound design would be, and went about creating some very specific sound effects recorded using the onboard camcorder mics and mixed in Premiere. I am doing the Music and Effects mix now (M&E) for sales and distribution, and I am amazed at how much I have used music to hide mixing problems with sound effects and vice versa.

We were shooting and editing simultaneously for 18 months. I work evenings and could edit at the office on my laptop, but I could only ever shoot days - I would shoot three days a week with Alistair (the guy who played *Colin*), and on Sundays we would shoot pickups and the occasional bigger sequence.

When Alistair was not available for shooting, I would be editing. Or I would spend time recording weird sound effects, like chewing fruit pastels to get the sound of zombies chewing flesh. I edited every single sound effect into the movie, even footsteps, which was an enormous job. I recorded and edited every footstep Colin took, and man, did he take a lot.

One of the things we could not control when shooting was the audio for the exterior scenes, so there is traffic sounds and planes etc. So on Guy Fawkes Night (a national fireworks celebration in the UK), I pointed my camcorder out of the window and recorded all the sounds of the fireworks in London. I then edited out the whizzes, leaving only the bangs, which created a sound bed for the film that resembled distant gunshots.

Q – Did you do several re-edits?

Marc – Not really, but that is in part due to the fact that we took so long to edit in the first place. I always had a clear idea of what the ending should be and worked hard on it, constantly evolving it and shooting more. I did take some stuff out and re-order after the first few screenings, just to help the pace a touch.

Q – Did you do any 'post' VFX in say 'After Effects'?

Marc – There are a couple yes, done by a friend who worked out how to use After Effects. The rest are simple compositing shots which I did myself in Premiere, using alpha channels.

Q – Did you do the picture grading?

Marc – Yes, and I learned how hard it is! The film suited a very contrasty look, which was also de-saturated. I did it all in Premiere, but my approach was quite simplistic and I am not sure it could be called colour grading! (laughs)

Q – We first came across **Colin** *when it exploded onto the media scene in Cannes. We checked out the website and watched your trailer – we thought it was great a trailer, who cut that?*

Marc – I did. I had been contacted by Sky TV who wanted to show a trailer as part of a film making show. So I cut it very quickly.

Q – It's around this time that Helen Grace got involved?

Marc - Helen is our sales agent, but in reality she is so much more. She really has become a partner. She saw *Colin* at Abertoir, a Welsh Horror festival, and we had a chat – she wanted to sell the film and she sent contracts through. I then referred to *The Guerilla Film Makers Handbook* (laughs) and we asked for changes based on what we read – and Helen agreed! Helen is good at getting the film in front of people, something I am not as good at.

Q – Helen is also a film maker, as well as a new sales agent. Does that help?

Marc – Yes. She has worked on bigger budget films, where I have worked with zero budgets, and we have had a meeting of minds in the middle.

Q – How did you feel when the plane touched down in Cannes?

Marc – All I could think is, what am I doing? I am broke and can't afford to come here. Why am I trying to compete with thousands of other films, with huge budgets and stars? It didn't make any sense to me at the time. Helen said we needed to go, to be visible and to get into published trade magazines, which would then make it easier to do deals with distributors. At the time, like most people, I didn't know that Cannes is both a sales market AND a film festival. Most non-film people think it's just a festival, so when you say you are in Cannes, they think you are in the festival and some press actually erroneously referred to us as being in the Cannes Film Festival competition.

Q – So your misquote of a £45 budget and non film journalists thinking you are in the Cannes Film Festival, combined to create a great credit crunch David and Goliath story?

Marc – I guess so, but we did not engineer that. We only had two screenings, the first was OK, though a lot of people left during the film, which is pretty standard for market screenings. But the second screening happened after the press hit, and that was packed, and everyone stayed to the end. The credit crunch didn't affect me as I was broke when I made *Colin* and I am broke now, but at least I am out of my overdraft (laughs!).

Q – The film, at one point, was reported as costing $800,000?

Marc – Yes, and we all laughed, thinking that if people were to read that cost then see our movie they'd think we embezzled the money and bought a boat instead! But it did highlight the fact that Helen didn't actually know what the budget was – she guessed £500 and I said 'I don't have that kind of money...' and that's when I said it cost 'about £45...' We decided to let people know that was what the film cost. Helen initially thought we should avoid highlighting the low-budget aspect as it would be detrimental to potential sales. I felt it would put an audience's frame of mind in the appropriate place.

There wasn't much happening in Cannes that year and I ended up being interviewed by a TV crew, and they asked about the budget - I said 'about £45...' and from that point, the phone started to ring as more and more people got wind of this story.

The media interest was much bigger and broader than we knew while we were in Cannes, and that created a buzz which led to a UK deal.

When we first approached one big distributor, they were not interested at all, but after the press, suddenly they were interested. They wanted to change the title and artwork, and I thought that didn't make sense, given that it was the press, based on the title and artwork, that had got them interested in the first place.

Then a distribution company called Kaleidoscope came along, and they embraced everything, and worked with us to create a great campaign. So we signed with them.

Q – Did they offer a minimum guarantee?

Marc – Yes, though I can't disclose the amount. It wasn't life changing, but it helped enormously.

Q – How did you find Kaleidoscope?

Marc – We had sent a DVD screener and heard nothing, but after the attention in Cannes, they called us. It is a shame that for *Colin*, it has taken a twist of fate to deliver us some great press - press which has resulted in our amazing success and distribution. I know of so many other film makers with great movies who should also get this great exposure and distribution. Of course it doesn't work like that, which is a shame. I know there are thousands of films out there that I will never see simply because no-one will distribute them. So often it feels like it's about who is in the film, and not about the quality of the film and story telling. They want stars.

Q – Maybe you have a star now? Maybe the story behind Colin *is the 'star'?*

Marc – Yes, I hope that's right. We now have a hook, but the film needs to deliver as well. We have worked hard to get as much as we can on the DVD, about the film making process, so that maybe other film makers can see what happened to us, and be encouraged to have a go themselves. Just like your books have done, and in particular, I read one article by Shane Meadows which really inspired me to make movies.

Q – The film came out on DVD recently. How well has it done?

Marc – We have sold about 30,000 copies on DVD now and we are very happy about that. We have not had a lot of marketing, but we have had a lot of press. We released theatrically a few days before the DVD release, to help build awareness quickly and grow as large as possible. We didn't have a 35mm print, we only screened on DVD and DigiBeta in a few selected theatres.

It seems to me that the holy grail for film makers is getting your film released in cinemas – and to me now, that's crazy as I know how easy it is to get your film into theatres. You just need to get the film booked and send them the film and some posters. It's damn easy really. I did attend as many screenings as I could, and when the screening was marketed well, it would be a sell out. These were selected screenings, not a solid week of screenings. That scarcity of availability created more interest in coming to see the film at a single specified time.

Q – Have any doors opened?

Marc – Yes, I have an agent now. It's very exciting. I still have my evening job though.

Q – How important has the partnership with Helen been to the success of Colin?

Marc – Helen pushed the film with so much more confidence than I could. She convinced me to go to Cannes, and that was the catalyst for our success. We are still working together and the next film will see us collaborating.

Q – What did you get right while making Colin?

Marc – Refining and working on that ending. We worked on that for about a year with several pick up shoots. The other thing we got right was doing research before signing with a sales agent, and ultimately working with a partner like Helen, and not just ending up a shelf with a bigger company. As we did not owe any money, we did not NEED to make a deal based on the money alone. We could make choices based on our careers and what we felt were the needs of the film.

Q – What mistakes did you make?

Marc – We could have had more and better marketing. The press was fantastic, but that only raised awareness of the film. People needed to know where to find it. I still get emails from people saying "hey I didn't know your DVD was available, I just bought it!" When we had a good turnout for a screening, it was just because we had a little bit of marketing. It was the difference between three people in a theatre, and a line going around the block.

Q - What advice would you offer a new film maker?

Marc – Do it now! Don't wait for permission. Tell a story and don't worry about the format, use your mobile phone, anything! We are at a point where anyone can get the technology, so get out there and start making movies.

'INK'
JAMIN & KIOWA WINANS

Q – How did you come up with idea and then approach writing the script?

Jamin – When I was four, I always thought there was a monster in my room that looked like the witch from Snow White. My fear was that she would grab me out of bed and take me somewhere. That kept brewing in the back of my mind for all these years and around 2002 took that idea and fleshed it out a bit. Every six months or so I added a bit more to the concept and eventually I had an outline for Ink. That is my biggest part of the screenwriting process. I like to have a solid and extensive outline before I go to script. That way the writing goes quickly and I hopefully don't have to do many drafts. I usually outline extensively and like to work it out thoroughly before I get to script. I did this on Ink and then rewrote it about five times.

Q – Do you think character first or structure first?

Jamin – For me, so much of a story being interesting comes from understanding your character and how to get them into a conflict that's going to affect them the most. So character is first and foremost and then I built the structure around that.

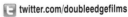 kiowa@doubleedgefilms.com    twitter.com/doubleedgefilms

www.doubleedgefilms.com   www.doubleedgefilms.blogspot.com

www.facebook.com/pages/Ink/55404284537

264

Q – Who did you get script notes from and what were they like?

Jamin – Kiowa and another writing partner of ours gave me the script notes. The biggest thing we learned early on from the first draft was that there wasn't enough character development before things start taking off. Most standard structure will set up character first, get the audience familiar with them and then throw them into a world of conflict, but a lot of times I like to start on the conflict. I realized we needed to give the audience a little bit more to latch onto before we took them through this maze.

Q – Were you ever writing with the budget in mind?

Kiowa – Not really. Jamin was ambitious so the story could be the best it could be. It kind of seemed impossible at first, but we just made sure we had enough time to come up with a way to make it happen. We knew we weren't going to have enough money to throw at problems, in order to make it work.

Q – Once you locked the script, what was the next step?

Jamin – We hadn't intended on being really low budget. We always hoped we might get some real money. So the idea was that we'd try and get some name attached to it, but it's a horrible problem for indie filmmakers. You can't get a name without money and you can't get money without a name. So we just carried on and wrote a business plan to get private investment. We also wanted to invest in it, so we re-mortgaged our house. That was key because by being the first in with money, it was easier to get people we knew to part with theirs. The investors were more willing knowing that our money was on the line as well.

Kiowa – Then we set a date to start shooting. I think it was around

September or October of 2006, we said we'd be shooting this film starting July 1st 2007. We didn't have any money, cast, or crew but just knew that we had to set a date and work backwards. So we started calling our crew and actors and doing fund raising at the same time. And guess what? We started shooting on that exact date. I feel that setting that kind of goal really lights a fire under you and you make it happen.

Q – What was your tipping point?

Kiowa –We live in a very small bungalow but for a lot of scenes in the movie we needed a big house. This way we could use it as multiple sets and a production office, so we decided to rent a large house in the suburbs. But the thing was we didn't sell our house, so by moving out we had double rent. Taking that bold step made us realize that we had to do it now and within two months of moving into that house, we had wrapped up our investment, hired everyone and were off to the races.

Jamin – Everyone committed at the same time. It was very apparent we were going to make the movie no matter what. I think if people feel that the film is going to happen with them or without them, no matter what, it makes a big difference. Plus we'd made a couple of films so they knew we were going to do it.

Q – How did you come up with the unique look of the film and how did you keep costs down?

Jamin – The key to keeping costs down was having a year of prep time. We started location scouting a year in advance in order to make sure we found the right forest with the leaves falling at the right time. We started working on the make up nine months in advance which was helpful because neither of us had ever done prosthetics before. So by the time we were really in production, we knew what we wanted to do and how we were going to do it. As for the look, let's start with Ink himself.

Remember, I wanted him to look like that old witch because one of the characters' main flaws is his vanity. So when he transforms into Ink, I wanted him to be hideous and have a very large nose. We worked with several make up artists in town and did tests so we knew how long the process was going take each day. As for how the fights looked, again, we took a long time choreographing them. We hired a very talented friend to be our fight choreographer. He had done various martial arts, wrestling expos and spent time as a bouncer at a bar so he's been in lots of fights. But the one thing he really knows is Parkour (free running)and we were able to put that into the fight sequences, which made them look fantastic.

Q – What about the color scheme and overall atmosphere?

Jamin - My cinematographer, Jeff, and I knew that with the many locations we were going to have there was a chance the audience might get disoriented. So we decided to make each one incredibly distinct visually so the audience would know where they are at every point. Giving them different color palettes in each world or dimension helped tremendously.

One key decision we made early on was that we wanted to shoot with a very small camera. We knew there would be an enormous amount of set-ups and shots and a lot of tight spaces, so we found the smallest HD camera we could find – the Sony-V1U. It allowed us to move quickly and if we needed to rig it to a car mount, a jib or a Steadicam, it could be done cheaply. We knew that would knock down our resolution a bit, but we did a test printing it to film and it worked really well.

This was also a very effects-heavy film. The most we've ever done and I was doing them myself. So we tested a lot there especially with the Storyteller's intro and exit into the world and the Incbui. Their look is a combination of visual and practical effects, so we had to do a lot to make sure they looked scary. And that was a good thing because on set they looked ridiculous. I thought I had made a horrible mistake. But it looked great and ironically the Incubi are the iconic images of the film.

Q – What program did you use to create their effects?

Jamin – Most of it was rotoscoping, which is why post took fourteen months. It was brutal. So for example, the Incbui have this screen in front of their faces with data moving across it. That was a combination of an actual plate of Plexiglas and then rotoscoped the effects in with After Effects. The glowing eyes are rotoscoping as well. It started with practical lighting on set and then I went in and animated them.

Q – Costuming was very elaborate in this film. How did you approach that?

Kiowa – We had three distinct things to create: the Storyteller's look, the Incbui's look and then Ink himself. Ink was very clear from the script, which says "He's wearing a cloak of rags that looks like an Apocalyptic bag lady." Very descriptive, but I also knew it was going to take a long time to make it. The Storytellers were harder because we had to come up with a concept outside of the script. So we put up pictures of things in magazines that inspired us. We knew going in that we wanted them all to look unique and conversely we wanted all the Incbui to look the same. So for the Incbui, we went sterile and plastic – where they are wearing rubber gloves up to their elbows, a plastic smock and this plate glass thing in front of their face. A lot of the look came because of cost as at one point we had to outfit a number of guys. But it probably made us be more creative. The Storytellers were my favorite part of the process because once we had the actors together I could design them individually. They are supposed to be angels that died at different points in history so their wardrobe reflected that. But the trick was they had to look cool individually as well as together so we couldn't overdo it. And then there was a practical issue, especially with the women. Because of all the fighting throughout the film, the costumes had to be such that everyone could move well or hide stunt padding - so no skirts!

Q – Did you go to thrift stores (charity shops) for these costumes?

Kiowa – Yes. But I had to go to regular stores too in order to get multiple sets of the costumes. If something got shredded or grape juice spilled on it without a back up, we would have been in a lot of trouble. I bought three exact replicas for each person. The troublesome one was the most elaborate – Ink. It took me nine months to create because it's a hand-sewn collage of old rags, sheets and curtains that I threw in the bathtub and dyed dark black. The shoulders of the cloak are hockey pads. I shredded it and did all sort of other things to make it look used. I also sewed other things onto it like the drums and shackles. It was the least functional costume to fight in. One particular drum would always hit him in the face! I had a tool belt on set every day with tons of safety pins and they would get so embedded in there, I would have to pull them out with pliers to make repairs and change the costume for continuity.

Q - How did you approach the art direction?

Kiowa – Jamin again had very specific ideas in mind, ideas that revolved around differentiating each world or dimension. For example, the Incbui hangout at the end had to be cold, sterile and somewhat modern because that's what they are.

We built it in a warehouse and the background were different sized squares that were backlit plastic. I connected them with the two-inch binder rings and hoisted them up on wood frames. The scene with the bride was a set built in the garage of our "production" house, where we lived during the shoot. We bought every pink sheet and curtain in about every thrift store in town for that set. We had no money, so what we lacked in money we made up for in time.

Q - How did you go about getting locations?

Jamin – We got everything for free, except for the required permit to be in the forest. For 99% of our locations we just made a pact that said we wouldn't pay for one and if someone didn't give it to us for free, we moved on.

Kiowa – We looked for places that were already dressed. Props can become expensive especially if you only use them once. So the place where the Collector lives was this old warehouse with tons of metal. We knew we couldn't build that so we had to find a place that was ready to go.

Q - How did you organize the production?

Kiowa – It was mostly my computer and I. An important thing we did was set up our office in a room in the house we rented, which was also used as a set a number of times. I didn't have the luxury of a line producer so I did it. I figured out what our weekly cash burn was and worked to stay within that range. One thing I did to minimize the pain on my side was to set up automatic payments for various things like salaries. The actors I would have to pay individually because they didn't work all week long. But it worked well and also took pressure off my crew because I knew they didn't have the time to get to the bank. I didn't have time to print out checks and put stamps on them and people appreciated that we paid them on time and frequently.

Q - What about call sheets?

Kiowa – We had an AD/Production Manager who would create them based on our schedule. But in order to be efficient, I created a Flash website where all the PM had to do was drag a PDF call sheet document onto a server. The rule was all cast and crew had to check the website after 9PM where they could download the call sheet for the next day. It was a huge time saver.

Q – Did you get film insurance?

Kiowa – Yes. Liability and worker's comp (UK, Equipment, Public and Employers liability). You need that to rent equipment and get permits. We shot the whole thing in Denver and around Colorado. It's really not expensive. It was $300 for the liability and a little more for worker's comp. At least for the size film we were doing.

Q – Did you get film permits?

Kiowa – 90% of the time. We got to know the city engineer really well. It's very easy to shoot in Colorado. Film production isn't big business in Colorado so there isn't a lot of bureaucracy.

Jamin – The car accident scene was shot in the busiest downtown Denver intersection on a Sunday morning and we didn't pay anything for the permit. All we had to do was rent a few cops, get some barricades and pay for a traffic control plan. It cost about $2,200 in total but that's nothing!

Kiowa – The only time we got hassled by the cops was when we shot a fight scene in an alley. They were walking by and stopped. They wanted a picture with Ink. For the most part when shooting downtown we always got permits because we couldn't afford to lose a day.

Q – How many shooting days did you do?

Jamin – 83. 65 with our whole crew, which was around 10 people depending on the day. Most of them were on the grip and lighting crew. We also had stunt coordinators occasionally. That is where most of the budget went – salaries.

Q – What did you do about food?

Kiowa – It was not luxurious and we didn't have a dedicated craft service person. We had a cooler with water and energy drinks on which people got totally cracked out. We had a cooler of snacks – granola bars, etc. And then we would get lunch from a local place. It was different every day because we moved around so much. Food gets so expensive! In fact, we had so many people who wanted to come down and help, but we had to say no because we couldn't afford to feed them.

Q – How did you do the car wreck?

Jamin – A green screen sequence that was partly shot in our back driveway. The front shot had the camera inside on the passenger side of the Mercedes. We hung a green screen outside the driver side window and mimicked the wreck. We blew rubber glass and compressed air at our actor and then built an airbag that actually activated. Then we went to the actual intersection location and filmed a car hitting us. The way we did that was to have a car start at the car and go backwards, so when we played the footage in reverse it looks like the car is coming towards us. That was the back plate that went on the green screen. We did the same thing generally for the things that broke and reformed throughout the movie.

Q – Did you cut the film and if so in retrospect, would you rather have had someone else cut it?

Jamin – Yes, I did cut it. I have been an editor since I was a kid. It's the one part of the process I like and don't find stressful. It's always nice to work with a great editor and get their take on something, but in this case I had a very specific vision for the editing. So it was easier for me to do it. It took me about three to four months to get the first rough.

Q – What was your post-production like?

Kiowa – Well, I didn't know anything about post sound and yet I became the sound designer by default. It was by far the largest thing to tackle. It started with me just placing in the ambience. We recorded all the Foley ourselves. We made a sound booth in our basement by stapling up mattress foam. Jamin did all the color correction. We did everything over fourteen months, back to back, in our basement, over networked computers. We were so finicky because we knew we had to get it right. A lot of filmmakers don't do this because the experience has already been so painful up until that point. But there is so much you can do in post to make a project look polished. I'm glad we did it.

Q – Was it hard to work together even though you are married?

Kiowa – It was great! We work great together. We have the same tastes. And if he had gone through this stressful situation by himself, I wouldn't have been able to understand the why of it. But being part of it was really cool. There were very few occasions where we got fed up with one another. Also I have no idea how to be a director so there was no competition.

Jamin – It was unifying to go through it together and only solidified us, which is odd because stress doesn't always do that.

Q – What was your strategy with film festivals?

Jamin – We played at a lot of film festivals with our short films – over 80 – and they can and can't be helpful. For us, they didn't really help us. Having the shorts on YouTube did more. So when we were making Ink, we knew festivals wouldn't be our primary focus mostly because we didn't want it to play festivals for a year and become old news. To kick things off, we went to the first film festival that took us: Santa Barbara. It was close enough to LA to get that kind of exposure. We sent out postcards and e-mails to distributors. And one night an agent from UTA came to see it. Then the Ain't it Cool News review came out, which got us more attention. Then we opened theatrically in Denver.

Q – What happened there?

Jamin – It played for eight weeks when it was supposed to play for two. And then it went to two other theaters in Colorado where it played for an additional four weeks a piece. We brokered the deals with the theater owners ourselves. We have gotten offers for around $5,000-$10,000 from distributors, but we think the film is worth a lot more and know you'll never see any money outside of an advance. So we are hanging onto all the rights.

Kiowa – We decided to take the film out ourselves to independent theaters around the US. It's done well – at least 15 cities. But it's a lot of work. I have to show them our reviews, get them a screener and follow up. But we get a lot more people to see it this way and the buzz is better. And we earn some cash this way instead of wasting money sending formats and marketing materials to festivals so they can take your box office dollars. I think filmmakers have to embrace the fact that they are their own distributor due to the state of the indie market.

Q - Ink is now selling on DVD and iTunes to your fans, but it did get ripped and uploaded to torrent sites. How did that happen and how did it impact on your sales?

Jamin - We don't know who put the bit torrent up. We were told by someone very familiar with the file sharing world that as soon as Ink was available someone would definitely rip it within a day or two. Sure enough, it popped up right away. What we didn't expect was how it climbed to the top of Pirate Bay in about 48 hours. We certainly didn't push it, but we recognized it as a good thing. On IMDB, *Ink* went from a ranking of #12,991 to #16 in a week and then to #14 the following week. We were open with everyone that we were happy about it and that made news all over the piracy sites. I think the community appreciated our stance and thus came back to donate and support us. Pretty cool really.

Q – How do you avoid the trap of not working on your next project as you are so busy of the current one?

Jamin – Kiowa and I talk about that all the time. The way I get around it is that most of the promotional stuff falls to her. I spend some time on it, but mostly I am writing scripts, taking meetings, and mentally preparing for the next thing.

Q - What doors opened for you career-wise following 'Ink'?

Jamin - A lot of doors have opened. We're now represented by a large agency, UTA, and have had numerous meetings with studios and production companies that we never would have gotten before. However, because we intend to keep making independent films in which we have creative control, those meetings are less important than the fan base we've been building. Fans are always the most important thing to us. They're who we're making our films for and their support makes it possible for us to continue with or without Hollywood support. *Ink* has created a fan base we never thought possible.

Q - What advice would you give a new filmmaker?

Jamin - I think it's really important to be sure filmmaking is what you want to do with your life. Filmmaking is extraordinarily difficult, competitive, and painful contrary to the glamorous image it has. It's very hard to do and even harder to do well. You can't half-ass it, so be absolutely sure it's what you want to do. If you decide to pursue it then stay focused and persevere. It takes a lot of endurance and a lot of failure to have any successes. We're still learning that every day.

'TEN DEAD MEN' ROSS BOYASK

Q – What is Ten Dead Men?

Ross – It's *Get Carter* meets *Commando*, shot on half a shoestring budget. I love martial arts and action movies and wanted to make that kind of movie. I think I will keep making *Commando* like movies until I get it right. It was one of the films that first made me want to make films.

Q – What was the format and budget?

Ross – It was shot mainly on Sony Z1's in HDV. The cash budget was just under £10k, but with deferred fees, it totals £25k. The money came mostly out of our pockets, off the back of our first no-budget film, *Left For Dead*, which made a very modest amount of money. The intention with *Ten Dead Men* was to make a better movie on every level – script, acting, editing, directing, camera – every level.

Left For Dead was shot on miniDV and was a straightforward martial arts revenge film. It was lots of fighting with some talking between fights (laughs). It sold in around 18 international territories. The film is now with a sales agent called IFM, based in LA and Australia, who handle both *Ten Dead Men* and *Left For Dead*.

 rossboyask@gmail.com

 www.stealthmediagroup.com

Search for Ross Stuart Boyask

www.myspace.com/tendeadmen

Q – How did you approach the stunts and action?

Ross – I knew a stuntman called Jude Poyer who had spent time out in Hong Kong and was now back in the UK. He got involved and brought a group of stunt players along. We had professional armourers including the excellent Mike Knights, and all manner of physical effects help too. One of the things that attracts this caliber of expert is that they are able to do things on our film that they are not able to do on bigger films – we didn't have any insurance, and as long as we were very careful, everyone knew we could take bigger risks than what would normally happen on other productions.

Q – You also had a diverse cast, some of whom bring their own group of fans, or 'tribes', in this Facebook world?

Ross – Yes, we got the *Cage Rage* guys involved and that brought us cage fighters like Tommy Gunn, as well as getting us in to shoot at Wembley in front of 7,000 fans. We also had Pooja Shah from Eastenders, Lee Latchford-Evans from Steps, and Doug Bradley who played Pinhead in the Hellraiser franchise. I am not sure how much this helped sales, but I am sure it had an impact.

Q – Given this is a ten grand movie shot on Z1's, how did you get everyone involved?

Ross – The budget never really came up. I think people knew it was micro budget, but they still got involved because of our level of enthusiasm. We also worked very hard to accommodate actors, often rescheduling so we could shoot all of their scenes in one or two days. So they were able to come onto what might normally be a difficult production, shoot their scenes quickly, and be done with it. We would always be very clear with people, don't do it unless you really want to do it, as it's going to be a tough production.

Q – How did you approach writing the script?

Ross – Chris Regan who wrote the script had been working with producer, Phil Hobden, and myself on an online comic, called *Night Warrior*. He is a very diligent and hard working writer. So we would brainstorm a treatment and he would write it up, then we would make changes, and then he would make changes and so on, from draft to draft. Between shoots, we would rework the script too, as and when required. So there was never a definitive script, it was in constant development in order to improve it as we went along. All the way up to the final day of voice over recording with Doug Bradley.

Q – Did you get any help from any official organizations?

Ross – Sadly no. Sometimes it's better not to ask, especially if you can do it without their help. If you ask for permission, people will often say 'no'. People love to say 'no' if they have the power to say 'no'. Just go and do it.

Q – What did you spend the money on?

Ross – The pyrotechnics were expensive, but we got a lot of bang for our buck. The general expenses were catering and transport, some costumes, some on people, some locations, but we already had cameras and editing equipment so there was no real cost there.

Q – The action is bone crunching in places. Did anyone get hurt?

Ross – Only one injury where Tommy Gunn landed hard on the ground and messed up his hip. He carried on filming that day and even did a stair fall before we wrapped.

Q – What were your biggest problems?

Ross – Time. It's always time. As it's an action film, we would film and Jude (stunt coordinator) and I would be editing in our heads as we went. So we were able to move very quickly, but even so, we never had enough time.

My one regret is that we didn't have better sound recording equipment, and so we ended up doing a lot of ADR which was time consuming and costly. But on balance, if we had better equipment and a more experienced sound recordist, maybe we would have spent more time on set and actually got fewer shots each day. So it's hard to say.

Q – How did you deal with post production?

Ross – I cut it at home in Final Cut Pro, with Phil providing notes on edited sequences. Grading was done with 'Color' by our D.O.P and post supervisor Darren Berry, and there were some After Effects shots too. The original cut was 107 minutes and we brought it down to 87 minutes. It was always our intention to get the film down to under 90 minutes. It's an action film, so don't hang around, particularly on a low budget. IFM (the sales agent) demanded that we deliver the film for MIP-TV (Cannes TV market held before Cannes Film Market), which meant we had to cut four weeks off the sound schedule.

Q – So you had the sales agents onboard before you completed?

Ross – Yes, because of our relationship with IFM on *Left For Dead*. And they were trying to sell it as we were making it. I regret that we were rushed as I now believe that you shouldn't even think about selling or marketing until your film is ready to be delivered.

Q – In retrospect, should you have missed that deadline and kept your four weeks to do the sound properly? You would then start selling at the next market?

Ross – Definitely.

Q – Did you enter any festivals?

Ross – We did Phantasmagoria in Swindon, and it's a great genre festival, but no, we haven't entered many more. We decided not to pursue the festival route.

Q – So sales... what happened at MIP-TV?

Ross – I didn't personally get to MIP-TV, but IFM did sell it, and we have now sold over 20 territories. MTI Video in the US did a rental release and they were so surprised by how well it did, they are now putting it out in retail too. I have had reports back that show we are now in the black, so a payment is now due from the agents.

Q - So you have made a profitable film, or more accurately, you have not lost money. How do you feel when asking for money for the next film now?

Ross – Yes it's great, I don't have to apologise when I speak about the last film. It puts me in a very strong position.

Q – So what happened with the UK release on DVD?

Ross – BritFilms acquired the film from IFM and released it on DVD in the UK. We have found BritFilms to be very passionate about what they do, they care about the film makers and they care very much about the packaging of the films they release. Unlike other distributors, they keep very much in contact with the film makers and that is great. They even did TV spots for the film. What they did was unbelievable.

Q – Did you have any inkling at how successful the film would be in the UK?

Ross – No, aside from being impressed by the passion and creativity that BritFilms were putting into it. They're not based in London and I think that may give them some perspective. Dare I say it, but make them a little more human?

Q – The film has done very well in the UK. How many DVDs has it sold?

Ross – Around 20,000 units on DVD. The deal that was struck between IFM and BritFilms was not in our favour, so part of me finds it hard to hear how well the film is doing as very little of that money will flow back to us. IFM were seeking a minimum guarantee (MG) and not royalties, so it's frustrating for us all. But yes, we are secretly delighted of course.

Q – It's the age old problem of having a sales agent in the USA or Australia, it's so hard to get a call returned let alone a signed cheque!

Ross – Exactly. I also think that sales agents, with the greatest respect, exploit rights that they understand, and work with people they have existing relationships with. The whole world is changing and there is tremendous room for innovation, but right now, it appears they are all playing catch up.

Q – What is it, do you think, that your film has, that has made it the success it is right now? Given that it has no stars, no budget and is a genre film?

Ross – That's a question I need to start asking other people as I don't really know. I would like to think it's because the distributors did a good job. It does look like a hard and gritty action movie, so it's clear what it is from the artwork.

Q – I think your title is bold and simple, and bang 'on genre'.

Ross – Maybe it's that simple. But it is misleading as it's more like a hundred dead men (laughs).

Q – What do you think you got right?

Ross – We had the right attitude in just getting it made. To keep going, and blagging, to get speed boats, Cage Rage and blowing up cars. We also got the balance between action and drama right, with respect to the genre.

Q – What did you get wrong?

Ross - We should have had more time to get the sound right, more cameras on set, and a generator for some locations would have made all the difference. More prep and real rehearsal time too. As a director, the only time I really felt I was directing was during the ADR sessions at the end, it was the only time I could concentrate on performances. During the shoot, I was worrying about everything else and I know the film suffered for that lack of focus on performances. And I wish we had loads and loads of more money (laughs).

Q – What did you learn?

Ross - There are a lot of people out there who will help – if you ask. And even when there is no money and things are going wrong, as long as you remain enthusiastic and determined, people will see that and will get onboard. So asking people for help has been a big learning experience. And when people say no, go back and ask again.

Q – What advice would you offer a new film maker?

Ross – If you really want to do this, then be prepared to give up virtually everything. It absolutely must come first. If it doesn't come first, it just won't happen. If you are lucky, your friends and loved ones will support you too.

'TREEVENGE' JASON EISENER & ROB COTTERILL

Q – How did you come up with the concept for your short film **Treevenge**?

Jason (director) – My family goes nuts over Christmas - they decorate the house from top to bottom. In fact, they actually have a separate storage locker for some of the decorations because they don't all fit in the attic or basement. One year, my Dad brought home a Christmas tree that must have stood 15 feet tall. We screw it into place, my Mom puts on Christmas music and I get up on a ladder and start decorating it. As I am doing that, I look at the tree and think this must be the most horrifying experience from its perspective. It's cut down and taken away from their quiet home in the forest, then sold off to these strange humans. I pitched that idea to Rob and he liked it.

Q – How did you approach writing the script?

Rob (producer) - We always saw it as a short. If it were any longer it might become tedious. Then we hashed out ideas for things that might be good for the story. At that point, We went off and put together an outline. We read it, gave our notes and then hashed it out again. I think Jason and I went through four drafts

---

 rob@yerdead.com   www.treevenge.com

 http://www.facebook.com/group.php?gid=40232300048&ref=mf

before we started shooting, but in the end what we shot was very different from the script. It ended up being more of a template.

Q – You built the humor and tension in levels. How much of it was in the script and how much came about on set?

Rob – Most of it was in the script. The guy getting tree raped was not. We like those kind of movies that keep building the story beats in that way. It creates an event-like atmosphere in the theater.

Jason – Yeah. When you see *Evil Dead 2, Army Of Darkness* or *Dead Alive*, you go and people are screaming and hollering. It's like being at a fun rock show. Even though you get gore and blood all over the screen, you know it can't possibly be real. And that freedom allows you to have a visceral reaction.

Q – What did you do about money and how did you keep the costs down?

Rob – We begged, borrowed and stole. A lot of our friends work in the industry in Halifax (Eastern Canada) and we got a lot of support from rental and transfer houses. They all supported us for free. Really, our biggest expenses were special effects and food. Everyone worked for free and what money we did spend came out of our own pockets. In the end, we shot *Treevenge* for about $1500 CAN and when you include post and music rights it was closer to $5000 CAN.

Q – Did you get any Canadian grant money for the film?

Rob – No. There aren't many financing structures for that here and the ones that do exist are application based. We didn't have time for that.

Jason – Christmas was coming. There were going to be Christmas trees in Christmas tree lots around for only a short period of time. So we decided to just go for it.

Q – How did you organize the shoot?

Rob – When we did our short *Hobo With A Shotgun*, it was sort of catch as catch can. But we took *Treevenge* more seriously, so I tried to create an atmosphere of a traditional film crew.

Jason – It was important for me to experience that because we plan to make features and I needed to see how that worked. And it was challenging because it was the first short I didn't shoot myself. Usually, I know where the camera will go or I do the lighting. At first, it was a big struggle to convey my ideas to the camera operator, but I got the hang of it.

Rob – And knowing that it might be an issue, I got a camera operator that would work well with Jason's mindset. However, most of the organization fell to me and I used a lot of friends. I know a great location scout and he found us the tree farm. In fact, that sequence wouldn't have been in the script if he hadn't taken us there that day. We were just looking for a place where lumberjacks cut down trees and while we were doing that, he took us there. It was amazing! It gave us great production value because it was so industrial. When we were there they said they were shutting down in a week, so we came back two days before they stopped.

Jason – We went there with a crew of four. Me, Rob, Pat, the camera operator, and one of the actors. There was not time to organize. We just went out and shot.

Rob – We got that location for a bottle of rum. They totally helped us out and didn't want anything, but I thought we owed them something. They even turned that conveyor belt on for us on the day.

Q – How did you approach bringing the trees to life – especially their language?

Jason – A lot of the tree movement is from friends lying on the ground and puppeteering a tree by its stump. The scene where the tree steps out of the house – that was a guy standing out of shot, holding it by the trunk.

Rob – One of our inspirations was Joe Dante's film, *Gremlins*. There's a scene where Corey Feldman walks into a house wearing a Christmas tree suit. Our friend Jason Johnson used it as a model, got a couple of fake Christmas trees and built a suit in a couple of days. Basically, it was a hula-hoop, a Christmas tree, a webbed body suit and a hat. And for the arms of the tree, we cannibalized the suit. So when the arms came out the branches looked like they were alive. We took the arms off a sweater and attached tree branches to them with wire.

When we wrote the script, we wrote the tree's dialogue. On set, we had the actual puppeteers saying the lines in English. After a couple days of shooting I realized that the trees shouldn't speak English. They had to have their own language. Plus it made the situation seem more dire as they didn't understand what the lumberjacks or family were saying. It seemed scarier for them.

Jason - The voice of the Christmas trees was inspired by Jason Johnson. We had him in the suit at the tree lot when the trees attack the lot owner. He put the axe in the air and screamed this dolphin sound. It was so cool and interesting, we decided to build upon that. Also, the voices were inspired by Ewoks. So we had some friends come in and do some voice acting inspired by them, dolphins and raccoons.

Rob – But we wanted it to sound like a human language. So we had them run through emotions and it was tough. We had John Dunsworth, who is on a show up here called *Trailer Park Boys* do it for an hour and I thought we were going to kill him. The squealing and the screeching sounds he made were incredible!

Jason – His daughter got in there and helped too. So I would cut up the sound effects and mix them together and change the pitches. And that's how the language was born.

Q – How long was the shoot?

Rob – We shot on weekends when we could, so we prepped a two-day shoot for a weekend and got everything together for that. Then we would have a couple weeks off until the next weekend shoot. So we got everything together in that time. We did that for four weekends, so 8 days plus one for pick-ups.

Q – What camera did you use?

Rob – The Sony F-900. We shot on HDCAM. For the most part, the camera worked great – especially with all that white of the snow. We had one nail biting moment where we really wanted these extreme wide shots as the perspective of the trees. On the first day of shooting, the lens hadn't arrived so it looked like we were going to get boned. But it came in at the last minute so we did a crew split to go get it at FedEx.

Q – Were there any surprises on set that you had to be creative to get around?

Jason – When we shot the opening sequence with the trees, we weren't expecting it to snow. And we didn't have time to wait for it to stop for continuity sake. So in the shots with the lumberjacks, it isn't snowing. In fact, it was in bright sun. So I had to shoot things close up and less wide so as to reduce the continuity issues.

Rob – There was another challenge on that day too. The DP hadn't worked with us before and he didn't realize that we shoot continuously. So he hadn't brought enough tape and at one point he said we only have 10 minutes left. And we had planned on doing these slo-mo Steadycam shots.

Jason – But we never ended up doing that because it took too long to set up. That was kind of sad because we got the Steadicam for free and when does that ever happen?

Q – How did you do the spurting blood?

Rob – In the scene where the girl gets killed, we cut off some of the branches from a tree and had two people standing behind it acting as the arms. Meanwhile, three of us stood behind the camera with syringes and water bottles with a nail hole in the cap filled with fake blood. On the cue, they grabbed her and we let loose. She was such a trooper because at one point she swallowed enough fake blood that she puked. But she wanted to do it again. Her Dad was there making sure she was OK and she said she was.

Q – Did you rehearse with the actors?

Jason – Yes. I like to have things down before we bring in the camera. That way I can shoot as much coverage as I can as quickly as possible.

Rob - Most of the actors knew our style so when we explained the world; they got it right off the bat. And we did that with the crew, too. In fact, we sat them all down and made them watch DVDs of the films that were inspiring us.

Jason – One of the actors, the father played by Jonathan Torrens, and I talked at length about his character. At first, I was going to get a normal Dad to play that role, but the more we spoke about it and the fact that I loved *Pee Wee's Playhouse Christmas Special*, I realized that I wanted a crazier, over the top kind of father - almost maniacal. We did that with every character in the film so even the nice, saccharine family is screwed. They all wear the same thing. They smile a little too much. We were always telling people to give us more, which is usually the opposite of what normally happens.

Q – How did you handle post?

Jason – I cut it at home on my girlfriend's iMac with Final Cut Pro. Surprisingly, that computer was able to handle the 1080p HD footage. It was hard because I was cutting it in the spring and close to summer and there was always that temptation to go out and be in the sun. Plus my girlfriend's office is painted pink and has trinkets around it – it's a girl's room. So I blacked out the windows like Sylvester Stallone did when writing Rocky. All together it took about 2-3 weeks to cut it. But then I was also working with several composers and handling the sound design for the tree voices.

Q – Did you have anyone watch the cuts or did you keep it internal?

Rob – Jason would go into his cave, do a cut and then show me what he had done. Then we would sit and talk about it. I might ask him to see if we have a better take of a shot and see how it works. Sometimes it would end up better.

Jason – We have the same mindset so it's great to have Rob come in see what I am doing. Sometimes I might not be sure of something and Rob would come in and give me his notes. It was reassuring because most of the times I was leaning toward his point of view.

Q – Did you do anything special in post?

Rob – Our biggest craziness was in post. We had a deadline to get it to the Fantasia Film Festival, which was going to be our premiere. We had to do the whole sound mix in 2-3 days. We had to do it after hours at this place so we were there from 6PM to 8AM three days in a row.

Jason – And we had a major problem with our final export. We shot it in 24p, but I was cutting it in a 29.97 timeline and when we went to do the up-rez, we had to bring everything back in at 24p. It created gaps between each cut so I had to go back and put it back together. Most of the time it was just a frame or two off, but that makes a huge difference. And I had one day to fix it.

Q – Did you have to kill any darlings?

Jason – Yes. There was this epic scene that we shot where a tree witnessed a boyfriend proposing to his girlfriend. The tree got sickened by it, stuck its branch into a light socket, catches itself on fire and then jumps on the boyfriend. We had a stunt guy. We had a pyro guy light the tree. We built a whole set for it. But when I was cutting it, the scene did not work with the pacing of the film.

Rob – It took over. We were working on it for days and then we both looked at each other and said, "This has to go." We were trying to get to the climax of the story and this scene was one too many.

Jason – I'm pretty good about cutting things that don't work, but it sucks when you have a guy that is risking his life for you and you don't use it.

Q – What was your plan for getting Treevenge *out into the world?*

Rob – I had never submitted a film outside of the Atlantic Film Festival here in Halifax. I would have been jumping for joy if it got into the Fantasia Film Festival or the Toronto After Dark Film Festival. But we submitted it and it got in both and won the audience award in both. Then it kept going. It got into South By Southwest and New York Horror. And we were winning the audience award at most every one. Then one of our friends said that we should submit it to Sundance. Yeah, right. No way. But this friend knew someone there so we sent a copy and never expected to hear back from them. A couple of months passed and I was working on a prison movie and it was a loud set. So when I got the phone call from Sundance saying that we got in, I couldn't hear the voice on the other end and I said, "I can't hear you because I'm in jail." So I got her to repeat it and I was flabbergasted. I called Jason right away.

Jason – At the time I was grocery shopping. I dropped my groceries and ran outside and started calling all my family and friends. I was almost in tears. So a crew of us went to Utah and had an awesome time. We made a presence. We had tee shirts made. All of our shows were sold out and people outside were throwing chairs when they couldn't get in. There were pools of blood outside the theater. It looked like a riot. The people at Sundance said it was the craziest reaction to a film they had seen at the festival. We won an Honorable Mention, which is a big honor. In fact, we went to the ceremony to cheer on this other filmmaker that we met that made *I Live In The Woods*. He gets nominated and I celebrated, then we got called and we both were shocked.

Rob – This was the first time it played to a mainstream crowd. Normally we preach to the converted at genre festivals, so it great to see it hit them like it did everywhere else.

Q – Has anything business-wise come of that?

Rob – Before Sundance we had agencies talking to us. It was getting good buzz on the internet.

Jason – The Hollywood Reporter put us on the 2008 International Watch List as well. So we've been out to LA a few times to meet with producers and studios. We got repped by UTA. It's helped to get our foot in the door.

Rob – All the people that we've met along the way have been great. They are like-minded and it's great to make relationships with them.

Q - What advice would you offer a new film maker?

Rob - Probably what everyone else will say - beg, borrow and steal everything you can to make your movie - you have to WANT it, because making movies is not easy, you have to have the fire and desire to forgo everything else in your life to get it done, and it will mean pain, tears and anger - but it will also make you laugh and feel full of life - and that first moment that you are in a theater watching your movie with a crowd and they go off, reacting to what you have made - it's amazing - the best drug in the world! So advice? Just get a camera and do it with what you have. Stop talking about it, and do it. We all have stories to tell.

'THE BLACK HOLE'
PHIL SANSOM & OLLY WILLIAMS

Q - What is The Black Hole?

Olly – We decided to make a short for the Virgin Shorts competition in the UK, so it needed to be less that 2 ½ minutes and rated PG, and we came up with *The Black Hole*.

Phil – It's about a guy in an office, working late one night with stacks of work to do. His photocopier stops working and spits out a piece of paper with a large black dot on it. He discovers he can put his hand through the dot and use it as a portal...

Q – Don't say anymore as people can track it down on Youtube and watch themselves. How many ideas did you come up with before going with 'The Black Hole'?

Phil – We had about a week to get it together as the deadline for the film competition was so close, which actually gave us a kick up the backside. Until you have a goal, it's easy to sit back and talk about it, but the deadline got us into action. We only had one other idea which was 18 certificate, so we couldn't do it. We actually wrote the script in three days.

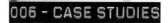

Q – How did you fund it? What was it shot on?

Phil – Having made lots of music videos, we had a close knit team of people we could call on for favours. We put some of our own money in, and the production company we work for put in some money too. The budget was £4,000 and was shot on VericamHD with a pro35mm lens adaptor. We shot it in a disused office below the production company where we work, and we had a week to post produce it in order to meet the deadline for Virgin shorts.

Q – How did you go about post?

Phil – I cut it in FCP, so we didn't need an offline/online as I worked in native HD. We then used 'Shake' to finish the film.

Q – So a lot of what made your film look so good was the fact that you had lots of contacts through your work as music video directors?

Olly – Yes, we are used to making stuff look aesthetically great for our clients.

Phil – Neither of us went to film school, our film school has been making lots of cheap music videos for god knows how long.

The Black Hole

0:10 / 2:49

★★★★★ 21,009 ratings   **5,850,523** views

Olly – We pitched it to our team like this… 'There is this film competition, we are going to make a film and win it, and then make another film, and we need your help and support…' It was very arrogant (laughs!)

Phil – We thought this would be a great chance - if we put all our eggs into one basket, we might have a chance of winning. We never expected it to do as well as it has, we thought it would just be a stepping stone to a bigger film.

Olly – They had a big awards and when we find out we had won, we were amazed. Part of the prize was a screening on Virgin TV as well as a small theatrical release in cinemas, supporting feature films.

Q – And you have great reviews from amazing people?

Olly – Yes, many of those people were on the judging panel which gave us great publicity – reviews from Kevin Spacey, Richard Branson – that's very valuable!

Q – Has it helped with managers and agents and stuff?

Phil – No-one has been phoning us. We still need to push ourselves. We got one random phonecall from LA that didn't lead anywhere. We get lots of internet feedback though, from all around the world.

Q – Most films struggle to find audiences, you have had nearly six million views and twenty one thousand comments on YouTube. How does that feel?

Olly – It's totally unexpected. There was one statistic that said we were the 97th most popular film with animation (laughs)

Phil – Is that true? I don't think that's true (laughs)

Olly – Well number one is probably a dog on a skateboard so it's not a league table of quality (laughs). But it's great to see that so many people have seen it.

Q – And YouTube can be used to monetize it too?

Olly – Yes. It's a tiny amount per click, but when you have six million hits, it does start to make a little money, only in the hundreds though. A lot of unexpected groups picked it up and started forwarding it, like Midwest American Churches who were asking to show it as it's a great parable of 'greed'. Within a week of going on YouTube it had a life of its own as it virally spread.

Q – Has this success made you think of the internet as a new way to get your work out there?

Phil – For shorts it's an excellent way to get out there.

Q – And has it acted as a good calling card?

Olly – Yes. We now have funding for another film.

Q – Have you put it into festivals?

Olly – It has played at lots yes. Usually you have to push your film to get into festivals, but this film has a life of its own and it keeps getting invited. We just did a recut today for the one minute film festival!

Q – Have you sold it?

Olly – We are not out there to sell it, it's being used as a stepping stone. We want to have it seen by as many people as we can.

Phil – It always seems to play very well. I guess it's just an engaging film about a guy – and there is no dialogue which makes it universal.

Q – Which is an important point – it's cross cultural and works on everything from a cell phone to a cinema screen.

Phil – Exactly. As long as it looks like it was meant for cinema, it will play well on both a big screen and a phone. We did not want to make something on a handycam, we wanted the feature film aesthetic.

Q – What advice would you offer a new film maker?

Phil – Do something you believe in. That will pull you through.

Olly – Set your sights high and believe you can achieve it. Don't sell yourself short.

Q - What is Dead Wood?

David – It's a supernatural horror film that we made over a couple of years, shot on a micro budget.

Seb – It's not really micro budget, it's no budget. It's a nano budget actually.

Q – How did Dead Wood come about?

David – We are a three man team, myself David, Seb and Richard Stiles. The three of us had been working together on all sorts of media related jobs, from low budget music videos to corporate work. We had the idea of making a low budget horror after we saw an online competition to make a horror short. We thought we should just go and make it, which we did for £200 – we were runner up in the competition, but thought, why not expand that idea into a feature film? We had no money ourselves, we didn't know anyone with money, so thought... let's just do it with what we have available.

---

 seb@menanfilms.com   www.dead-wood.com

 www.menanfilms.com

 www.facebook.com/group.php?gid=57346593370

Seb - And at the time, we didn't know anyone who made films aside from each other. The three of us just had this common dream of making a feature film.

David – We thought a feature would be like the short, only scaled up. It didn't actually work out like that (laughs)!

Q – So how much did you spend?

Seb – The most expensive element was the petrol. I did crash the van too, so we had to pay that insurance expense.

David - Yes, to be clear, we did actually manage to raise 'no money' (laughs). We just wrote the script around what we had - a camper van, the woods… We didn't want to shoot interiors as that means lots of art direction. In the woods, no matter where you point the camera, it looks good.

Seb – We had a crew of three. There was no-one else involved. We had two cameras which we owned, so usually two on camera and one on sound. We could also split up and shoot two scenes at the same time with different actors. We didn't want to have other people involved as they would slow us down. There was never any discussion as there was no-one to get into a debate with. It was the same with funding – we had no money so we had no-one to answer to. We took as long as we wanted to do everything and get it right.

Q – How did you get your cast?

David – We had a bunch of actors cast. We had one day filming ahead of the main shoot and two actresses fell out with each other, and another actor got a job on a big film, so we lost almost all our cast. We talked about delaying but we chose to go for it, and madly scrambled to get a new cast.

Q – Were you actually in the woods?

David - Yes. Well no. Not really. My parent's house was a few miles from the woods. So my parents moved out for a week for the shoot. The actors had a room each and the three of us slept in the hallway. We shot for a week, and both weekends on either side. That was the plan. But it just went on and on and on. We would arrive at 6am and leave at 2am the following morning.

Seb – There was a Tesco just down the road so we would clear them out of sausage rolls when things got hairy (laughs). Shooting in the woods is probably the worst place to shoot. You put anything down, it gets ruined or lost. At night, when the light is switched off, you can't find the light to switch it back on! The generator will sometimes fail and suddenly you're in complete darkness. And because you are under the canopy of the leaves, and because we were shooting video which does not have much latitude, during the day, the bright bits were really bright, and the dark bits really dark. It was a problem.

Q – What lessons did you learn from the shoot?

David – Schedule. We packed too much in. What we learned in our reshoots is, shoot it until you get it right. Don't plan to shoot too much in any one day. Allow yourself enough time to get it right, because if you don't, you will need to go back and do it again. Perhaps we also lost focus on what we were trying to capture in the race to just get it covered in the first place. We had the mentality of get it done, not necessarily get it right.

Q – So did you do lots of reshoots and pickups?

Seb - When we watched the first cut, we decided to do pickups. So we would redo a couple of shots in a scene, and as we were much better at getting what we wanted by then, those two new shots looked so much better, we would end up reshooting the whole scene. We even shot some scenes more than once and still ended up cutting the scene in the final edit. Luckily our actors were really great. There are scenes with shots that were filmed literally two years apart. Luckily, with the heavy grading, it just about cut together.

Q – What editing system did you use?

David – On an old FCP. It worked well, though it was groaning by the end.

Seb – We had made lots of micro budget music videos which had taught us to squeeze everything possible out of the FCP system. We had also learned while making these videos that shooting on the long end of the lens gave more attractive images. Richard, our third team member, spent two years on and off, doing the visual effects, learning how to use After Effects, and rendering effects and grades. That stuff just takes so long because of the rendering. A lot of the work was heavy grading, or simple shot fixing, like removing stuff from the frame (such as kit that was accentually left on set) or adding an attractive sky to what we had on tape which was a horribly burnt out sky.

Q – How did you deal with the sound? It's very professional for a small film.

David – There were so many reasons why we had to do lots of post sound work, from leaves rustling and generator noise, through to not having mic cables long enough to reach the camera when shooting on the long end of the lens (the camera would be some way from the actor), plus nearby roads, planes overhead... most of the sound needed to be replaced in the end. We found a small studio basement and we brought the actors in, one at a time, and re-recorded the dialogue, line by line.

Seb - Then we had the problem of the dialogue sounding wrong, just all the same and too clean. We had to work on it to sound more like live dialogue from the set. We also did all the atmospheres, effects, foley etc and mixed it in 5.1 ourselves at home.

Q – How did you get your film onto a format that you could sell?

Seb - We pulled in favours to do the online onto DigiBeta. I was unaware of how much we needed to do to make the film conform to broadcast standards, like TV safe areas (not having titles too close to the edge of screen) or making sure our whites were not too white (making video levels 'legal'), by passing it through a video legaliser. If we hadn't done this, we would never have been able to sell it.

Q – Did you enter festivals?

David – Yes, but way too early. It was taking so long to complete that we started sending rough cuts and of course, kept getting rejections.

Q – You have a great sales brochure that sets the tone of quality.

Seb - We did a course here in London about marketing films and we were really unimpressed with what we were shown as examples. We knew we could, and should, do better. So we put together a really polished full colour sales pack, cut a trailer and got to work on a cool website.

Q – So how did you proceed?

David - We trawled the net and started posting on all the horror film fan sites about *Dead Wood*, asking people to come to the site and watch the trailer. The advantage of making a genre film, like a horror film, is that there is this ready made audience that you can reach via the internet. Those guys love to discover something new so they will always take a look. We had so much success that the traffic crashed our servers! All the horror sites loved our website and trailer and linked to us – and somehow, someone noticed. We got an email from a company called Grindstone, a US based DVD distribution label owned by Lionsgate and they said, *'Hey love your trailer, do you have a screener?'*

Q – So you didn't even have a sales agent at this point?

Seb - No. It was before we even started looking. I think the website and trailer got them interested, as well as the buzz in the horror film online community. Grindstone need to acquire horror films regularly as they have a quota to fill, and if your film is good, if it delivers on the horror genre and if they can cut a trailer and make a poster, you could be in business.

David - They initially asked *'What will you take for it?'* We spent some time worrying about how much we should say, hundreds of thousands...? Would that scare them off? We had no reference at all. We just didn't know what to ask. But we did know that you want to be the person who opens negotiations by starting with the first number. Aim high, close high. But they beat us to it by offering $25k. We said, *'You are Lionsgate, is that the best you can do?'* We made a counter offer of $70k and they came back saying, *'The most we can go to is $40k'*, and so we accepted that. This was for North American rights, which included Canada.

Q – Did you get that money?

Seb - We have all heard of sales agents who never pay the film makers, but there was no middle man involved, and so yes, we got the whole $40k, less a few expenses in getting an NTSC transfer done. This was all a big surprise as we had planned to spend six months promoting at film festivals and then maybe find a sales agent. Once Lionsgate were involved, we started to get into film festivals, suddenly people were interested. When we thought about it later, we could not have been luckier – we always wanted Lionsgate as they are the perfect label for *Dead Wood*.

Q - So now you had Lionsgate, how did you deal with other sales?

David – We started getting offers from other distributors in other territories – clearly having Lionsgate distribute our film in North America had given us street cred. We also went to the Berlin Film Market with a press pack that said *Dead Wood* was being released in America by Lionsgate, and that generated a lot of interest from Sales Agents. We finally signed with one and got great releases in the UK, Germany and some other territories.

Q – And have you seen any money from the sales agent?

Seb – We have seen £1k.

Q – Isn't it ironic that you got all the Lionsgate / Grindstone sales money but only a fraction of all the other territories? Have they sold more than the Lionsgate deal?

David – Yes, they have sold more than $40k. But they also have all their costs to recoup, as well as their fees. In retrospect, I think if we had done all the sales work ourselves, we could have made more money. But that is of course in hindsight, and we just don't know if we could have sold it as we are not sales agents. I would certainly consider doing it on our second film, but on *Dead Wood*, we had no clue. We needed that experience to know what to do next time. We now have relationships with all the companies who bought the film and if we make another film like *Dead Wood*, we could go straight to them with the completed film and cut the sales agent out.

Q – What advice would you offer a new film maker?

Seb – Don't wait for anyone to give you permission to do it, just get on with it. Even if your film is very cheap, you are going to be living with it for many years, so make sure you are very passionate about it.

Q – What is your background?

Oren – I have no film background – *Paranormal Activity* was the first thing I did in film. I'm a computer games programmer which I did growing up as a kid in Israel. With games, you're dealing with the placement of lighting, actors, choreography and the visual representation of things on a screen. You have to deal with camera angles. There is some storytelling, but in video games it's more interactive. Plus I was comfortable with computers, which helped with the editing and visual effects.

Q – How did the idea for the film come about?

Oren – I moved to a new house and I started hearing noises at night. My first instinct wasn't that the house was haunted, but it did get me to think about what was going on. It lead me to the idea of what if someone did think their house was haunted and wanted to prove or disprove it, so they set up a video camera. Then what if they let it play all night and the next day saw something scary in the footage. I was inspired by slower paced horror films like *The Blair Witch Project* and *Rosemary's Baby* where the audience has to use their imagination more to get the scares. I didn't tell anyone I was making the movie. Not my neighbors. Not my co-workers. Only my small crew, my parents and my girlfriend knew.

Q – How long was your screenwriting and prep process?

Oren – About a year. I did a lot of research on filmmaking and ghosts. I had to learn how to do everything. What kind of camera should I use? How do I mix audio? I practiced with the editing software and learnt what I could and couldn't do with visual effects, then I wrote the plot around that. I also read a lot of books and web articles on the process of filmmaking so that when I got to set, I was like an automated machine. I also bought a lot of books and watched a lot of movies and documentaries about ghosts, hauntings, demons, possessions and exorcisms. I tried to make myself an expert so the story was credible.

Q – Was it difficult taking the leap to making a movie?

Oren – It wasn't that tough because my life was going on as it would and this was something I was doing on the side. I figured if nothing happens because the movie turns out horrible or it's good but nobody does anything with it, at least I did something fun. Plus a lot of people spend a lot more money on their hobbies and still don't have something that could change their lives. There was never a script. It was more like a simple treatment. In the film, all the dialogue was improvised. The treatment was like: a couple goes to sleep, such and such happens and then they investigate... As we were getting closer, I refined it more and as we were shooting it was really brought to life by the actors.

Q – This was the first time you auditioned actors. How did that go?

Oren – The idea was to use improv. I had to make sure that they were quick on their feet. In the audition there was no script to read, it was more like an interview. So I would ask them why they thought the house was haunted or tell them to get into an argument about whether they should bring a psychic over. We went to LA (I'm based in San Diego) and rented a theatre for the auditions.

Q – Where did you get your money to make the film?

Oren – It was my own money from working so I paid for things as we went along.

Q – I understand the shoot only took seven days, is that right?

Oren – The original schedule was set for five days as that's how long I thought it would take. And it did. But I kept the actors and crew on for two extra days just in case we needed to reshoot. When you don't have to worry about lighting and don't have a large crew, you can be very nimble. I took a week off work.

Q – Did you have any other crew?

Oren – The crew consisted of myself, my best friend whose experience in film was the same as mine – none, and my reluctant girlfriend at the time. We lived together so she didn't have a choice! The only thing I couldn't figure out on my own and needed professional help with was make-up. So I hired a make-up artist for one day to do make-up effects such as the bite marks on Katie.

Q – What did you do about the camera and audio?

Oren – I shot on the Sony FX-1. It was an HDV camera that shot to tape. As for sound, that was part of my research. I wanted everything to be natural, so I didn't want to use lavs (tie clip mics) because the characters wouldn't be wearing them in their everyday life. But I had to find a way to get better quality audio so I had a boom mic attached to the camera which is obviously the one Micah uses in the movie. We used the excuse that they needed that mic to catch all of the little sounds from within the house at night.

Q – You shot the film in your house. Did you modify it in any way?

Oren – Yes. When I got the video camera I did test shots around my house and noticed how lame it was. All I had were these bare, white walls and carpeting. I wanted it to look normal and not like an eerie castle. So I put in hardwood floors and replaced the stairs and banister, painted the walls, built an archway between the living room and the dining room and put some artwork on the walls. I didn't include this stuff in the budget because I was going to do it anyway as my own home improvements. The hardwood floors alone cost more than the whole film!

Q – Did you do a lot of takes?

Oren –There were sequences where we only did one take. The one with the foot powder and they go and investigate was the first and only take we did. When scenes didn't work or if it didn't make sense, we would stop, confer and try and fix it. It was a very collaborative process with the actors. I experiment a lot, and when I see it I say, "No, that wasn't such a great idea. Let's try something else," or "Yes, that works great. Let's move on." So it was a lot of organic trial and error.

Q – How did you do some of the special effects in the film?

Oren – We have been very careful not to give away any secrets on how we did the special effects, but I will say that everything we did was in-camera.

Q – How long did post take?

Oren – Close to a year and I did all the editing on Sony Vegas. I chose Vegas because I use PCs not Macs. Also I read that Vegas is the easiest to use and very intuitive. I downloaded a trial version and found that I could move blazingly fast with it. It really helped when I got a page of notes from the studio as I could go through it in about an hour. I bought a dedicated editing machine and put all my 70 hours of footage on the internal hard drive. I didn't want to use external hard drives because they slow everything down. I had so much footage because I would let the camera just roll while Micah and Katie were making dinner, plus tape is cheap. And if I got a minute of useable footage from that, then great. I also did all the visual effects at home too. I went into forums online to get ideas. It might not have been the most efficient way to do it, but it made sense to me.

Q – How did you come up with the title?

Oren – For the longest time there was no title and I was forced to come up with one because I was submitting to festivals. *Paranormal Activity* wasn't even one that we were all crazy about, but it didn't suck and it's dry and accurate.

Q – From the test screenings you did, what kind of feedback did you get?

Oren – The one that kept popping up was that the beginning was too slow. I kept shortening it, but what I learned was that if I kept it slow then people would say it was the scariest movie they've ever seen. But when I trimmed the beginning and made it flow well, then people would say that the pacing was excellent and the movie was kind of creepy. It just didn't generate the same visceral terror. So, in the end, I didn't care about the slow pacing. People are used to horror movies that start with a big bang at the beginning so when you break that structure, it's very unsettling for them. They don't even know they are watching a movie and then when you start scaring them, it really works.

Q – I understand there are multiple endings?

Oren – At the beginning I was very married to my version, which had the police coming in at the end. I got some criticisms, but I didn't care. But it was too slow and didn't have a big punch at the end. I then shot another version where Katie slits her own throat, but it didn't fit with the film to be so gory. But when we experimented and tested the endings, the one that is in the theatrical version is the one that went through the roof, so there was no question what to do.

Q – What was your film festival strategy?

Oren – I hoped I would get into Sundance and then there would be a bidding war. But I finished too early and I didn't want to wait. So I submitted to Toronto and a bunch of other festivals and got rejected by all of them. The only one we got into was Screamfest. But I knew if we went there we would lose our premiere at prestigious festivals. But I gambled and took the bird in hand. At the screening, I was as nervous as hell. I knew Screamfest was a smaller festival, we didn't even do a Q & A, but a lot of press and distributors do go there. So I thought it was a good way for the film to get noticed. The screening was incredible! The audience was screaming and shifting in their seats and covering their faces. This was the first unbiased audience that the movie had played to, so it was the first time I realized it could work on a larger scale.

Q – Did you do any special marketing for the film like Blair Witch did?

Oren – I didn't go that far. I created a simple trailer and website and before Screamfest I bought TV ad space and ran the trailer in LA. Then I stood on street corners and handed out flyers and went on a lot of bulletin boards and websites of film and horror fans to tell them about the screening.

Q – What was the tipping point at Screamfest that made the film do well?

Oren – We got a lot of good reviews and won a few awards, which got the attention of CAA. So they sent it out to producers as a directing sample. One came on and he took it to Dreamworks who loved the movie and they made a remake deal.

Q – How did that feel?

Oren – It was great but really we were more focused on getting a theatrical release. But Dreamworks had had a hard time trying to sell and market the movie as it was low budget and no stars. Even though *Blair Witch* was a huge example of how it could work. It took 2 years until they decided to release it themselves, instead of doing the remake, so we were happy for that but it was a difficult 2 years as I'm not someone who's blessed with patience.

Q – What was it like dealing with agents?

Oren – They were very cool. I met my personal agent at a restaurant. I was excited to meet him because we had spoken on the phone and he was very complimentary about the movie, saying it kept him up at night scared. Most of my dealings with them have been over the phone and via email because I'm in San Diego. In fact, I didn't even meet the agent who sold my film until very recently.

Q – How much did Paramount spend to release the film?

Oren – Once I delivered the film, it was out of my hands, so I have no idea.

Q – I heard that you met Steven Spielberg?

Oren – Yes. It was incredible! We had an amazing conversation. To meet your childhood idol and have a talk about our movies, it was surreal and exciting.

Q – What do you think was one of the biggest things you learned?

Oren – I underestimated the time needed for post production. I thought you'd just slap it all together and you're done, but there's a big difference between having all the footage in order, and having a movie that works.

Q – What advice would you offer a new filmmaker?

Oren - Casting. Get it right. It can make or break a film.

Q – Why did you choose to make Gone Fishing?

Chris – I had made three feature films, with some measure of success, but I wasn't breaking through into the business in the way I had hoped. I knew I needed to make another film, something current. But I could not face another low budget feature film as there are so many compromises on that kind of production. Often, at the very end of production, you look back at it and in some ways, it's a disappointment. It's just the obvious impact of having an inexperienced cast and crew, being severely underfunded and therefore forced to be underscheduled. Compromise, compromise, compromise. I had also seen a few of my friends make extremely polished short films, and I realized that many of the compromises thrust upon me with a feature film just didn't happen on a short. It's still hard work and very tight, but it's so much more doable. And so I chose to make *Gone Fishing*, a film about a boy and old man sharing memories about catching Goliath, the biggest pike ever caught.

Q – Why choose that story?

Chris – I had a very simple strategy. I was going to win an Oscar®. I figured out that every year a bunch of film makers walk away with an Oscar® having made

---

✉ chris@guerillafilm.com   🐦 www.twitter.com/livingspiritpix

🏠 www.gonefishingseminar.com   🅱 www.chrisjonesblog.com

📘 Join our Facebook group 'Guerilla Film Maker'

essentially entry level films. That's Short Narrative, Short Doc and Short Animation. These are amazingly produced films, but essentially, they could be made on a shoestring, with no stars and no studio backing them up. I could make one of those I thought. And winning an Oscar® is a surefire way to get your calls returned. I figured a heart warming story about life and 'letting go of loss' would be a universal and resonant theme, and *Gone Fishing* was the result.

Q – What did it cost and where did you get the money?

Chris – It cost around £20,000 ($30,000) and I raised it by being very unreasonable. I asked every person I ever met for £50 ($80). Some people gave us £50, some £100, one guy even gave me £5,000! This was just around the time when the phrase 'crowd sourcing' was being phrased, though I had never heard of it as a concept.

Q – Why would people just give you cash? What's in it for them?

Chris – I was very clear about the deal. I think with something like this, it needs to be clear, pitchable fast and sexy as hell. So my pitch was this… 'Give me £50 and help me win an Oscar!' If they read on through my document, they would get all the other stuff like 'Come to our Oscars® party if we get nominated, get a signed DVD, come to the world premiere, get a credit as an Associate Producer…' I think people who contributed weighed it up and thought, 'Heck, he does have a chance of winning an Oscar®, and if he does, £50 for two tickets to that party is pretty cheap.' I also think people just wanted to come on the journey with me, they wanted me to succeed because if I succeeded, they would be a part of that success too. Who wouldn't want to back an Oscar® winning film maker for £50 if you really thought they had a good chance? That was my pitch.

Q – You also wrote a blog?

Chris – Yes, I promised I would detail everything I learned on a blog, and that became my way of communicating where 'I was at' all the way through the production process. This was good as no-one ever called or emailed me for updates, they just went to the blog, and as we ended up with 175 contributors, plus maybe 50 cast and crew, managing communications to that many people could have been hard work. The blog made it easy. For those who were sitting on the fence, reading the blog and seeing me take action and get results finally sealed the deal, so there was a flurry of contributors when we announced we were locking the titles and 'closing the offer'.

Q – How did the project develop?

Chris – It all came together very quickly. Producer Ivan Clements and myself just hit the phones, asking everyone for help. It seemed the more we asked for, the more people were prepared to offer assistance. Of course we were always very polite, but also a little pushy, with a smile. We managed to get pretty much everything we needed for free, cameras, stock, processing, grips, make-up, everything. The shoot went extremely well, even though we were shooting in British summertime which is notoriously rainy.

On the shoot, I forged a new and important relationship with our DP Vernon Layton. Vernon is an old school cinematographer with decades of experience and heaps of big movie credits under his belt, and he brought a cinematic magic to what we captured on film. When I saw the rushes I was truly breathless. I knew we were making something extraordinary.

Q – We heard that you used keywords on your script?

Chris – Yes, it's something I wanted to do, to make sure I kept my head clear when things went a little crazy around me. I put the words 'Cinematic', 'Sensitive' and 'Confident' in large letters on the front of my folder so that I would see them every time I opened the script. Under pressure, it's easy to make snap decisions, and these three words kept my decisions consistent under pressure. I am happy that the film actually ended up being all of those words, it is very cinematic and sensitive too. And when I used the word confident, I didn't mean I should be more confident on set, I meant the story telling should be confident – not tricksy or over flashy for the sake of it. It really helped me.

Q – It's an ambitious film as it has a king size killer pike and also has period flashbacks. How did you manage to pull that off?

Chris – I began work many months before the shoot, buying all the hero props off eBay. I had learned from past films that one bad prop can kill you dead. And I also knew we would have no prop rentals budget. The advantage of buying props is that you can keep them too, and I am glad we did as we used the large fishing reel with chain fishing line in a subsequent reshoot. So, many of the props were in place before we got to production which was a relief as that was one area I had been forced to compromise on past films.

Costume designer Linda Haysman looked after the period costumes and the big fish ended up being a mix of practical effects, with stunt man Jude Poyer under the water, and digital effects created by a very talented new FX guy called Russ Wharton who was working from home in mid Wales at the time. Every night we were FTP'ing frames back and forth! Then there was the location, a stunning English lake lit by sunlight at the tail end of summer. Combined, it created a rich sense of time and place, and not a single prop, costume or location is weak. That was great for me as I never needed to worry about covering up problems. It all came together because we gave ourselves ample prep time to get it right.

Q – You had two units on set?

Chris – Yes. Because we had a backup camera as part of the camera package, I asked a director friend of mine, Simon Cox, to shoot second unit. This allowed me to let go of some of the smaller but technical shots – close ups of photographs, the stunt duck scenes (!), close ups of winding fishing reels etc. These are shots that must be perfect and they take a long time to setup and get right - but it's also crazy to have a full crew standing around while we shoot a close up of an inanimate object, so I gave those shots to Simon. He had a long shot list and story board and just worked his way through it. It really took the pressure off me so that I could concentrate on performance and story.

Q – How did you approach post production?

Chris – Eddie Hamilton cut *Gone Fishing* on his laptop using Avid. During the shoot, I was unable to view rushes as we were on location, but Eddie saw them and reported back to me. It was quite liberating to not have to add an hour to every day to view rushes. If there were any problems, Eddie would tell us. And because Vernon, our DP, was so experienced, he was also quite comfortable not viewing rushes as long as he knew there were no technical problems. In fact I didn't ever see the rushes. I just viewed the first cut that Eddie had done. Again, it was liberating to know that a second set of very experienced eyes had watched the footage and made initial choices for me. We could always go back and look at alternative takes, but whenever we did, Eddie was always right in his initial choices. I am a strong believer that film making is a team effort and one should surround oneself with talent and enthusiasm – if you are going to do that, why dominate that talent and squash the enthusiasm by dictating what should be done?

So, Eddie did the first cut and we watched it, then he did another cut, and we held a test screening, and then did another cut, and another test screening and so on. Finally we did a day of pickups where we filmed about 20 new shots and inserted them into the final edit. All in all, the film was cut over three months. It was only a few days work, but spaced over those three months. That space gave us time to reflect on the edit and make the right choices. I remember the night we locked the edit, we were so excited because it is so rare that you have the time to really fine tune the edit down to the frame. Even now I look at the film and marvel at the editing. There really isn't a single frame that could be removed, and that is the product of Eddie's hard work and taking the time to get it right.

Q – People who have seen the film do call it a rollercoaster of emotions.

Chris – I wanted it to be a very exciting and emotional experience for the viewer, and many reviews have said that we managed to pack more into 13 minutes than many Hollywood features do in two hours.

Q – So the Oscar®?

Chris – The Oscar® qualifying rules are quite odd and it's easy to fall foul of them, so check their website before you complete your film to make sure you don't screw up your chances. The big one to look out for is TV and internet screening. If you do either, you are disqualified from the Oscar®. So keep it off the web. But do check their rules as they constantly change. To get on the long list for the Oscars® you need to do one of two things. Either win an Oscars® qualifying festival, and there are about 100 around the world (again a list is available on the Oscars® site). Or you can screen commercially in LA for three consecutive days, which most people do with the Laemmle theatres. We did both.

Then you are on the long list. How that gets down to the short list is a little bit of a mystery, but we found out in December of 2008 that we were in the final ten films, the official shortlist, which would be taken down to the five nominated films. It was a very exciting email to get from the MPAA, especially as we had made getting an Oscar® our goal from day one. Suddenly, it all looked like it could happen. At that time I also found a manager in LA who had seen *Gone Fishing* and wanted to represent me. And before I knew it I was back and forth to LA every few weeks as my career moved forward very quickly. I flew into LA the night before the Oscar® nominations were announced, and stayed with co-guerilla film makers Genevieve and Zee. I didn't sleep at all that night. For the last year I had been working toward this moment and the following morning, I would find out if I was going to the Oscars® or not. In a moment my life could change forever.

Sadly, we didn't get the nomination, though I heard from Academy insiders that this particular year was such a close call that all ten shortlisted films could have been nominated, there were fractional percentages to separate them all.

Q – How did you take the news?

Chris – I was of course disappointed. But at the same time, there I was in LA with a new manager and with agents wanting to meet me to discuss projects. So in the moment it was quite rough, but I quickly bounced back. And while I could not say *Gone Fishing* was Oscar® nominated, I could say '*Gone Fishing* was Oscars® shortlisted...'

Q – What doors has it opened?

Chris – I have been surprised at how the film has been received, especially in LA. People just LOVE it. And that is reflected in the awards we picked up, over 40 now, with the vast majority coming from the USA. Even though it's a British film, I believe it has a commercial and mainstream sensibility that just goes down well in Hollywood. I am now attached to a feature project in LA - we will see how that goes. I head back out there several times a year now, for meetings to see what else I can hustle.

Q – What did you do about film festivals?

Chris – I knew that if we didn't get an Oscar® nomination, the second best thing would be a bunch of awards from film festivals. So I began a fairly large scale campaign to enter as many as I could, choosing festivals that I thought would accept the film, and where it would play well. Broadly, Europe rejected the film and America embraced it. We ended up winning around forty awards, and I spent six months traveling the world. It was a huge job, almost as much work as making the film in the first place. I really underestimated the time and money it cost. All in I spent around $8,000 on our festival campaign as I ended up having to hire someone to work the office and campaign while I was attending festivals. I cash flowed that by selling DVDs of *Gone Fishing* and we sold around 1,000 disks which pretty much covered the festival work.

I had attended festivals with my other films, but the festival run for *Gone Fishing* was something different. Something quite magical. I had a great time, met some amazing film makers, went to some breathtaking places and saw really wonderful movies. Most of all, the ability to meet the audience is what I found most gratifying. Unlike musicians or stage actors, where you get to feed off other human beings who are witnessing your work as it unfolds, film makers are in a vacuum. You do your work and send it out, often never getting any interaction with audiences aside from a few words from a snooty critic or a bizarre review on Amazon. So to actually meet and speak with people, to hear their own stories of how the film touched them and moved them, that was awesome. I believe this is a vital element to a film maker finding a kind of spiritual balance to their work. It was so moving when people came to me, laughing and crying, holding hard onto my hand and saying how much they connected with the film. Really amazing responses.

Q – Do you really need a big crew and 35mm to win an Oscar®?

Chris – For the Oscars®, yes I think they are seeking a very specific look and feel. There are HD films that were shortlisted, but that bigger budget feel and high production values are essential. But for other awards, big awards even, it needn't be that larger format. Cannes, Berlin, Torronto, Venice, Sundance etc., they can all choose winners from much lower budget backgrounds. While I was in Australia with *Gone Fishing*, I met some amazing film makers who made a short called *Mankind Is No Island*. It's very moving and shot entirely on a phone. That film had collected a bunch of awards, including one big one with a cash prize of $20,000!

006 - CASE STUDIES

Q – You built an online workshop out of your experiences?

Chris – We filmed a workshop that I ran at BAFTA and then built a whole online training experience around that. It's basically about making a world class short film in order to launch a career. I wanted to create something that would really help film makers get the most out of their resources and give them as good a crack as possible at winning an Oscar®. And it's worth saying again, every year, a new film maker wins the Oscar® for best short film. You can check out the workshop at www.gonefishingseminar.com

Q – What common mistakes do you see?

Chris – Part of the online workshop tackles a big problem I see over and over. Very few film makers develop a long term career strategy. They just run headlong into making films. They can only see success in their future. And they see that success as being just around the corner too. I understand why they don't really think too much about career planning, no-one else has ever told them they need to make a long term strategy, and the film myth seduces them with the promise that if you 'make a killer low budget feature, it will make tons of money, you will get funding for the next film and the rest will be history…'

Consequently, they end up making over ambitious films before they are ready. And then they have blown that 'first movie' opportunity – remember you can only fund and produce your first feature film once (they have also spent the money from that one 'soft investor' they know personally). The career strategy that I have been teaching film makers to use is in four basic stages, and knowing where you are in those stages will inform what choices you should make. It doesn't take long to go through these stages either, but most skip some critical experience and fall into a trap on their first big film. When people take the workshop and do the career planning module, its like a light bulb is switched on, suddenly all the anecdotal stories they have been hearing have a defined and clear structure and it all makes sense.

Q – What advice would you offer?

Chris – Enjoy the journey. It's probably going to be a long one. And in reality, even if you get 'there', wherever 'there' is for you, I suspect you will already be considering another destination as 'there' didn't real turn out to be what you expected.

**FROM SHORT
TO FEATURE
JONATHAN NEWMAN**

Q – You are working on your first big budget feature, tell us what has happened to you over the years.

Johnny – Many years ago I made my first feature film, called *Being Considered*, which was shot on Super16mm for £10k. Like a lot of film makers, I expected the doors would then open for me, and when they didn't, I realized I needed to be more in control of my own destiny. I thought long and hard, and chose to make another film, something that would demonstrate other sides to what I am can do as a film maker.

I made a short film called *Foster*, about a young orphaned boy waiting for a family. My starting point was to make a film that was touching and heart warming. The film was shot on HDCam and completed on a budget of £1,000. I was amazed at the response it received, it won awards and was picked up by the BBC and HBO. And then I got a call from Pete Farrelly, one of the Farrelly brothers, who had seen it at the Rhode Island Film Festival. He said he loved it and asked if I had thought about developing it into a feature film. Truthfully, I hadn't, but of course I said 'Sure!' Within days I was on a plane to LA to meet

Pete, then I found myself at Fox pitching to execs, then DreamWorks where Steven Spielberg walked past me and said 'hello!' At that time, I couldn't figure out a way to make *Foster* work as a feature, I couldn't find a structure as my creative mojo had disappeared. And so that opportunity fizzled out. But we will come back to *Foster* later.

I then had an idea for another short called *Swinging With The Finkels*, about a bored couple who decide to spice up their sex life by swinging. We shot it on the Red camera and produced it for a few thousand. Then I entered it into a competition called *Behind Closed Doors*, run by a company called Filmaka, which in turn is run by Deepak Nayar, a prolific producer based in LA. The winner would have their idea turned into a show for the FX network. It was shortlisted to the final two, but ultimately it didn't win. But it did catch Deepak's eye, though he didn't contact me then.

Soon after, there was another competition to make a Ford commercial, the winners being screened before each new episode of *Knight Rider* on US TV. There would be ten winners, each of whom would be given $5,000 to produce their film, based on their winning scripts. The ten films would air alongside *Knight Rider*, and there would be an overall winner selected. I wrote a script called *Fathers Day*, which was shortlisted, became a finalist, and then to my delight, won first prize. I was flown out to LA for the unveiling of the new Ford Mustang (which featured in *Knight Rider)*, where they screened my film, and that's when I met Deepak.

FROM THE AWARD WINNING DIRECTOR **JONATHAN NEWMAN** AND THE PRODUCERS OF **BEND IT LIKE BECKHAM**

Swinging with the Finkels

It's Certainly Not Boring Anymore!

Martin Freeman & Mandy Moore

Deepak had then seen *Foster*, *Fathers Day* and *Swinging With The Finkels*, and he thought *'clearly this guy is more than a one hit wonder'*. He suggested developing *The Finkels* into a feature, which I was delighted with as I had always had

313

that idea too. He said, *'Go write the script, and in six months we will be on set...'* Having had a lot of carrots dangled in front of me before, I took it with a pinch of salt. But there was something interesting about Deepak, he was very charismatic and he had an amazing track record.

So I agreed, and true to my word, I wrote and delivered the script on schedule. Deepak had 100% faith in the film, went away, and amazingly, raised the entire budget in four months. Suddenly I found myself on set shooting a feature film based on my short film (the budget is approximately $3m). I am so used to guerilla film making that it was luxury (laughs!), though it was still very tight. It seems that no matter how much money you have, there is never enough of it, or enough time. We shot for 26 days, 6 day weeks, which was relatively tight.

Q – So you made three shorts beforehand. Do you think that was a good way to develop your skills and show different aspects to your abilities?

Johnny – When nothing was happening after *Being Considered*, it took me a while to realize I had to take action myself. I think a big mistake many film makers make is they expect people to come to them. What I chose to do was to continually generate my own work, and while I was doing that, I was getting better at my craft, and developing my own voice. With *Foster* I discovered I could tell a story that was both funny and heart warming, and that concept resonates throughout my work. It's something I am interested in. I learned that if you approach a story in a way that is truthful, you can capture the full breath of human emotion, and that is a great place from which to tell a story.

Q – Anyone who knows you, will know you are a consummate networker and hustler. How important is that?

Johnny – Your work must speak for itself, and if it can't speak for itself, no amount of networking or hustling will help. You could be the greatest talent on earth, but if no-one knows who you are, then you have no chance. So, yes hustling plays a part, as does chance and luck, but for me, it's a chain of events – had I not got off my butt and made these short films, the chain of events that followed would not have happened. So taking action is by far the most important thing to do.

Q – So in the absence of a great opportunity, you can create your own great opportunities, and if you repeat that pattern, eventually something will happen?

Johnny – Yes. That's why I love the expression, *'You can't wait for the cow to back into your hands so you can milk it'*. You need to go into the field and get the cow! After *The Finkels* feature film I had an overwhelming feeling that I would never make a film again, and that got me to write another screenplay while I was in post production. I have a lot of friends who are successful, in that they have made great films, but they are still struggling, and that is the challenge we all face until we get into the studio system. And so I choose to take action and aggressively self generate my own opportunities.

Q – What doors has the Finkels opened?

Johnny – I now have an agent in LA at ICM. People no longer consider me a new film maker, even though before when I was thought of as a new film maker, I already had a feature film, several shorts and commercials under my belt. That was very frustrating. It's an economic concept. Money attracts money. I had to make a fully budgeted film in order to be considered for a fully budgeted film. I am now perceived as a different commodity. I am now going up for open directing assignments in LA.

The other door that has opened is the relationship with Deepak. For years I have worked with other producers who have failed to deliver on promises. The relationship that we have cultivated is probably the biggest door that has opened, perhaps in my entire career. Deepak has the ability to make films happen, and he believes and commits 100%. Deepak and I are already working on the next film, even though we are still in post production on *The Finkels*. Extraordinarily, it could be in production within a few months.

Q – What is it?

Johnny – It's *Foster*! With the break from the Farrelly brothers, and after *The Finkels*, I got my creative mojo back and I was able to crack the structure of it.

Q – What are the big lessons you have learned over the years?

Johnny – I was very prepared to make *The Finkels*, to bring it in on budget and on schedule, and that is important for studios and producers. Coming from a guerilla film making background I have learned to focus my resources on what is important, on the story. By making many mistakes on the shorts, when making the feature, I knew how to get the coverage, how many takes I needed, what I didn't need etc. My goal was always to get what I needed and to stay on schedule. Here's the thing. If I went past the wrap time by ten minutes, it would cost the production £5k per hour. If we went over by a day, it would cost the production tens of thousands. So I was conscious of the schedule at every moment. Many film makers do not act responsibly with regard to time and money, and unless your work is exceptional, you may not be invited back for the next one.

Q – What advice would you offer a new film maker?

Johnny – Short films are a great place to learn and to show off your skills. If you have had one success, don't rest on your laurels, continue to generate more material and create relationships. If you can write your own material, that puts you in stronger position. In my experience, when you get an opportunity, when someone sees your film and they like it, they will say… *'that's great, so what have you got?'* And at that point you need a project. You need a script. The odds are very much stacked against you in regard to being hired to direct a feature off the back of a short. Producers are already looking at directors who have made several feature films, possibly very successful feature films. Why would they take a risk on a new and unproven short film maker when they don't need to? So you need your own screenplay so that you become necessary.

Keep the dream alive. It's taken me ten years between my last feature film and this one, and there were times I considered doing something else for the sake of a stable career, but if you believe in your ability, you will keep going. Every rejection makes you stronger and hope keeps you going.

Ultimately, be self generative. Go milk the cow!

(To watch Johnny's films, log in for free at www.guerillafilm.com)

UPDATE - As this book goes to press, so Johnny walks out onto set to shoot 'Foster'! INCREDIBLE!

INDEX